DEATH
of the
SWEET
WATERS

Also by D O N A L D E . C A R R — *The Breath of Life*

DEATH

of the

SWEET

WATERS

DONALD E. CARR

W · W · NORTON & COMPANY · INC ·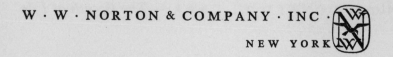
NEW YORK

*To the League
of Women Voters of
the United States*

CONTENTS

ILLUSTRATIONS are between pages 130 and 131.

FOREWORD

IN PREPARING a book about water a writer must have a good deal of nonchalant impudence, since the libraries are full of learned books about water and unlearned ones too. Originally I had planned simply to write about water pollution and to stress some new phases on this subject which had concerned me in my profession as a chemist.

It became rapidly apparent that a book on water pollution, designed for the general reader, is nearly without meaning unless the reader is already familiar with some of the facts of life about soil management, river basin behavior and the patterns of rain. How can one write of one of the most dangerous kinds of pollution—the silting up of rivers and lakes—unless a background is laid down, for example, on the relationships between farming and forestry practices and the water erosion of the soil?

Silt and salt have ruined ancient civilizations and are remorseless enemies of modern ones.

This book consequently covers the water front. The theme nevertheless emerges in a crescendo toward the end—the theme that water pollution is a scandal to the modern world (and especially to the American world) that should arouse us all. If my Scottish tendency to abstract indignation betrays me and has caused me to hurt the feelings of certain politicians who have been friendly toward me, I hereby apologize to them. I can only excuse my slashing about on the grounds that the people must know.

The best country-wide job that is being done in educating the people to the importance of the water problem is, in my opinion, that of the League of Women Voters. Indeed, I must acknowledge the help of many charming and busy League members (one of whom is my wife) who have made available to me material from their abundant files. Water pollution has long been one of the League's continuing national responsibilities. It is on their current agenda for concerted action.

Nevertheless, the *views* expressed in this book are mine and have no connection with the League's consensus on the problems of water pollution. The League is cautious and reasonable. I am rambunctious. I do not use its skirts for drapery or for hiding.

DEATH
of the
SWEET
WATERS

"MY GRANDDAD SAYS THIS SEWER USED TO BE A RIVER."

The Lord God took the man and put him in the garden . . .
to dress it and to keep it.

—GENESIS 2:15

Sennacherib king of Assyria came, and entered into
Judah. . . . So there was gathered much people together,
who stopped all the fountains, and the brook that ran
through the midst of the land, saying, Why should the
kings of Assyria come, and find much water?

—II CHRONICLES 32:1, 4

1 LORDS of the ANCIENT WATERS

As DID ALL living creatures and plants, man came originally
from the sea. Even after millions of years of evolution, we still
carry with us the mark of the oceans in the fact that the plasma
of our blood has almost the same mineral composition as sea
water and our bodies are 71 percent composed of water. It is an
embarrassing biological fact that the useful aquatic habit of
being able to ingest salt water instead of fresh water has been
lost by land animals and virtually all land plants. Otherwise we
would not be in the spot we're in.

Very early in man's precultural history he became concerned
with a childlike sort of water control. Between the hunter and
the true prehistoric farmer there was a period of some thousands
of years of what anthropologists call the "food-gathering" age. In
addition to killing occasional animals and catching an occasional
fish, men collected wild edible vegetables and thus had a more
balanced lunch than most modern teen-agers who subsist on
hamburgers. Since such succulent green stuff grew near springs
or brooks, men began trying to spread it about a bit. The simplest
of all devices was used to raise water—the hollow of the hand.

Thus there grew up a primitive sort of handicraft dribble irrigation.

It is noteworthy that the transition from pure paleolithic cave man to the early farmer took place in a semiarid region, somewhat similar to Southern California in the fact that rains came in the winter rather than the spring and summer. At the very end of the paleolithic period, the Natrefians of Mt. Carmel, who still lived in caves, reaped grain with a sickle consisting of a grooved bone-haft set with flint teeth—the earliest agricultural instrument known. From the viewpoint of geologic time it was hardly an instant, from the cave-dwelling farmer to the vast ancient farm communities with reed, thatch or wooden houses, located mainly near great river systems.

The Fertile Crescent (Mesopotamia) of the Near East, the Nile Delta, the Indus, the Hwang Ho of China all became the breeding places of great populations: Where no rivers were at hand, water had an even more haunting aspect in man's life. In Southwestern Asia, the ancient Arabians are believed by some scientists to have started the institution of polygamy because of the problem of hauling water. The primitive sheikh lived an average of nine miles from a water hole. It took the wife all day to get home with one bucket. This was not enough on a summer day. The answer that seems to have appealed to the Arab mind was not to move nearer to the water hole but to accumulate more wives.

In comparing the river civilizations, it is possible to make a good case for the character of the river in determining the nature and the pace of the culture. Thus a large factor in the early blooming sophistication of the Egyptians is the fact that the Nile has always been known as a gentlemanly river. For the most part it rises and falls precisely according to the calendar. When, as most gentlemen do, it goes on an occasional binge, it really hangs one on. When contributions from the Blue Nile and the Sobat swell the central river simultaneously, colossal inundations occur.

The loss of life in the floods of 1874 has never been more than approximately estimated but certainly amounted to tens of thousands. On the other hand, catastrophic droughts have occasionally through history dried up the farm lands and resulted in horrifying famines. The avoidance of such catastrophes is one of the justifications of Nasser's great Aswan dam.

Irrigation from the Nile actually has amounted to a sort of controlled inundation. As early as "King Scorpion" of 3200 B.C., before the Pharaoh dynasties, a dike was ceremoniously cut to inaugurate the majestic flows of water. Wide basins surrounded the river, with elaborate series of revetments and canals. Manuring was unnecessary since the great river's silt was rich in decomposed vegetable matter and phosphates—a gift from Middle Africa. Artificial drainage was not needed. The river was simply allowed gently to cover all the arable soil in the basins, sink in as deeply as it would, and the overflow drawn off to the river mouth. Enough water for another year of vegetable growth had then been delivered. The "Night of the Drop," when the heavenly tear fell and caused the Nile to rise, is still celebrated on June 17.

This one-shot irrigation system satisfied the fellahin and gave them bread, but the Pharaohs themselves and the aristocratic families were not satisfied and invented what is called "perennial irrigation." This consisted of diverting the river into small ditches or conduits to palace gardens and lovely estates of the elite, so that water could be applied to a variety of exotic plants the year round. The Pharaohs were avid horticulturists and, on their travels to other lands, the royal cortege would invariably return home laden with all manner of foreign trees, bushes and seeds. The quantity of water they often used is indicated by the fact that they employed as many as 1,600 home gardeners.

Since the Nile was the aortic artery of a great civilization, it was measured scrupulously, ever since recorded history, with

"Nilometers"—simple depth gauges. These Nilometer records are almost as old as writing. Nilometer records for the 1,300 years from the Arab conquest to the present show that the silt in the Nile Valley has raised the land some 8 feet. Thus in the days of the Pharaohs the level would have been about 20 feet lower than it is today.

In the more turbulent and unpredictable rivers, such as the Tigris, the Euphrates and especially the Hwang Ho, the load of silt was far greater. Furthermore, in dealing with the Mesopotamian torrents a far more virile and subtle degree of expertise in water management had to be developed than that required for the predictable, gentlemanly river, the Nile. These were fierce, implacable and irresponsible rivers. The control exerted over them by the Sumerians, the Chaldeans, the Babylonians, the Phoenicians and the Assyrians represents perhaps the most dramatic instance of heroic engineering in history. Such control in Mesopotamia gave birth to a thriving population of 40 million people, who were the envy of the ancient Mediterranean world.

There is perhaps no more theatrical instance of Nietzsche's concept of the "pathos of distance" than a comparison of those robust cultures with the present shabby handful of half-starved human rats in the same part of the world (with the exception of Israel, where modern techniques coupled with indomitable resoluteness have turned but half a page back toward the ancient hydraulic glories). Let us take a look at these incredible Mesopotamians of the past and try to perceive the reasons not only for their ancient lordship of the waters but for their fall from hydraulic grace.

In the great alluvial river valleys of Sumer and Akkad temperatures were much more extreme than in North Africa, varying from 30° F. to 120° F. The flows on the Tigris and Euphrates were quite whimsical. Their rises would occur without warning, and these rivers had no intention of watching the calendar. In another sense, too, the waters were ill-behaved, since they carried five times the silt load of the Nile and annoying amounts of salt.

Irrigation for food crops in Mesopotamia was combined with the problems of drainage, water impoundment for the constant control of floods, and the very serious question, which was also a desperate one in China, of preventing the rivers from changing their course. When the Tigris and the Euphrates reached flood stage at the same time, which rather frequently happened, there was all hell to pay. The Sumerians, contemporaries of the predynastic Egyptians, lived in a fog of fear of colossal inundations. One of these, which gave birth to the legend based partly on truth and inflamed by the constant nightmare of poets, was said to have destroyed all but one of mankind. This Sumerian best seller became the story of Noah.

This story of the Great Flood, of course, is not a peculiarly Near East tale. All early cultures in flood-prone lands, including those of South America, China and India, have legends passed down through countless generations about a monstrous flood. Only the more romantic students of antiquity believe this was a worldwide catastrophe that happened during the same week. It is the habit of human societies to construct a giant prototype that stands for common fears or even common joys. In forest lands there has always been the legend of a gigantic tree—the Tree to Heaven, so to speak. There are prototype bears as big as the chief's cottage and deer whose antlers could bear the weight of a squad of men. There are prototype giants of incredible strength and resource, such as Hercules and Paul Bunyan and even the mighty Casey whose career was marked with final poetic tragedy worthy of Euripides. There have been gods who, in cultures like that of the pre-Christian Greeks, were simply powerful and immortal prototypes of men and women with unusually risky temperaments, lordly lack of moral sense, and enormous whimsicality—all qualities that the Greeks admired.

It is not surprising that one of the most potent gods of Sumeria was Ea, "the lord of the sweet waters that flow under the earth." This was a most practical sort of godhead, since it involved a very modern type of concept of the underground water table, which is not stationary but moves. The Sumerian god Nur, the dragon of primeval waters, represented floods and wild waters in general and was a very naughty god indeed, in fact, a fearful enemy of mankind. Happily, in Sumerian theology, he was conquered by the warrior-god Ninurta, who created the world and made it habitable, mainly by water management.

The Sumerians from the beginning of their history as we know it practiced a kind of perennial irrigation. They liked to keep the soil covered with a few inches of water from the time of sowing in November until harvest in May. This was done by building a complicated network of water channels from the rivers, with land divided into fields and fields into small plots bounded by little parallel ridges forming the walls of temporary dikes. Archaeologists have discovered the remains of a series of great waterways intersecting the area between the lower Tigris and the Euphrates, each surrounded by a network of canals which watered the surrounding district and brought prosperity to its people and dues to the local temple. There was a monstrous canal, Nahrwan, the greatest of antiquity, 400 feet wide and 200 miles long, from which riparian temples received a sort of toll tax. The priests made a good thing of it.

The Euphrates, more manageable than the Tigris, carries only about half its volume of water and recedes more slowly into its bed, which lies higher than that of the Tigris. Thus the people could drain surplus water off into the lower river. It is in the southwestern part of Iraq, a flat plain of mud and marshes, with its superabundant water, that the oldest city sites of Sumer are found.

The water of the Tigris, like that of the Colorado, was too muddy to drink and thus water treatment arrived on the scene.

Conduits carried the raw river water to city catchment basins where the silt could settle out.

The conquest by the great Babylonian king Hammurabi (2038 B.C.) of the entire Tigris and most of the Euphrates Valley led to a strong centralized control of irrigation. Several of the laws in the famous Code of Hammurabi deal with irrigation. Certain laws which survive have to do with water claims and the obligations of "rivals." This word derives from the Latin *rivus* (river) and refers to those who shared the water of an irrigation channel. Thus there were involved jealously guarded water rights which in the Near East have been more basic than land claims.

During the reign of Hammurabi the production of barley, wheat, emmer, sesame and flax grew to standards comparable to those of our Kansas wheatlands. The Babylonians sowed their seed-grain thickly, allowing four fifths of a bushel to an acre, so that a return of at least three bushels was not unlikely. The use of perennial irrigation allowed two or even three harvests a year. During this period reed thickets as canal arresters grew so densely that countless lions lurked in them.

For one who has traveled in or over Mesopotamia, it is incredible to realize that in the millennia before the birth of Christ the population of this part of the world was about that of modern France and, during the peak years of Babylon, the western Mediterranean peoples, such as the Greek, burned with envy at the lushness of the crops and the proud life of the people of Babylonia. The Greeks in their rock-strewn islands and peninsulas had no opportunity for agriculture on this prodigious scale.

The Babylonians, luxuriating in the midst of their bumper crops, could, like the Pharaohs, afford to play around with new plants and indulge in rather fancy horticulture. The date palm was imported and dates became a sort of rich, concentrated staple food for soldiers and, for the folk in general, the equiva-

lent of American apple pie. The date palm is said to grow with
"her head in hell-fire and her feet in the river." A horticultural
wonder of the world was the Hanging Gardens of Babylon in
the royal palace estate of Nebuchadnezzar. This was "hung"
only in the sense that it was built over an arched cellar in which
there was a well, worked by water wheels, which irrigated the
garden. The cellar roof was heavily waterproofed by layers of
reed and asphalt, stone slabs, brick and mortar, and sheet lead.
Over this was placed a deep layer of earth in which trees were
planted. As the aristocracy gulped its wine and indulged in its
immemorial follies, relays of stout slaves turned the water
wheels beneath.

In this immense irrigation society, it turned out that the Assyrians were the absolute technological masters. One always
thinks of an ancient Assyrian as a sort of wolf man with a rec-
tangular beard and a massive sword, about to behead a child.
The Assyrians should more accurately be enshrined with Theodore Roosevelt and Goethals. Their skill in hydraulics has seldom been equaled, even in modern times. Ambitious land reclamation schemes were carried out. Reservoirs were built in
the mountains. Sennacherib, the engineer-king, built the Greater
Zab canal to Nineveh, which was not only 50 miles long and
wide as a road but was paved with masonry and partly covered
with a roof. This was the most impressive piece of hydraulic
engineering until Roman times. The most astounding feature
of an age when it was not unusual to take a generation to accomplish any constructional feat is the fact that the project was
completed in fifteen months, which is perhaps better than could
be expected of our Army Corps of Engineers.

Aqueducts had also been built by the Phoenicians in Lebanon to tap mountain streams. The ruined aqueducts of Pal-
myra, 135 miles northeast of Damascus, tell of that city's van-
ished fields and gardens, and traces of canals can be seen in
other parts of what is now desert—haunted by mean little men

with guns. Underground conduits, or *ganaats*, were often built to solve the evaporation problem. An ancient subterranean conduit still supplies Aleppo and its famous but somewhat faded gardens.

Assyrian irrigation laws distinguished between rain water and water from natural springs, wells and cisterns. Regulations dealt with the rights and duties of land owners whose properties were irrigated from a common source. They provided for cooperation in maintaining the supply, keeping the canals free from silt and pollution, and ensuring that the farmers farthest from the source got a fair share. In case of flooding, each farmer had to pitch in and help and there was a special court to deal with recalcitrants. If a farmer proved too stubborn, he was beheaded or stoned to death.

The Assyrian's control of water was more than systematic conservation. They handled the waters as a great general manages an army. In fact they often used water for military purposes. They would divert a river or a tributary overnight to engulf an enemy city. When Sennacherib of Assyria in his fury destroyed the hated Babylon, which had been responsible for his son's death, he pulled down temples and palaces and dumped the debris into the canals, flooding the city.

(Water was important also for armies on the march in the arid lands. Scouts had to be sent ahead to search for likely spots for digging wells. In the Near East water can usually be reached in the wadis if at all, by very shallow wells, averaging from 12 to 15 feet. Herodotus relates that in the Persian invasion of Egypt in 525 B.C., huge wine jars were used to store water along the invasion route. Hefty sums were paid to local sheikhs for the use of camels and water skins. The army engineers of antiquity were prepared, however, to drill quickie wells through solid rock. They would heat the rock, then pour cold water on it to split it.)

The Old Testament is full of stories involving water. The

Pools of Solomon, great stone-cut cisterns, were used to supply Jerusalem. The huge size of these reservoirs showed knowledge of the fact that stored water must be deep, otherwise evaporation is so fast in such a climate that the summer ends with only a small brackish remnant in the cistern. Town planning in those days usually involved placing the citadel on a hill, for defense purposes, with a tunnel leading down to a spring. Best known is the tunnel by which Hezekiah, King of Judah (740-692 B.C.), made the waters of a spring in the side of the hill Ophel at Jerusalem available to the garrisons besieged by the Assyrians. An inscription marks the spot where two gangs, burrowing from either end, met. This was a remarkable achievement, since the passage twists and is 1,760 feet long.

In the Book of Ecclesiasticus, Wisdom is made to say, "I came out as a stream from a river and as a conduit into a garden. I said, 'I will water my garden, I will water abundantly the soil of my garden. And lo, my stream became a river, and my river a sea.'"

Wisdom indeed taught these energetic ancient people of the Near East the techniques of irrigation, and they used these techniques as no other people before or after had used them. Under their hand the desert bloomed as the rose, and the hillsides became hanging gardens.

Why, then, did it all end up as a desert again? Why have the roses disappeared and the hanging gardens become ghostly legends? Why, in short, has a great center of antiquity become a sort of broken-down dust heap?

There are numerous theories. One of the more romantic and least sensible is Arnold Toynbee's contention that the Mongols in their invasion killed some 40 million Mesopotamians and hence there was a century of essential void, where there were not enough able-bodied men left to do anything, let alone carry out reclamation projects and maintain complicated irrigation systems. Some modern authorities maintain that salt incursion ruined the water. As we shall see in a later chapter, there is some danger in certain highly irrigated soils that the water may concentrate salt by leaching action so that the runoff or the water table becomes too salty for many kinds of food crops. There is little proof that this happened in the Near East.

There is no doubt that the Mongol invasion destroyed the delicate balance of water control. A sort of preview of what could happen later was the invasion of Southern Babylonia in 2100 B.C. by the wild hillmen from the Zagros, who did not appreciate irrigation. During their thankfully brief ascendancy the irrigation ditches were used only to urinate in and the country became disorganized almost overnight. The much more serious arrival of the Mongol hordes, who were as vicious and subhuman as mad curs, resulted in complete neglect of the canal banks. Overflowing and flooding ruined the land's fertility. But this was the fourteenth century and the region had been going downhill long before.

The best hypothesis is that of Paul B. Sears, who attributes the decline to the gradual silting up of the whole water system. The great rivers had always been silty but the load increased because of the imprudent practices of overgrazing and overcutting of the vegetation on the highlands whose runoff supplied the rivers. Water erosion of soil and denuding of watersheds had from remotest antiquity been recognized as dangers and been met by such expedients as terracing. This was mainly to protect the upland farms themselves. The deadly peril of silting up the downstream waters because of soil erosion was not fully appreciated. Besides, the pressure was on for the quick buck by sheepherders or lumbermen or row croppers. Thus a very modern American dilemma faced the Mesopotamians. So much labor was required for the cleaning of canals that little leisure remained for anything else. Finally the tired civilization said, in effect, "The hell with it!" and dropped back into the hammock of history.

Although not so much is known about it, evidently the sophisticated hydraulic civilization of the Mohenjo-Daro in the
Indus Valley went through somewhat the same cycle and at
about the same time. Five thousand years ago these mysterious
people enjoyed well-designed water supply and drainage systems
and even public pools and baths, tanks and irrigation canals.

Somewhat before the great centuries of Roman aqueduct
building, the Chinese in the Tukiangyien system diverted the
Min River, a tumultuous stream that rises on the high plateau
of Tibet. A series of dams and dikes was built to irrigate half a
million acres. These structures were for the most part composed
of bamboo frames weighted down with rocks.

There is recent evidence of a very ancient hydraulic civilization in Arizona and New Mexico since scattered remains of
about 1,000 miles of irrigation canals have been excavated. The
1965 discoveries of Dr. Emma Lou Davis of the University of
California at Los Angeles in the desert lands of Southern California give some hint that a water-minded culture, perhaps the
same one, existed there. Unfortunately no way has been found
to date these remarkable early North American populations,
since no wood is associated with the remains, and "carbon-dat-
ing" is the only positive way of placing a people in archaeological
time.

The Greeks paid little attention to irrigation or water management, although from time to time they made a few half-
hearted efforts to drain their swamps and marshes. Agriculture
in the Greco-Roman world consisted almost entirely of dry
farming. However, the Romans had need of bountiful water
supplies for domestic and industrial use and proceeded with
great vigor to build aqueducts not only in the Campagna around
Rome, but in the colonies, such as Gaul, Spain and England.
They took steps to prevent flooding of the Tiber and the Arno.
In Holland Drusus in A.D. 12 laid a breakwater in the Rhine west
of Cleves to keep excess water from flowing through the Waal.

A canal was dug between the rivers Rhine and Yssel to shunt floodwaters from the Rhine.

The Roman aqueducts, many of which remain visible, were marvelously engineered. Since the eye is attracted to their superb arches, it is seldom realized that the course of these conduits is mainly underground. The aqueducts of Merida and Segovia still stand nearly intact. Others were at Nîmes and Arles; Cologne, Bonn, Mainz and Treves; Lincoln, Dorchester and Worcester.

Eight aqueducts led into Rome. From springs or rivers the water was led to settling tanks. Since many of the springs tapped were fairly hot, the Roman aqueducts suffered from serious incrustations of calcium carbonate. Part of the supply was undrinkable and was used for mills, fountains, and sewer flushing.

In the troubled days of the later Republic (first century B.C.) the aqueducts were neglected. Augustus had to repair many channels and ducts that had fallen into decay and build others. The huge aqueduct of Claudius took fourteen years to build. During the tremendous expansion of Imperial Rome, the flat marshy land by the Tiber was gradually drained and its streams were enclosed in sewers of which the Cloaca Maxima still survives.

The ancient world was conscious in a vague way of water pollution and water contamination. (In this book we shall distinguish between the two, pollution being defined as anything that makes the water undesirable for various reasons and contamination consisting of pathogenic bacteria which threaten human beings with disease.) Ancient physicians, including Hippocrates, and engineers stressed the need for pure drinking water. Galen, Vitruvius and others denounced the use of lead in lining cisterns or pipes, but lead was a very popular material and lead poisoning continued. Crusting of the surfaces with calcium carbonate reduced the number of poisonings where the water was hard and relatively warm.

To purify water, ancient recommendations range from mere exposure in the sun and air to filtration through sand (the latter being still popular in modern times). The water of the Karschen River, which flows by Susa, was boiled and stored in silver flagons for the Persian kings. Herodotus, a snobbish writer, highly approved of this practice for royalty. Porous filters of tufa, wool, lengths of wick were sometimes used, but Athenaeus of Attalia in his book *On the Purification of Water* (A.D. 50), was strong for sand filters. However, one must include the most popular of chemical treatments, which persisted for many centuries —the addition of wine to the water. A dictum which was nearly universal was "Certain waters can bear a little wine." It is possible that by dosing water drop by drop with a strongly colored wine the Romans were estimating roughly the lime content of their water—a sort of procedure which chemists call "titration."

We shall treat the subject of sewerage in the third chapter, but it should be said that the ancient peoples were not too specifically concerned with pollution or contamination from this source.

By far the most severe pollution problem was silt. As we have seen, it wiped out a nexus of great Mesopotamian cultures. It gravely threatens our own.

Water is insipid, inodorous, colorless and smooth; it is found,
when not cold, to be a great resolver of spasms and lubricator of
the fibres; this power it probably owes to its smoothness.

—EDMUND BURKE

I am the poem of earth, said the voice of the rain, Eternal I rise
impalpable out of the land and the bottomless sea.

—WALT WHITMAN

Let the most absent-minded of men be plunged in his deepest reveries ...
and he will infallibly lead you to water, if water there be in that
region. . . . Meditation and water are wedded forever.

—HERMAN MELVILLE

2 THE WETNESS of WATER

LIFE IS possible without oxygen in the atmosphere, as we
know from the existence of the so-called anaerobic bacteria,
but life without water is inconceivable to us. Water is the basis
of the blood of animals, the sap of trees; and the very texture of
life at its rawest and most ancient (in single-celled protozoa)
consists of structures in which water is used as a mortar, as a
minuscule pool for digestion, and as a means of carrying chemical and electrical information from the outside world to the
nucleus, so that even the tiniest bit of life may be organized
and may strike its small spark of struggle against the oblivion
that surrounds all creatures.

Water is very rare in the part of the universe that we can
observe. For the benefit of English listeners, Chet Huntley in
the first communications satellite broadcast said that our planet
might well have been called "Shakespeare." Imaginary Latin-
speaking astronomers in deep outer space would probably call

it "Aqua." In our own solar system, Earth has secured virtually all the water rights. It is a monopoly that increasingly depresses us, since man's instinct is to people the stars in imagination with a brilliant zoo of life, so that we have our assurance of *alternatives*: surely someone better or kinder or wiser than we must make his home out there—if not someone who will help us in our planetary sickness, someone who will at least inspire us or even fight us. The bleak news that Mariner IV gave us of Mars, picturing a world seemingly dead since birth, was followed by the most severe epidemic of flying saucer reports of any year— as if mankind were determined in its pathos to deny the plain evidence of its scientists.

Water is not only so rare in the observable universe that Earth is an oasis separated by inconceivable deserts of space from any theoretical water-rich brother planet, but water is fundamentally a very strange substance. It behaves so peculiarly that chemists have not yet succeeded in explaining its chameleon structure.

Compare a molecule of water (H_2O) with a molecule of methane (CH_4). Both have the same weight. Yet water boils at 212° Fahrenheit while the methane becomes a vapor at 258° F. *below zero*. The amount of heat required to evaporate water and to melt ice is far greater than for other seemingly simple substances. This behavior is attributed to the fact that water molecules form semichemical bonds with each other (so-called "hydrogen-bonding") so that more heat energy is required to get water or ice molecules to unclasp.

This property is important to life. It means that water evaporates relatively slowly and when it does evaporate it cools its surroundings. Life in or around bodies of water is kept at rather modest temperature ranges. The high heat of melting makes ice a remarkable refrigerant. Water is thus a cushion against both rising and falling temperatures.

The fact that ice is lighter than liquid water is almost unique.

This has its advantages and its disadvantages. A pond freezes from the top down rather than from the bottom up: icebergs float away rather than sink to the bottom of the sea. Yet, since ice formation results in expansion, radiators and water pipes burst, soils heave and mountains are gradually worn down. This property of water is what makes ice skating possible. The pressure exerted by the skates lowers the melting point of the ice (in accordance with a famous law that pressure favors that form of a substance which has the highest density), so that the skate runners are lubricated by a film of water.

Water is a remarkable solvent. The fact that it will dissolve such inorganic compounds as ammonia, salt, potash, phosphates, etc. makes it indispensable as a fluid for feeding both plants and animals. But still more important than its solvent properties are what might be called its qualities of wetness. Giant molecules, such as proteins, which water cannot truly dissolve, it can *disperse*. The incalculably complex colloidal (or dispersed) systems that make up living matter are due to the wetting power of water. Wetness also manifests itself in capillary behavior—the tendency of water to cling to soil and to run up surfaces against the pull of gravity. If it were not for this surface-wetting behavior, it would be impossible to cultivate the soil. Water, having fallen as rain, would either run off immediately or would all sink far too deeply through the soil for the roots of common plants to find it.

The wetting properties of water are connected with the same molecular habits that make water hard to evaporate and give it high surface tension. It is surface tension that enables one to float a steel needle on the surface of very still water. Because of its high solvent power and high wetting power, absolutely pure water is seldom found in nature. The purest form of natural water is snow. Most people find melted snow and artificially purified water disagreeable to the taste. This is because of their *absence* of taste. The water from a gurgling

spring in the viny coolness of a forest tastes good because it is
usually high in mineral content.

It is of course the mineral content of water that determines
whether it is "soft" or "hard." "Hard" water contains calcium
and magnesium salts which form insoluble curdy precipitates
with old-fashioned soap. Such soaps are usually the sodium salts
of fatty acids, but the calcium or magnesium salts are water-
insoluble. Dirt containing fatty material also reacts with hard
water to form precipitate—the reason for the ring around the
bathtub. Hard water can be softened very simply by passing it
through ion-exchange columns, which substitutes sodium for
calcium and magnesium in the water.

The degree to which the higher animals depend on water
for their substance is shown by the fact that a newborn calf
contains 80 percent water. This goes down at maturity to 60
percent in a lean animal. In very fat animals the water content
may be no more than 40 percent. Aside from the fat deposits,
most of the soft tissues of the body average from 70 to 90 percent water. Animals may lose nearly all the fat and about half
the protein of their bodies and still survive, but the loss of one
tenth of the water from the body means sure death.

Many smaller desert mammals thrive without any visible
sources of water except that obtained from dry seeds and plants.
Yet they do not seem to have any peculiar body structures
that conserve water. The answer is that they burrow and remain inactive in the shade during the heat of the day. The
Arabian camel, however, like its master, works during the heat
of the sun and will carry a load of 500 pounds, 25 miles a day
for three days without drinking. Contrary to popular misinfor-
mation, camels do not store water. During nondrinking periods
water is manufactured in the camel's body, chiefly by oxidation
of fat.

Sheep on pasture can go for weeks without drinking and
may actually live and grow to maturity without ever taking a

drink, provided that the grass is not too dry. The water consumption of cattle will be reduced on good pasture but not to the same extent as that of sheep. The most damaging effect of droughts on livestock is the effect on plant growth and food intake, not the reduced intake of water as such.

Man is one of the few animals that can lower body temperature by perspiration. He is surpassed, however, by the horse, which sweats heavily.

The cycle of water from the oceans that cover 71 percent of the surface of the earth to the sweat from a horse is a vast and zigzag chemical route. But how did the oceans arrive in the first place? It is easy to find a geological explanation for ocean basins, since they are common on solid planets. They are seen on the moon. But how did the ocean basins of earth come to be filled with water?

In the first place, water is a chemically bound constituent of many minerals. Molten rock such as lava holds much more water of composition when liquid than when it hardens and cools. Over the billion years of the earth's early life, as the crust solidified, water vapor was given off to the atmosphere. The process is still going on today on a minor scale, as shown by the analysis of gases from volcanoes. The amount of water freed in this way over geologic time was enough to cover more than two thirds of the surface of the planet. Something like this must have happened on the moon, yet the moon has no ocean. The explanation is that gravity on the moon is much weaker than on earth. Gas molecules in the earth's atmosphere behave just as does any other moving body with respect to gravity. If the escape velocity of 7 miles per second is reached, the body (or molecule) can escape to outer space. At the boiling point of water the average speed of water molecules is only about half a mile per second and the probability of any one molecule reaching escape velocity is infinitesimally small. On the moon, where a temperature of 212° F. is regularly exceeded on the face presented to the sun, the escape velocity is only about one and a half miles per second. An important fraction of water molecules reach this speed, and hence the moon fails to hold water vapor or indeed any of the other light gases that make up an atmosphere and hydrosphere, and hence it lacks an ocean.

Another reason for the stability of our oceans is that the temperature of the earth's surface averages much below the boiling point of water. On a planet such as Venus, which is comparable in size and gravity to the earth, the surface temperature is too high for any water to condense. At the 700-800° F. temperature recorded by Mariner II, the water would always be in the vapor state and the average velocity of the molecules would frequently exceed the escape velocity. Thus Venus would not be expected to hold water.

Why is the ocean salty? The salts in the ocean are the result of two billion years of disintegration of the igneous rocks of the earth's crust. The soluble materials remain in the ocean; the insoluble precipitates have formed the young rocks that we call sedimentary rocks and have also formed the deep ocean sediments. The ocean therefore contains all the elements, including gold, originally present in the igneous rock to the extent that they are soluble, are not absorbed on clay particles, or are not removed by marine life.

Suspended matter (all too often, good soil) and dissolved salts extracted from the rocks of the continents are still being delivered to the sea by rivers. Much of this eroded material is from sedimentary rocks that have passed through the same cycle, although new sediments are being laid down at the same rate. The result is that the salt content of the sea remains steady. It has probably been at virtually the same composition for millions of years.

When changes in drainage pattern and climate cut off lakes from their outlets to the sea, they soon become salt lakes. The

Great Salt Lake in Utah is an example. Evaporation keeps it from overflowing, the salts leached out of the mountains remain behind, and in the 100,000 years since its parent Lake Bonneville became isolated, the Great Salt Lake has become about ten times as salty as the ocean. Most of the world's other salt lakes, such as the Dead Sea, the Caspian Sea and the Aral Sea, have built up salt in the same way, independently of the ocean. They represent oceans in miniature.

When one recalls that the total volume of the ocean is 328,-750,000 cubic miles, that it is stable and virtually inexhaustible (lacking some unimaginable cosmic catastrophe), it is ludicrous for modern man to talk of "water shortages." As we shall continually emphasize in subsequent chapters, our shortage is not of water but of *clean* water. We can regard the ocean as the ultimate in a polluted water reservoir, both in size and in degree of pollution. Any broad consideration of the future water management of the planet must necessarily include taking the salt out of sea water.

We have mentioned previously that water, although surrounding us within and without, is regarded by a chemist as a rather off-beat substance. One should also be reminded that some people consider water to be responsive to witchcraft. Underground water is thought to exert a mystical force which can twist a forked twig in the hands of the initiated. Thus, this silent, almost violent message calls the water seeker to a spot where a fruitful well can be dug.

The U.S. Geological Survey has published a learned monograph on the divining rod and the history of water witching, which it regards with ill-concealed disdain. The durability of this incredibly lunatic notion, which persists now into the late twentieth century, is shown by a book by the novelist Kenneth Roberts, who insisted with eloquence and passion that skeptics who doubted the reality of water location by dowsing should be in the same sheepish company with the opponents of Einstein and even Kepler. But the supporters of water witching also include at least one professional forester. Arthur M. Souder, in a publication put out by the U.S. Department of Agriculture, admits that he has the arcane power. He believes that such a gift, like extrasensory perception, is given to only a few chosen by God. He believes one person in a thousand has dowsing ability and one in ten thousand has his wizardry sufficiently well in hand to become a consistently successful dowser.

He describes the simple act. Forked twigs of many species of trees will work but those from the peach, apple or maple are best. He grasps the ends of the twigs firmly with palms up and the butt of the stick pointing skyward. As he nears water he feels a pull as the butt begins to dip downward. This is no gentle suggestion from the insistent waters. A stick of brittle wood will break under his grip as the butt dips. Pliable twigs will bend despite efforts to hold them straight, and the dowser who resists this irresistible summons may go home with blisters.

As one who long in populous city pent,
where houses thick and sewers annoy the air.
—MILTON, *Paradise Lost*

Whose hopes are water in a witch's sieve.
—ELINOR WYLIE, *Farewell, Sweet Dust*

3 DEAD WATERS THAT KILL

THE AVERAGE American city dweller, perhaps living in a seventeenth-floor apartment, never gives a thought to what happens to his urine and feces once he has flushed the toilet bowl. As far as he is concerned, this organic matter has suddenly disappeared from the face of the earth.

This is not true of India, and other backward countries because there human excrement is everywhere. As realistic observers of that great country have noted, the lower-class Indian is likely to defecate literally any place—on the street, on the shore of a beach, on a railroad track, in a rose garden, in a river. Subsisting predominately on high-residue grain foods, his bowel movements are massive and frequent. He takes some pride in them. It proves he is not starving. This must have been true in the great grain civilizations in the past, such as Babylonia, Egypt, China and the like, since no such thing as a separate sanitary sewer was constructed in the world until the eighteenth century.

This is not to say that fecal matter was left lying around to fester in the streets of sophisticated antiquity. It was seweraged but in sewer systems that had not been built primarily for this purpose; they had been designed to handle rain water. They were "storm sewers." Domestic wastes were dumped into this

tempestuous flow that reached the rivers. In the summers, however, things got rotten very suddenly. It is seldom realized
that in our country we are saddled with approximately the
same system—the so-called "combined sewer." Since practically
all American cities of a certain age have grown up with this
incredible abortion of a system, it is well that, in our examination of the past, we do not too complacently absolve the present and the future.

During the Akkadian supremacy in Southern Mesopotamia
(3000 B.C.) and in the Mohenjo-Daro culture at the same time
in the Indus Valley, ample drains were used to handle both
domestic sewage and rain water. This was satisfactory, at least
when it rained, as in the monsoon period in the Indus. In the
Akkadian palaces all bathrooms and water closets were ranged
along the outer side of the building so that the drains discharged directly into a vaulted main sewer, running the length
of the street beyond. They were of baked brick, jointed and
lined with bitumen, with open inspection chambers at their
principal junctions. The bathrooms had a pavement and a surrounding revetment of bitumen-covered brick. The water closets were raised pedestals with the occasional refinement of a
shaped bitumen seat. It must be emphasized that only the
patricians enjoyed such accommodation.

The palaces of Minos at Knossos in Crete had elaborate
drainage systems (before 1500 B.C.). Stone ducts and terra-cotta
pipes conveyed rain water from the roofs and terraces to spouts
in the outer walls. A latrine on the ground floor connected to a
main drain and provision was made for flushing it with rain
water, whence the raw sewage wound up in the Mediterranean.

In spite of its magnificent water-supply network, Rome had
a rather spotty sewerage system. In the sixth century B.C., Rome
built an elaborate combination of sewers leading into the
Cloaca Maxima. This was originally an open canal, but four
hundred years later it was roofed in. Lavish public baths partly

made up for the lack of sanitary provisions in the tenements, which had no means of heating, cooking and no drainage. Some of the larger private houses had cesspools. On some of the roads leading out of Rome there were public toilets at which a small charge was made. The public toilets near the Forum were incredibly chi-chi. There were twenty carved stone toilet seats, each flanked by graceful marble dolphins. A neighboring fountain flushed out the drains. There were also public latrines near the Forum at Ostia entered by a revolving door and provided with marble seats.

Refuse other than sewage, instead of being thrown into the Tiber, was collected by rag-and-bone men. This was unusual in the ancient world. Usually everything, including dead babies, went into the storm drains.

With the fall of the Roman Empire, not only did the water-collecting systems collapse but all pretense at sanitation was abandoned. In the towns of the Middle Ages people gaily hurled night soil out the windows into the street. There was no systematic drainage. It was an era when cleanliness was theologically suspect. The infrequent cesspools and latrines were located close to water wells. Open gutters in the midst of the street carried a fantastic regatta of refuse. The streets were never paved and consisted mainly of a succession of mud pools from which the excrement of pigs and cattle leaked into wells and private plots.

In the later Middle Ages filth caught up with medieval Europe. The Black Death wiped out an estimated one fourth to three fourths of the population in 1348-1349. Still the lesson had not been learned. In London the plague had recurred from time to time. Scavenging birds such as kites and ravens were protected by law and they and the pigs which roamed about grew fat on the offal of the streets. Evil-smelling dogs were innumerable. Scavenging officials were appointed, including Izaak Walton, the immortal fisherman.

In the records of Paris for 1412 reference is made to the "great drain," the brook of Ménilmontant into which drainage from the street gutters was discharged. Later this was walled in, then still later arched over. In 1513 the *coutume* (common law) in Paris decreed that every house should have its own privy. This seems to have been the least obeyed law in the history of mankind, since as late as the eighteenth century it was still a common habit to throw refuse into the street.

A survey carried out in Madrid as late as 1773 disclosed that the royal palace did not contain even one privy. When one talks of privies of those years, it is important to remember that the privies did not usually connect with a flowing sewerage system. They were the equivalent of "backhouses," which persist today. In many towns the contents of privies and domestic ashpits were collected at the same time as street sweepings. Some of the refuse was sold to farmers. By 1800 the houses of the well-to-do in England usually contained at least one privy, but for the poorer classes a common privy served a number of houses and became a place for gossiping, like the communal water fountains. Until well into the Victorian period there was little bashfulness about intestinal functions. Great nobles and even dames often held long conversations with their friends while seated upon the cloacal throne.

The privy population was significantly higher in Britain than in Europe on the whole, as we can learn from the writings of the terrible-tempered Tobias Smollett, who complained bitterly of the scarcity of privies in France and of their filthiness. Night-soil men emptied the privies of the wealthier houses but, as the first traces of Victorian fastidiousness began to be apparent, the London County Council prescribed that these collections should be made only between the hours of 4 A.M. and 10 A.M. from March to October and between 6 A.M. and 12 noon from November to February. This allowed enough daylight to discourage accidentally spilling all the slops on the stairway or the front stoop but, since these were hours when the people of quality were usually still in their beds, the offensive sight and smell and the dreadful possibility of brushing shoulders with a night-soil collector were avoided.

By the end of the eighteenth century the valved water closet had been developed in various forms, not dissimilar to that of today. This revolutionary apparatus was considered such an advance in sanitary mechanics that the people who could afford having them installed gained a false sense of purity. The closet was usually built into an enclosed cupboard and connected by an unventilated pipe directly to a cesspool, often located in the basement. The net result of such an arrangement was that foul gases were conveyed directly into the house from the evil-smelling cesspools. The houses of the wealthy stank worse than ever and were actually less healthful than before.

In order to prevent the passage of odors, traps containing a water seal were introduced. John Gaillait's patent in 1782 described his device as a "stink trap." This helped a great deal. Fancy water closets became popular but the problem of connecting them to cesspools or sewers remained, since one had the complication that bath water and the flow from kitchen sinks had to wind up in the same place as the toilet flow. The two-pipe system of house drainage (separate outlets from the W.C. and from lavatories, sinks and baths, but flowing into the same drains) was found to prevent all dirty smells from penetrating into the house, but it did not come into use in England and the civilized world in general until near the close of the nineteenth century.

As has been pointed out by discerning critics, Victorian and modern English literature is pervaded by the underlying guilt of sewer smells. Wilfrid Sheed observes "the mystic silence surrounding the post-Victorian bathroom [affected even] George Orwell, who brought the smell of excrement into almost everything he wrote."

Water closets were increasing in numbers in the early 1800's but drainage authorities at first insisted they should be connected to cesspools, not to sewers. As in the civilizations of antiquity, the main job of a sewer was believed to be to handle rain water. Since the cesspools were seldom emptied, the contents frequently overflowed and the surrounding ground became sodden, stagnant and covered with flies. However, this regulation in favor of cesspools did not last long. The domestic sewage was diverted to the shallow storm sewers and in large towns this became compulsory. The result was the transfer of sewage contamination from the ground on which the houses stood to the nearest river.

This was one of the most critical and perhaps disastrous decisions ever made in our civilization. We shall see later in more detail that, if *separate* drain systems for domestic sewage and for carrying off rain water had been instituted at this time, the great American cities would probably have continued such a design practice and we would not now be faced with an astronomically expensive and almost impossible problem of urban redevelopment. As it is, every time it rains hard in most of our cities, our sewers overflow or back up and sewage is left strewing the streets. In one particular storm in one of our major cities pollutants were entering the receiving stream at a rate nine times that which would have occurred *if the city had discharged all its sewage untreated.* This was because the storm not only made bypassing necessary but flushed out the sewers as well.

However, the die was cast in London. Sewage began to fill the rivers and a series of great public catastrophes took place. Now the problem of sewage was mixed up inextricably with the problem of supplying drinking water. Bacteriology was not yet existent as a science. Nobody could distinguish a typhoid bacillus from a sand flea. In England in 1843 the Poor Law Commissioners investigated sewage and draining and twiddled their thumbs, even though the banks of the Thames in the wider reaches between Waterloo and Westminster bridges became covered with a vast accumulation of foul mud exposed at low tide. It was going to take some killing to get anything done, and indeed killing promptly ensued. Cholera in 1849 and 1853 killed 20,000 people in London. In the Western world this was the greatest pollution disaster of history. John Snow did a classical piece of detective work on the 1854 cholera outbreak in the Soho district, where he found that nearly every one of hundreds of victims had drunk water from the same pump on Broad Street, which got its water supply untreated from the sewage-infested Thames.

Paralyzing typhoid epidemics hit the town of North Boston, New York, in 1843, Plymouth, Pennsylvania, in 1885, and Hamburg on the Elbe River in 1892. There were innumerable smaller epidemics of typhoid and paratyphoid fever, all traceable to sewage-contaminated water. Even today sewage-infected water causing typhoid and cholera accounts for over 20 percent of the hospital beds available in India, China and the Middle East. Infectious hepatitis from sewage-polluted water or from eating oysters or clams in filthy rivers became a widespread disease and is now the worst danger of all in the United States. In 1956 one of the greatest water-borne epidemics of hepatitis ever recorded took place in Delhi, and less widespread American occurrences are quite common. A bad epidemic from eating oysters occurred in Mississippi in 1961, in Sweden in 1958; in 1961 from infected clams from the interstate water of New York and New Jersey and the coastal waters of Connecticut. More recently typhoid broke out in Florida from the consumption of polluted oysters. Viral hepatitis is tricky, since the chain of infection can be extended by merely handling or contacting infected articles such as toilet seats, flush tank handles and bathroom doorknobs.

It is interesting to note that among famous victims of water-borne diseases were Louis VIII of France, Charles X of Sweden, Prince Albert of England, his son Edward VII and his grandson George V. George Washington suffered from dysentery from bad water. Abigail Adams, the wife of John Adams, Zachary Taylor, and (ironically) Louis Pasteur's two daughters died of typhoid fever, caused by contaminated water.

Because of all the large European cities London had suffered the most, it took the most vigorous steps to control the sewage-contamination problem, although the authorities were working in the dark until the discovery in 1880 by Eberth of the typhoid bacillus, in 1883 Koch's isolation of the cholera microorganism and Pasteur's studies of sterilization. In 1885 Franklund began the routine biological analysis of water supplied by the London water companies. He showed that slow filtration through sand would reduce the bacterial content by 98 percent. This dates the modern period of water treatment.

London's first and brilliantly successful step to reduce sewage contamination of the Thames was to lay large sewers running parallel to the river and to divert the sewage into the river far downstream. The city became almost a wholesome place to live in.

Of course, people still worked and dwelt near the outfalls, and the London Metropolitan Board of Works, after being besieged through many years of complaints, considered the adoption of land irrigation to purge the water. It was decided that the buying of land to let sewage filter through the soil would cost too much. The Board finally constructed works for the precipitation or chemical clarification of sewage at the outfalls. London wound up early with a much more sophisticated sewerage system than most American cities have today.

The great sewers of Paris have been made the scene of dramatic novels, but perhaps no more curious class of people existed than the "toshers" of London in the nineteenth century, who spent all day underground searching for metals, money, etc. ("tosh"). One would expect such men to be hollow-eyed and to give the general impression of the pale twitching bellies of dying fish. On the contrary, the toshers were strong, robust, generally florid in complexion and very well satisfied with their job. Some men of eighty had followed this trade all their lives and believed that the sewer odor contributed to their health and longevity. It must be pointed out, however, that sewermen, unless they were very careful, were liable to attacks of leptospiral jaundice (Weil's disease), due to the presence of rats. The disease is contracted through abrasions in the skin. Thus even in this paradise the serpent's tooth gleamed!

The average sewage is 99.9 percent water. The remaining 0.1 percent consists of approximatly equal parts of sand or grit and organic matter, such as feces, fat, and vegetable matter. Aside from contamination with disease-carrying organisms, the organic matter if not removed by treatment takes up dissolved oxygen and releases foul gases. When discharged into a river in large enough amounts, the sewage will use up all the oxygen in the water and thus kill fish or aquatic plants. As we shall see in a later chapter, this has become a desperate problem for the fishing industry and for sport fishermen in the great American rivers. Appropriately enough, the Izaak Walton League (recalling that this great fishing author was at one time an official scavenger) has campaigned heartily for giving the fish a break. Some of our rivers have zero oxygen content, on which not even trash fish can live.

As noted previously, the complete sterilization of drinking water and of sewage had to await the discovery of bacteria and the finding that treatment with chlorine would kill the bugs. Few sewage-treating plants to this day involve chemical treatment, although chlorine is becoming nearly universal for safeguarding drinking water.

Typical good standard practice in an American city or town involves, however, the actual use of bacteria to clean up the

sewage water to the extent that it can be released to a stream
or outfall to the ocean without gross contamination. The sewage is first screened to remove dead mice and condoms. (Sometimes this is *all* that happens to it.) It then is often treated
with "activated sludge." This is simply sludge that has settled
from previous treatment and has accumulated a lot of sewage-
consuming bacteria. The solids, still containing large amounts
of water, are digested in the absence of air for a period of
hours or days. The solids that are still left are dried on sand or
with filters and may be disposed of to farmers as fertilizer. This
residue no longer shows coliform bacteria but may contain some
animal parasites. The treated sewage water then goes to a river
or to the ocean or may be used in irrigation or for some industrial purposes. Without additional drastic chemical treatment, however, such water is not fit for drinking. Most of the
towns of this country, with the exception of those that have
grown up on the banks of giant rivers and have become ac-
customed to the river as a catchall, have tried to do a reasonable job of sewerage. Very often the towns have gone far beyond the requirements of the local state health departments,
whose specifications are frequently absurdly tolerant.

Red Wing, Minnesota (population 11,000), is a typical example of a town that treats its sewage far more thoroughly
than the state of Minnesota regulations would require. It removes 90 percent of organic wastes, although a simple "primary" treatment, including merely sedimentation to remove
only 30 percent of the organics would have satisfied the state.
Red Wing has sedimentation, bacterial digestion in the presence of air over trickle tile filters, and anaerobic digestion (in
the absence of air) to let a different type of bacteria consume
the waste, and finally chlorination in a four-hour basin. This
water is fit to feed Lake Pepin, a popular water-sports resort.
It is noteworthy that the Mississippi in the vicinity of Red Wing
contains raw sewage equivalent to that from a 660,000 popula-

tion. Hopefully this can be improved when sewage treatment at Minneapolis-St. Paul is reconstructed to remove 75 percent of the organic matter.

In some of the most modern city sewage plants, such as the one now designed for Chicago to handle 1.7 billion gallons a day, closed-circuit television circuits are spotted around the plant to send pictures of the various processes to the control room. Instead of hand-sampling water to determine the amount of treating chemicals needed, samples flow continuously through tubes to a laboratory, where a computer signals if treating instructions are not being followed with precision.

Yet some river towns, especially in the South, have no sewage system at all—not even septic tanks. So-called "honey-wagons" go from door to door and collect the shallow tanks of fecal matter and empty it into the river.

In rural homes and in some communities the only answer is the septic tank and, if well designed, it is not a bad answer. The septic tank is in effect a private anaerobic sewage digestor. The special bacteria in such a tank, acting in the absence of air and over a long enough period of time, destroy practically all the organic material. The overflow from the septic tank is conveyed over farm drain tiles laid in the top soil below the probable depth of any cultivating instrument. The overflow is suitable for plants but should not be allowed to percolate back into the farmer's well. Unfortunately, this often happens, as we shall discuss in the chapter on "White Beer."

In most countries the contamination of water with sewage increases as rapidly as attempts at correction. The pace of water purification barely keeps up with increased loadings in Western Europe and the United States. In the United States almost 20 million people still discharged raw sewage to waterways in the middle 1960's in spite of the fact that over 8,000 treatment plants were in service for some 80 million persons.

A new fright in water contamination was aroused by a discovery in 1960 of Dr. Shih Lu Chang of the Robert A. Taft Sanitary Engineering Center at Cincinnati. This was the fact that otherwise pure water from various American rivers contains microscopic worms called nematodes, which can carry pathogenic bacteria and viruses. These nematodes are able to withstand chlorination and other severe treatment and act as protectors of the microorganisms attached to them. Thus a nematode can slip through a whole water purification system, carrying in its stomach, so to speak, the undigested bacteria. The worms are known to breed in sewage-disposal plants.

Nematode infestation has been found in treated drinking water from the Mississippi in both Louisiana and Illinois, from the Missouri River in Kansas, from the Potomac in Maryland, the Colorado River in California, the Columbia, the Chattahoochee in Georgia, the Delaware in Pennsylvania, the Detroit River, the Rio Grande in Texas, the Merrimack in New Hampshire and Massachusetts, the Niagara in New York, and the Tennessee River.

Treated water from Lake Michigan was found to contain nematodes but water from Lake Superior was free of them.

This is so new a threat that nobody has decided just how serious it may be or how to cope with it. Water containing appreciable numbers of nematodes has a strange musty odor.

A new mystery in water contamination, which may or may not have anything to do with nematodes, came to light in the pleasant little city of Riverside, California, in the late spring of 1965. In order to understand the baffling and perhaps revolutionary nature of the puzzle, it is necessary to review the way drinking water is usually tested for sewage contamination.

A quick routine check is made for the presence of the coliform bacteria, which are harmless organisms living in the human intestine and are very easy to detect. If any are found in a sample of drinking water, the alarm is sounded, since it is then obvious that contamination by inadequately treated sewage has occurred. A more difficult and elaborate series of tests may then be made for pathogenic bacilli and viruses, including those causing typhoid, cholera, viral hepatitis, dysentery, and other water-borne infections.

In the Riverside case the worst epidemic of gastroenteritis in the world in twenty-five years, affecting 18,000 people, suddenly took place for no apparent rhyme or reason. The bug causing the diarrhea, fever and general malaise, with a few deaths, was identified as *Salmonella typhimurium*, an agent of ill-repute in food poisoning. But there was no common source of staple food that could have resulted in the enormous number of primary infections. Examination of the city's water supply, which comes untreated from deep wells, showed *Salmonella* in the water, and steps to chlorinate it were immediately taken. However, here is the sinister part of this epidemic: *no coliform bacteria were found in the water*. This was the aspect of the water-borne epidemic that started epidemiologists and public health experts flying to Riverside from all over the world. Thirteen investigators showed up from Atlanta alone, where the U.S. Public Health Service's Communicable Disease Center is located. Two tentative explanations have so far been advanced. A septic tank in an outlying area of the city was found to have leaked into one of the city wells. This would mean that *Salmonella* is able to resist the digestive treatment which eliminates the coliform bacteria. This is hard to believe, since the coliforms are normally more resistant than any of the pathogenic bugs. Another clue was a leak in the water line in a beet field which had been fertilized by chicken manure. This might produce the organism, but it would be a unique and unexpected phenomenon.

The Riverside case is still the weirdest and most important water-contamination mystery in modern times. It may result in a complete and expensive overhauling of the way domestic water is tested. It may add millions of dollars per week, in order to include worldwide the routine assay for a variety of specific bacteria and viruses instead of the one standard coliform test.

It is obvious that the problem of sewage and its contamination of city drinking water is far from solved.

In the United States our sewage-disposal plants are adequate to serve only between 70 and 80 percent of the people who use them, and a huge amount of raw, untreated sewage still gets into the Great Lakes and the larger rivers. The St. Lawrence Waterway has brought in more ships that dump sewage in the Great Lakes. Lake Erie can be regarded as one big sewage reservoir. The multiplication of large motorboats with "heads" that simply dump raw toilet effluent into the water is believed to have caused more than one minor hepatitis epidemic. Astonishingly enough, Uncle Sam himself is one of the worst offenders.

In 1961 various federal installations discharged over 46 million gallons per day of untreated sewage directly into surface waters or on the ground: this was 3 percent of the total estimated 1,500 million gallons of municipal sewage discharged without treatment, but it is a very dirty 3 percent. The Marine Corps base at Camp Lejeune, North Carolina, sewaged up the New River area so effectively that a serious epidemic of viral hepatitis broke out from people (including Marines) eating infected oysters. Chlorination of the camp's sewage was obviously indicated immediately but repeated letters from state authorities to the Department of the Navy in Washington elicited no replies.

The Navy has also maintained a stony imperturbability in regard to the incredibly filthy ship sewage conditions which it causes in Pearl Harbor, Hawaii. Under the present laws, lacking an official complaint from the Governor of Hawaii, all the Public Health Service can do is wait until the sewage drifts to the California coast, whereupon Governor Brown could summon in the Federals, who have express authority over *interstate* pollution squabbles. That could be quite a while, and in the meantime the principal harbor of our fiftieth state festers and stinks in the sunlight of the beautiful isles.

Other federal sewage scandals exist at: Hamilton Air Force Base, Marin County, California (only primary treatment, while all civilian sewage discharging to San Pablo Bay receives secondary treatment); Elmendorf Air Force Base, Anchorage, Alaska (raw sewage); England Air Force Base, Rapides Parish, Louisiana (raw sewage to the Red River); Philadelphia Navy Base (raw sewage and industrial waste to the Delaware River); U.S. Federal Penitentiary, Steilacoom, Washington (untreated sewage and wastes from cannery, laundry, piggery, slaughterhouse and milk-processing plant discharge to Puget Sound); U.S. Coast Guard Yard, Baltimore (sewage from urinals and toilets discharged to 15 septic tanks, 14 of which overflow to nearby water courses).

Although Congress has specific legislation before it to ring the bell on such disgusting practices, it is intrinsically more difficult to get the military authorities to move than to persuade the municipalities. Cleaning their own sewage is not part of their "primary mission." If the Bureau of the Budget narrows them down to a choice between a new football field and a sewage-treating project, they will always choose the football field.

A U.S. Senate committee has reported that we must spend at least $600 million a year nationwide merely to catch up with the need for sewage-treating facilities, civil and military. In order to meet present deficiencies and future needs it will require $1.7 billion a year until 1980 and increasing amounts after that. This is a very conservative estimate, since it does not take into account the installation of separate sewers for water run-off and for domestic and industrial wastes.

This problem of the combination sewer, referred to previously, may be pinpointed with St. Louis as an example. Not long ago St. Louis bonded itself to the tune of $125 million for

trunk sewers and treatment plants alone. But still during a summer downpour the city is a disgusting mess. You see toilet
paper and fecal matter out in the streets. Crews from the Metropolitan St. Louis Sewer District have to get out after a storm
and hose this stuff down the gutters. Peter Mattei, executive
director of the district, has testified that additional relief sewers
to handle the problem would cost a billion dollars. This is an
agonizingly expensive operation from the standpoint of both
direct and indirect expense since streets have to be torn up,
private yards invaded and buildings remodeled. St. Louis does
not have that kind of money. Neither do the scores of other
cities plagued with the disastrous combination sewer system.

One troublesome drawback to all present sewage-treating
processes must be emphasized. This is the fact that even severe
chemical treatments leave certain phosphorus- and nitrogen-
containing compounds in the effluent water. These are nutrients for aquatic life and, from that point of view, are looked
upon with some favor by the Fish and Wildlife Division of the
Department of the Interior. However, beyond a certain limit
they become water despoilers. They result in such a tremendous
growth of algae (miscroscopic water plants) that the available
dissolved oxygen is used up, and the water is again a dark and
unhealthy mess.

An interesting positive use of reclaimed sewage waters for
growing algae is in making food for animals. At Lancaster,
California, the North American Aviation Company has harvested algae, which are high in protein, and fed them to
chickens, which thrived.

A curious instance of the indirect effect of upsetting the
balance of nature by providing too much marine nutrient is
the disappearance of the once lush kelp forests off the coast of
Southern California. The kelp has been devoured by sea urchins. These ravenous pincushionlike creatures have multiplied in
unprecedented numbers as the result of the vast outfall sewage

increase from the Los Angeles Basin. Maybe we can find something that will eat the sea urchins.

One exciting new idea in sewage treatment has been kicked around in the past few years and has especially caught the fancy of the great conservationist, U.S. Supreme Court Justice W. O. Douglas. This is to combine sewage treatment with desalting and the recovery of potable water in general. A case in point is the Potomac River Basin. A typical old-fashioned grandiose solution to the horrible filth of the Potomac was the Army Corps of Engineers' program embodying an extremely expensive dam at Seneca, Maryland, the chief function of which would be to supply a load of water for flushing the river of sewage—a kind of giant toilet tank, so to speak. A brilliant analysis of this plan by A. W. Smith of the National Park Association demonstrated that the cost of installing a coal-fired water distillation plant to purify the river would be only three fourths of the cost of the dam; furthermore, the dam would not really do the job, since sewage effluent gathered in the embayments would not be measurably affected by flushing of the deep-water channels. The operating costs of the dam, according to Smith's estimates, would also be greater.

Who would want to drink reclaimed sewage? This has been a much-abused question, but is an essentially nonsensical one because millions have been doing it to some degree or other for years. Reclaimed sewage water can be as pure as a mountain spring.

Actually a large percentage of chemically treated municipal water throughout the country has been exposed to sewage contamination. Chicago's potable water comes from Lake Michigan, for example, a sink for innumerable small and large sewer systems.

A case where sewage water is directly and deliberately processed into drinking water is that of the Whittier Narrows water reclamation plant of the Los Angeles County sanitation districts. The plant takes millions of gallons of sewage a day from an enormous area. First the solid matter is settled out in the usual primary step; it is then exposed to activated sludge and is finished off with chlorine. At this stage the California Institute of Technology can find nothing wrong with it. But even so—in order to appease the nervous Nellies—the Whittier Narrows water does not go directly into local water lines. Instead it is pumped into spreading basins. There it settles into the ground-water supply of the county. Diluted by the natural ground water, it is then pumped into community faucets from wells.

Pennsylvania State University is doing some research work on the use of treated sewage water for use in irrigation. The 3-million-gallon-per-day effluent from the community of State College is put through filtration, aeration, an activated sludge step, and chlorination to remove 95 percent of the waste's biochemical oxygen demand (BOD), making it nearly pure enough to drink. It is then sprinkled through special nonfreezing spray heads to replenish ground-water supplies in the area. Percolation through the soil results in removal of 99 percent of the phosphorous and 88 percent of the nitrogen and practically all of the detergents. The success of this kind of treatment depends on the soil. If it is too porous, the percolation time is not long enough to use the soil as a treating material; if it is too impervious, waterlogging will occur.

We need not only an open-minded consideration of new concepts of sewage management, we need a new way of extracting money from the citizens. Bond issues and property taxes for sewers are reaching the end of their elastic breaking point. One solution would be to establish sewerage as a straight utility rather than as a tiny increment added to the water bill. A houseowner gladly pays $11 a month for a telephone service. Why shouldn't he pay a somewhat similar amount to have his household wastes disposed of in a thoroughly safe and foolproof manner?

And the waters shall fail from the sea, and the river shall be wasted and dried up. And they shall turn rivers far away; and the brooks of defence shall be emptied and dried; the reeds and flags shall wither.

—ISAIAH 19:5-6 (prophecy against Egypt)

The Sea of Galilee and the Dead Sea are made of the same water. It flows down, clear and cool, from the heights of Hermon and the roots of the cedars of Lebanon. The Sea of Galilee makes beauty of it, for the Sea of Galilee has an outlet. It gets to give. It gathers in its riches that it may pour them out again to fertilize the Jordan plain. But the Dead Sea with the same water makes horror. For the Dead Sea has no outlet. It gets to keep.

—HARRY EMERSON FOSDICK

4 LORDS *of the* MODERN WATERS— ASIA *and* AFRICA

THE LORDS OF THE ancient waters had for the most part only small pieces of land and parts of river basins to work with. The modern lords have whole subcontinents to engineer. Perhaps the most grandiose proposal of all the history of water is the North American Water and Power Alliance (NAWAPA), which would transfer surplus water from Alaska, Northern Canada and the Columbian Basin to the Great Lakes, the Southwestern United States and to Mexico. This would cost $100 billion and take 30 years to complete but would presumably solve the North American water problem for 100 years. We shall have more to say about such projects, which unfortunately involve nearly as much geographical word combat as they do engineering grandeur. First let us understand some world numbers about water.

The total amount of rain and snow falling on the earth

each year is about 380 billion acre-feet; 300 billion on the
ocean and 80 billion on the land (an acre-foot is enough water
to cover an acre of land to a depth of one foot; it is 325,872 gallons). The volume of water carried to the sea by glaciers, rivers
and coastal springs is 27 billion acre-feet per year. This water
is essentially uncontrolled. Even agriculture, man's principal
consumer, takes little of the available supply. A billion acre-
feet per year (less than 4 percent of the total river flow) is used
to irrigate 310 million acres of land, or about 1 percent of the
land area of the world.

It is evident that the world's water problem is not total
lack of water but scarcity of cheap water or clean water at the
places where it is needed.

In the first chapter we have mentioned the ancient Egyptian
hydraulic civilization based on controlled flooding of the Nile
in June and July. This wasn't good enough for Egypt to compete as a thriving nation in later centuries. In 1820 the population of Egypt had dropped to 2.5 million with 3 million cultivated acres. This was the year of a critical decision. Egypt went
to year-around irrigation and widespread planting of summer
crops, including cotton, corn, rice and sugar cane as well as
the time-hallowed winter crops of wheat, barley, beans, onions,
flax and clover. Low dams called "Barrages" were built across
the river, and the water thus backed up was diverted through
large new canals that flowed all year long. By 1956 the cultivated acreage had more than doubled and so had the intensity
of cultivation. Egypt was able to support a population of 27
million. As the great hydrologist Roger Revelle points out, from
the standpoint of crop yields per acre, although not per man,
Egypt is a developed country. Politically speaking, our dona-
tions of wheat to Nasser are not truly needed but are used by
that wily man to execute trade deals with Cuba and other nations unfriendly to us.

With the completion of the Aswan High Dam the river will

be under complete control. There will no longer be a Nile flood. The reconstructed river will become simply a huge feeder canal for irrigation.

On the other hand, an instance where modern hydraulic dreams applied to an ancient river basin have ended in ghastly disillusionment is the Indus River system in West Pakistan. This has turned out to be a classical case of what not to do in conservation. The Indus and its tributaries carry more than twice the flow of the Nile. Half this tremendous volume has been diverted into an intricate system of canals and is used to irrigate some 23 million acres—by far the largest single irrigated region on earth. In spite of this, the 50 million people of the Punjab and Sind areas are nearly starving. Food has to be imported to keep them half alive. What happened?

Primarily what invariably happens when megabucks are spent on a people so ignorant and socially degraded that giving them an astronomically expensive water system is like offering them a nuclear bomb to play with. They would not drain the farms even with the unsophisticated techniques used in America in the nineteenth century, hence the flatlands became waterlogged and covered with salt. Many of the farmers are sharecropping tenants whose landlords are living it up in Paris, hence incentive is lacking. Plowing is done by a wooden stick pulled by undernourished bullocks. Unselected seeds are scattered blindly to the wind. Pakistan uses only a hundredth as much fertilizer per acre as Egypt. The poverty is so crushing that the illiterate farmer does not dare to do anything newer than was done 4,000 years ago, because failure will mean total starvation. The irrigation canals look very formidable on a map but they lose so much water by seepage that when they reach the fields there is only enough water to irrigate half the land during each season. Thus most of the cropped area receives too little water even to prevent salt accumulation.

There is another kind of handicap to modern irrigation in

backward countries: disease and plant pests. The Western Asiatic peoples in nine cases out of ten will prefer malaria and bilharzia to the rather drastic steps necessary for the prevention of such diseases. They regard plant pests as traditional warnings from Allah, not to be argued with by way of chemical pesticides, and thus they are true Rachel Carson-ites, without having heard of that great lady.

Somewhat the same combination of problems of water, land and people now exist in the Tigris-Euphrates valleys, on a smaller scale with the sour string notes of religious hatred as an accompaniment. Obviously the once Fertile Crescent, a much smaller place than the Indus Valley, requires revitalizing as a river basin rather than as a collection of small belligerent nations. However, the Arabs are bound, as a matter of strategic warfare, to divert river water from Israel, and Israel is in a similar diverting mood. Thus a river system is pulled to pieces by Jews and Hashimites, with guns in their hands as they redistribute the forlorn earth that was ruined centuries ago.

The fact remains that if the flow of the Tigris-Euphrates could be fully put to work, if the soils were well leached of salt and drained, the irrigation area cultivated each year could be increased from about four million acres to twelve million.

If greater water usage were combined with year-round cropping, better farming practices and big shots of chemical fertilizers, the total agricultural production could be raised at least fivefold.

Israel, with a tougher problem, is doing a better job than Jordan or Syria. The philosophy of Israel's National Water Carrier Project is to make the best of almost impossible weather variations, where in a small country the rainfall runs from 40 inches in the Upper Galilee region to 1.25 inches at the southern end of the Negev Desert. Moreover, a wicked peculiarity is that the most rain falls at the lowest elevations of altitude, so gravity is of little use in moving water. Unfortunately the most important feature of the plan (to take water from the Jordan Fork in order to prevent the desperate drop in level of the two main water tables in the country) was violently objected to by Syria, the objections being punctuated by cannonades. The plan was referred to the United Nations and vetoed by Soviet Russia in the Security Council.

A Unified Water Plan proposed by Eric Johnston in 1955 would have given to Lebanon and Syria the full amounts specified by their governments for the irrigation of farms in the headwater region and to Jordan the water required for all of its irrigable lands; Israel would have received 40 percent of the entire flow. The United States offered a carrot in the form of a $200 million gift to start the dirt moving. This appeared to be satisfactory to all four parties involved, but the political committee of the Arab League tabled the proposal. Nasser has frankly admitted that he wants to goad Israel into an offensive war by keeping it thirsty.

Another area of the earth aching for intelligent water control is the lower basin of the Ganges and Brahmaputra rivers where 140 million people of East Pakistan and the Indian States of Bengal, Bihur and Assam live on 70 million cultivated acres. Soil and water in this land are insulted and injured. Each year, at the time of the monsoon, rivers carry a billion acre-feet to the Bay of Bengal and in the process they flood most of the country. Yet only one crop is grown a year and the land is left idle half the year because of the shortage of water and for six to eight months all the people have to do is manufacture babies on an insane and accelerating scale. These human beings are so antiquated in their agricultural traditions that they do not even approach the Egyptians of 6,000 years ago.

There is no doubt that a few billions of dollars spent on surface and underground storage of the waters that come with the monsoon could give them three crops a year over more than half of the cultivable area in the alluvial plain. A year-round water supply would make conditions favorable for the intensive use of fertilizers, higher yielding plants and better farming practice. Yields per crop and per acre could be tripled for cereals, pulses (the edible seeds of leguminous plants such as peas and beans) and oil seeds. A balanced diet could be provided for twice the population. What is more likely is that they will get twice the population anyway and that they will starve. They need some tremendous jolt that will educate 140 million Rip Van Winkles to be twentieth-century men. A sophisticated irrigation system, as in West Pakistan, would simply be more water down a rat hole. Without birth control it would be an expensive futility.

Perhaps the most dynamic instances of modern Asian lordship of the waters, long overdue, are in Soviet Russia. Between 1950 and 1960, 15 million acres near the Black and Caspian seas got their first irrigation water from the Volga, Dnieper, Amu Darya and Syr Darya rivers. Soviet engineers have outlined a gigantic plan, similar in scope and premise to the North American NAWAPA concept. They would build an immense dam on the Ob River, creating an inland sea about the size of Italy and a canal to connect the Ob and the Yenisei above the dam. The impounded waters would be led through an unprecedented system of canals, rivers and lakes to the Aral Sea and the Caspian Sea. Several hundred million acre-feet of water that now go to waste every year in the Arctic Ocean would thus be conserved and used to irrigate 50 million acres of crop lands and a somewhat larger area of pasture in arid western Siberia and Kazakhstan. Accompaning hydroelectric power installations would have a capacity of more than 70 million kilowatts. Major water storage, irrigation and hydroelectric works are under construction or planned in the northern Caucasus and in the Azerbaijan, Georgian and Armenian Soviet Republics.

Evidence that the Soviets are not kidding in this giant effort to build up agriculture by continent-carving is the fact that they are purchasing the know-how for chemical fertilizer manufacturing plants from Western countries at an unheard-of rate. It remains to be seen whether they can get Ivan the Muzhik to go along with all these dazzling agenda. It was not too long ago that Ivan's father could be taken out and shot for having more than one cow.

What about other continents, other peoples? Aside from Egypt, the prospects are ambiguous in North Africa. In the Maghreb countries—Tunisia, Algeria and Morocco—there is superficially not enough water north of the Sahara to irrigate more than 3.5 million acres of land, yet the combined population is already 26 million (equal to Egypt's) and will double in twenty years.

To indicate the ingenious extremities to which thirsty peoples will go, water in the Egyptian Sudan is stored in the trunks of large hollow trees. The openings are sealed with wet clay to keep the water pure. Thousands of these small reservoirs, which hold from 300 to 1,000 gallons each, appear along roads of travel. In one province all the trees are registered and the contents noted for information on the water content.

There is one exciting possibility that might completely reverse this gloomy outlook for North Africa. Recently an oil-drilling company was hired by the Libyan government to drill a water well near the village of Sokna, deep in the desert. Geologists said they should hit water at about 2,000 feet. Instead, at 650 feet the bit hit a high-pressure artesian zone that shot 52,000 gallons an hour of sweet water over the top of the derrick. Libya has never seen anything like it before. The water is expected to transform a whole region that once had to haul drinking water for more than 20 miles. This is one more piece of evidence that large areas in the Sahara may be underlain by an enormous lake of fresh water. In some places the water-bearing sands are 3,000 feet thick and appear to extend for at

least 500 miles south of the Atlas Mountains and perhaps eastward into Tunisia. If this proves to be the case, the amount of
useful water may be of the order of 100 billion acre-feet, sufficient to irrigate many millions of acres for centuries. All of
North Africa could become a garden.

Superficially, it would seem that great possibilities exist for
water control and large-scale agricultural civilizations in the Af-
rican and South American regions of the savanna climate,
which are characterized by an annual cycle of heavy rainfall
during one season, followed by drought the remainder of the
year and by hot weather at all seasons. In Equatorial Africa, for
example, many millions of what are now barren acres could
be brought under irrigated cultivation, provided that interested
farmers could be found, in the neighborhood of the great bend
of the Niger River in former French West Africa, in the basin
of the Rafifi of Tanganyika, and near Lake Kyoga in Uganda.

As in the Mekong River and Amazon River basins, however, there is an ugly and hitherto little appreciated worm in
the apple. This is "lateritic soil." It is becoming gradually realized that the catastrophically wide distribution of this soil type
may make nearly all tropical lands incapable of development
for modern agriculture.

Laterite is a mineral-rich earth that, when exposed to air,
turns into a brick-like form of rock (the name comes from the
Latin word for brick). It has been an important building material since prehistoric times. A lateritic soil is rich in iron and
aluminum, low in silica and chemically acidic. It is usually red
or yellow. Laterized soils occur most commonly in the tropical
belt between latitudes 30° North and 30° South, although laterization has ruined some soil in Ireland—evidence that tropical
conditions once prevailed, for example, in County Kerry. Laterite soil is formed primarily by high rainfall, even if limited
to one season, and by high temperature. Such a soil is rapidly
leached. Under tropical conditions overluxuriant growth of bac-

teria, insects and earthworms break down the organic material
in the soil and also aerate it to make it permeable to oxygen
and vulnerable to leaching.

A pathetic paradox arises. One always imagines that the
lush jungle, rain forests and savannas of the tropics are proof
of enormous soil fertility. One drools at the enormous yield of
food crops that could be raised if the Amazonian jungles, for
example, were to be cleared for agriculture.

Actually, because of laterization, these tropical soils are extremely poor, a fact veiled by the spectacular wild flash vegetation caused by superabundant water. That the tropical forests
and grasslands cover some of the earth's most inhospitable soils
has been proved by attempts to wrest cultivated crops from
them. Put to the plow, these lands yield an incredibly small return and soon become completely infertile. Once a lateritic field
has been laid bare to the air it may harden into brick of the
type used in the ancient walled city of Angkor Thom of Cambodia. In the Amazon Basin there are accumulations of lateritic
soil 70 feet thick.

At Iata, an equatorial mass of blazing green jungle in the
heart of the Amazon Basin, the Brazilian government sent in
tree-pulling and earth-moving machinery and planted seed in a
large clearing that was expected to furnish luscious crops for
an agricultural colony. But what had seemed to be rich land,
with a promising cover of humus, disintegrated after the first
planting. Under the brilliant sun the iron-rich soil began to bake
into brick. In less than five years the cleared fields became
virtually pavements of rock. Today Iata is a squalid, despairing
colony that has to have food sent upriver to it.

The small country of Dahomey, adjoining Nigeria in tropical West Africa, had the same experience. There the replace-
ment of forests by plantations resulted in deep leaching of the
soil and converted large areas into brick over a period of sixty
years. Small clearings in such a forest for the "milpa" type of

farming, common among forest people all over the world, will exhaust the soil within a year or so. Under native customs the forest community simply moves to another milpa and the original worked-out site returns to jungle-type shrubbery. This happens, however, only where the clearings are small. Large areas cleared for plantation farming are lost to agriculture after a few crop cycles have turned the soil to brick.

It is believed that the ancient, highly evolved Khmer culture in Cambodia may have perished because of lateritic soil. Probably for the same reason the Mayas, who flourished in Central America at the same times as the Khmers in Southeast Asia, and who used the milpa system of agriculture, were forced to abandon their cities and move north into Mexico.

The lateritic soils must be babied by experts. Sophisticated fertilizing, crop rotation and movement of plantations every few years are all absolutely necessary. Cuba is an example of a lateritic country going downhill because of inexpert soil and water management. The great sugar plantations will not produce much more than two successive stands of cane on a given tract.

This matter of lateritic soils in underdveloped tropical countries should be carefully noted by Peace Corps workers. There is some evidence that such well-meaning but frequently uninformed people may be inviting disaster by trying to apply the agricultural methods of the U.S. Corn Belt to Nigeria, for example. Deep plowing of the soil will accelerate leaching and quickly strip the soil of all organic nutrients. The opening up of vast tracts to cultivation, in order to make efficient use of tractors and other modern farm machinery, will lead rapidly to the laying down of the best sources of brick houses in Africa but it will certainly not help the Nigerians to eat better.

Some of the large river-valley plans now projected, such as the Mekong River system of Southeast Asia, the Amazon Basin of Brazil, the Niger River of Nigeria, the Volta River of Ghana, threaten to lead to complete devastation. This may appear strange in view of the fact, for example, that the Mekong Valley is now part of Asia's famous "Rice Bowl." The paradox is resolved if one examines the pattern of water and soil. Each year the growing of crops depletes the highly leached soil. But then in the monsoon season the overflowing rivers flood the land and replenish it with a new layer of fertile silt from the uplands. But what will happen when the designers of the Mekong River Plan stop the annual floods? One can expect the fatal cycles of permanent soil depletion and brick formation to ensue and to represent a ghastly disaster for this whole part of the globe.

The phenomenon of lateritic soils is one of the most serious that the planet faces. It is also a signal to the lords of the modern waters that there are times when one should hesitate to rush in with bulldozers and should wait until all the soil analysis data are in before building a dam. It may turn out that the tropical jungles, rain forests and savannas are the only wilderness we can afford ultimately to retain on earth.

Ye marshes, how candid and simple and
nothing-withholding and free
Ye publish yourselves to the sky and
offer yourselves to the sea!
Tolerant plains, that suffer the sea and
the rains and the sun . . .
—LANIER, *The Marshes of Glynn*

The moving waters at their priest-like task
Of pure ablution round earth's human shores . . .
—KEATS, *Last Sonnet*

5 LORDS *of the* MODERN WATERS— EUROPE *and the* UNITED STATES

IN THE gloom of the Dark Ages of Europe the only constructive
actions in water management were those taken by the invading
Arabs and by the Roman Catholic Church. The Arabs greatly
extended the irrigated areas in Spain and Sicily.

With the fall of the Roman Empire and the lack of central
lay authority and consequently of public funds, all public services went to pieces. In the early seventh century any attempt to
keep the aqueducts in repair was commonly undertaken by
bishops, but in many cases the clergy themselves were hard up
for water. The archbishops of Salzburg, for instance, obtained
their daily supply of fresh spring water by special messenger.
Solid citizens had private wells or cisterns. Water from public
fountains and wells was usually distributed by professional
water carriers.

Near Milan the Cistercian monks introduced the use of city
refuse and sewer water as fertilizers. At Canterbury in England
the priory had an elaborate water system for its own use. Re-

ligious orders were active in the revivifying of ancient drainage schemes near Rome and proposed, indeed, to drain the Pontine Marshes.

The greatest of all European projects, however, was of course in the Netherlands, and there the work was started by religious orders such as the Benedictines, the Cistercians and the Premonstratensians. Holland was caught in a mysterious long cycle of world weather. The 2,000 years from 1,500 B.C. to A.D. 500 represented a relatively dry two millennia during which the sea's encroachment on the land had not been very serious. After A.D. 500, however, the Dutch had to fight hard to save their soil. The saltings and mud flats were first consolidated, then marsh samphire and marram grass gradually raised the beaches. The grassy shores suffered less and less from periodic floodings and could be used as grazing pasture for sheep, who are easy to satisfy. With progressive drainage the land could even be plowed or used for the more exacting grazing tastes of horses and cattle.

By the tenth century the Dutch had gained much experience —but little soil. Until 1500 they actually lost more land than they gained. Owing to subsidence, the sea encroached more and more so that the Zuider Zee, for example, reached its largest area near the year 1300. During a storm on December 14, 1287, more than 50,000 people drowned in its swollen waters— one of the greatest natural catastrophes of history. By gradually encircling the threatened land by dikes, so-called "polders" were formed. These areas of reclaimed land discharged their water into the sea at ebb tide through gates or sluices which could be closed when the tide began to flow. The object of the polders was to shorten the coast and close the bays, creeks and gaps. the old sea dikes now became inner dikes. Soon after 1300 the great dike encircling West Friesland was finished. Between 1200 and 1500 over 285,000 acres were gained and held.

With the rise of cities peat was dug in the low country be-

hind the coastal dunes. The shallow lakes thus formed encroached on the land and had to be diked, drained and re-
covered as farmlands. It was to provide power for these drainage
operations that the Dutch developed windmills.

In France the biggest problem was to keep Paris supplied
with sweet water. The situation was improved to some extent
when Philip Augustus enclosed the city within walls about 1190.
The Abbey of Saint-Laurent had a reservoir at Pré-Saint-Ger-
vais which held water from springs at Romainville. This was
now piped to Paris in lead conduits. Paris today is one of the
few large cities in the world (in addition to Vienna and Munich)
which gets its drinking water entirely from springs. In 1865 and
1871 long aqueducts were built to bring water from additional
spring sources at Dhuis and Villeneuve-l'Archevêque. The system of dual water, reminiscent of ancient Rome, in which spring
water is used for drinking and domestic supply, while water
for industry and public services is obtained from the Seine and
the Ourcq Canal, is now one of the best in any great Western
city.

It was with the invention of water pumps (pistons driven
by undershot water wheels) that municipal authorities or groups
of citizens replaced ecclesiastics and monasteries in taking
charge of the water supplies throughout Europe. Joint stock
companies to build and manage waterworks were formed in
Great Britain under special powers conferred by private acts of
Parliament. London continued to be supplied by eight different
private companies, in fact, until 1902, when the Metropolitan
Water Board was set up. The trend toward publicly owned
waterworks was evident much earlier in the United States and
in Continental Europe.

The planning of services such as water was difficult before
the nineteenth century because, for one thing, nobody could
foretell the society's needs since nobody knew what the population was or even what the rainfall was. The first census of

Great Britain was taken in 1801 and showed the population to be 10,500,956 (about the size of the present city of Tokyo). By 1851, it had doubled. The first known rainfall records for the British Isles were kept by an eccentric private citizen, Richard Townley, in the eighteenth century. By 1800 ten such records were being kept, but the recording of rainfall was still regarded as nothing more than a hobby for amateur scientists and clergymen. Not until 1919 was rainfall recording made a national service undertaken by the Meteorological Office of the Air Ministry.

Water in the home tap was not a very reliable service during most of the nineteenth century. One would turn on the tap and nothing would happen. People got in the habit of leaving their taps permanently open so as not to miss the sudden gushes of water that enabled them to fill a bathtub or a kettle. Constant-pressure water main systems were not installed in Europe until the 1890's.

So MUCH for the old countries. In the remainder of this book we shall be dealing with the water problems of the United States, with only brief excursions to draw comparisons with specific analogous problems abroad. One of the reasons why the United States requires separate attention is that it is the biggest water hog in the world. On a per capita basis, poor tropical countries use less than 5 gallons per day. Small rural communiites in England use perhaps 20 gallons per day. Similar United States communities use twice as much. Large commercial towns in England use about 50 gallons a day while the average in the United States for such towns is closer to 200 gallons. The highest per capita water consumption of any city in the world is that of Beverly Hills, California (over 500 gallons per person per day), where in an arid climate immense lawns are kept sprinkled the year around and countless swimming pools are filled and refilled.

When the Pilgrims came to New England they nearly
starved because, although the new land was well watered, it
was dismayingly unproductive. Used as they were to British
soil enriched through generations by compost, they had to learn
from the Indians to throw in dead fish with seed corn.

As the settlers drifted westward they ran into land that was
very fertile, such as that in the Ohio and Mississippi valleys,
but at the same time was extremely sloppy. It needed draining
like the "fenlands" of England. Still farther west they hit the
prairies. Cultivation here was impossible until the development
of special "prairie breakers" (plows equipped with a long steel
moldboard for turning over the furrow slice) to rip through the
tough grass roots. Even then the crops that had flourished in
the humid east, such as corn and soft wheat, failed in Kansas.
What opened this area up for intensive agriculture was actually
the arrival of Germans and especially Russian immigrants. They
brought from the regions around the Black Sea varieties of hard,
red, winter wheats that had been grown under conditions like
those of the Great Plains.

Still farther west the settlers arrived at the arid intermountain states and finally the Pacific Coast. They were now faced
with the ancient problems of elder hydraulic civilizations. Irrigation systems became not only an agricultural way of life but
a political battle cry.

The rainfall of the country averages 30 inches each year,
but the extremes vary from over 81 inches in the Olympic
northwest (watershed of the Columbia River) to less than one
quarter of an inch in the intermountain deserts of the Rockies;
from over 55 inches in Louisiana to 8 inches in Nevada.
Another distinction is that, while in most of the United States
over half the rain falls during the growing season, most of the
rain in the Pacific Coast States falls during the winter. What
happens to the average 30 inches? Seventy percent of it is
either evaporated or transpired from vegetation. The latter is

usefully consumed if the vegetable itself is useful. All plants suck water from the ground and breathe most of it out through their leaves. The remaining 30 percent (or 9 inches) becomes either surface runoff to rivers or ground water. It is this 9 inches per year that we can do something about.

The volume of wild water, or runoff water, varies more than the rainfall. Volcanic soil, such as can be found in parts of Idaho, Oregon, California and New Mexico, acts like a sponge. Even when the rainfall reaches 100 inches per year or 10 inches a day, there is no runoff. The flow of streams that border such lava plains is also absorbed and they become "lost rivers."

There is a mystery involved in the water balances of the country in that some 40 cubic miles of water every year (equal to one fourth of the amount of yearly flow of the Mississippi River) is lost in the bookkeeping somewhere. It may be that the lost rivers take it unrecorded to the sea. Those lost rivers from volcanic watersheds that reappear, however, are beautifully stable, in fact, a water manager's dream. Thus the flow of the Deschutes River in Oregon is the most stable in the country. Billions of dollars have been spent in dams to make other rivers as well behaved.

Every great river basin of the country has its individual character. Most peculiar are those, like the Sacramento, in which the lower part of the basin reaches high water with the February rains while the headwater tributaries draining the snow-melt of the Sierra Nevada Mountains do not reach their crests until May or June.

Such behavior is very important for the control of floods and for irrigation programs. It is also significant for drainage of soil that has been more or less permanently flooded, and it was this problem which first concerned Americans looking for new, fertile farmlands. In our history the first problem was to get rid of water rather than to acquire more. In 1763 the Dismal Swamp area of Virginia and North Carolina was surveyed

by George Washington with a view to land reclamation and inland water transportation. The Dismal Swamp Company was
later chartered by the two states and a canal was constructed
which served for both drainage and boat traffic. This is still used.

In 1823 Professor W. H. Keating of the University of Pennsylvania and his party made an important trip to Indiana and
upper Illinois and found it in the spring a continuous swamp-
land. Where Chicago and Fort Wayne are now, the professor
and his friends met canoe traffic almost as lively as automobile
traffic would be in the years to come. Keating describes the
eeriness of sighting in the early morning mist of what might
now be the Chicago Loop countless Indian canoes gliding in all
directions, silently and purposefully going about their inscruta-
ble engagements. The mosquitoes, observed the professor, were
terrible. It is worth noting that in the Indiana-Chicago area today there are many more miles of public outlet ditches and
drains than there are miles of public highways.

For the effective drainage of existing or potential farm property not immediately adjacent to a river there was no very
good technique available, until in 1835 John Johnson of Seneca
County, New York, brought over from Scotland patterns from
which clay tile was molded by hand and laid on his farm. That
was the beginning of modern tile drainage in the United States.
(Tiles are similar to sewer pipe in composition and appearance,
except that lengths of the tile are not fitted together but gaps
are left between the pieces of pipe so that drainage along the
length of a trench can enter the tile conduit. Swinging gates are
left on all tile outlets to keep out small animals.)

Under the Swann Land Acts of 1849, 1850 and 1860,
about 64 million acres of public swamp and overflow land in
fifteen states was turned over to the states' ownership for reclamation. Few of the states did anything at all about these
gifts. However, in Louisiana drainage was a matter affecting
public health as well as crop production and remained a hot
political issue for over thirty years. Land in organized draining

enterprises is largely to be found today in the Mississippi Delta, the Corn Belt and the Lake States.

On farms where drainage is bad one will see stunted crops with yellowing leaves. If the water pools remain long enough, the plants will die. This is the result of root damage caused by lack of oxygen and an accumulation of carbon dioxide. The water itself doesn't kill plants, for they will thrive in pure water containing plant food if they can get air. Plants such as rice, which can stand long saturation of the soil with water, have specialized air-conducting tissues in their stems which bleed air down to the root system.

A dismal paradox is that some of the worst drainage problems, such as "waterlogging," occur in arid areas which have to be irrigated. We have seen such a land disease in West Pakistan. The biggest cause of this is too much irrigation water. Too many irrigation farmers are ignorant water hogs. They think that if 1,000 acre-feet is good, 10,000 acre-feet is ten times as good. Thus "wild" flooding, lack of drainage outlets and absurdly long irrigation runs bring on waterlogging. A second cause is seepage from canals, laterals and ditches. Of the 140,-000 miles of irrigation canals and laterals in the 17 Western States only about 7 percent are lined. Most of them are simply untreated earth channels. The seepage losses are horrible—up to 70 percent of all the water diverted into them. The seepage enters underground strata at elevations often higher than those of the irrigated lands and (as in the South Platte Valley in Colorado, the North Platte Valley in Nebraska, and the Big Horn Basin in Wyoming) becomes a direct source of waterlogging of the lower-lying farms.

A third cause lies in the structure of certain farmsites. Sand layers may be underlain by impervious strata of clay through which ground water will not percolate fast enough. Thus the so-called "perched" water tables are found notably in the Imperial Valley and the great San Joaquin Valley of California. There, however, the farmers are working with expensive cash crops and all have college degrees, so they take steps to avoid the waterlogging that has ruined West Pakistan and alarmed much of Arizona.

Still another cause is artesian pressure. Water wells drilled downward to penetrate underground aquifers (water reservoirs) often result in flowing wells which may or may not be used fully in irrigation. Entire valleys have become waterlogged because of the uncontrolled flow of artesian wells. Examples are the Payette Valley in Idaho and Weber Basin in Utah.

Utah is historically important in the history of water in North America since the first large-scale irrigation projects were set up by the Mormons in 1840 near the Great Salt Lake. As was their habit, the Mormons did this on their own and invented laws as they went along. Irrigation as a big systematic way of opening the arid West to agriculture did not progress very well, however, until under Theodore Roosevelt's inspired bossiness the famous Reclamation Act of 1902 was passed, establishing irrigation as a national policy.

The mind boggles at the stubborn and wrong-minded pressures that were exerted by congressmen and senators of the wet East against this historic legislation. Bellows of rage and ridicule echoed through the Capitol dome. One Eastern senator expressed the feeling of the opposition in the debate on the floor: "It is the height of irresponsibility—nay of fiscal folly—to propose another needless agency in our burgeoning bureaucracy to expend millions of dollars to build dams in a region inhabited only by jack rabbits."

The opposition of such men was overcome only by the frantic promises of the Western bloc to back pet projects of the East and South in return for their support of the reclamation bill. The strategy paid off, but to this day reclamation appropriations are regarded as being afflicted with a "pork-barrel" odor. We shall have more to say about this in the chapter entitled "Pork Is Soluble in Water."

Even in the semiarid areas, such as the Great Plains, many problems had arisen because of the plowing up of hard-to-farm grasslands. The cattlemen had basic cause to complain when good rangeland was broken up by plow to yield poor and unstable farms. Water erosion and particularly wind erosion disheartened the dry farmer. Millions of trees for windbreaks were planted in the Great Plains but this is now an antiquated practice, since the trees take up too much crop space. Fertilizer was very seldom used, since the trouble at first was not with lack of essential mineral elements. However, chemical analysis of soils in dry-farming areas of the Prairie States show 40 percent loss of nitrogen and a giant swing to chemical fertilization has been under way for several years.

The notion of farming according to the soil moisture supply is an idea that seldom occurs to the dry farmer, maybe because it requires a slight change in thinking habits. If such a farmer would plant a crop in season when he has an adequate supply of soil moisture and leave the seed in the bag when he is short on moisture, he would come out all right. A more sophisticated modification is to rotate the crops according to water content of the soil. True crop rotation is not possible in the Great Plains because there are fewer crops to choose from and few soil-enriching legumes that will grow. However, corn leaves the soil with a better supply of water than does small grain. Wheat exhausts the available soil moisture entirely by harvest time. One would think that the soil auger or the tile spade (simple instruments for measuring ground moisture) would be standard equipment for every dry farmer, but such is not the case.

One can see why irrigation in the arid areas farther west, as cheap water and virtually free reservoirs and canals became available, had an enormous appeal to the people who had been struggling with the harsh season-to-season decisions and weather gambles of the prairie farms. So enormous was the rate of increase in irrigation that by 1963 the total area of irrigated land in the 17 Western States was about 30 million acres. The present value of crops harvested from irrigated land rocketed from around 1 percent of the value of all crops in the country at the turn of the century to over 37 percent at present. Irrigation is now spreading eastward, and even the humid states of the Eastern seaboard have considered it, since it fits in with multipurpose reclamation projects aimed principally at flood and pollution prevention and the creation of recreation areas. Sprinkler irrigation is usually used in the East on rather fancy crops, such as cranberries.

In the struggle of arid areas for water no society, of course, has been more aggressive than Southern California. The Owens River Valley drama was typical and nearly as violent as the water wars of the Assyrians and the Babylonians or the more recent ones of Israel and Jordan. The Owens River Valley is 240 miles from Los Angeles, close to Death Valley on one flank and the great mountains of the High Sierras on the other. It had long been settled by people who had fought the Piute Indians for it. This land was acquired from the white settlers by the sort of villainous subterfuge that is associated with the widow's mortgage and the twirled black mustache. A former mayor of Los Angeles went into the valley taking up options on every other farm and leaving the impression that the government was about to begin a great irrigation project there like that of the Imperial Valley. No one outside of a small group, which included the Los Angeles newspapers, knew what was going on, not even the city council. The object of this secrecy was supposedly to head off speculation and holdups, but one of the results was that the insiders were able to realize enormous fortunes by buying up thousands of acres of land in the San Fernando Valley of suburban Los Angeles, for which the Owens River water proved to be destined.

The options on the Owens Valley land were taken up in 1904 and paid for by a bond issue of $25 million. A yell of rage swept the Owens Valley. A herd of speculators from Los Angeles whipped up their carriages to take government claims in the path of the aqueduct. Theodore Roosevelt immediately ordered all homestead land thereabouts converted into a forest reserve and granted the city a right-of-way across it. This was probably the first forest reserve in history that contained only sagebrush. Roosevelt had made these grants on the guarantee that the water would be used for domestic purposes only—not to irrigate ranches around Los Angeles. Later he withdrew this stipulation.

Thus, in effect, water was taken from the Owens Valley farmers and given to the San Fernando farmers—or, more properly speaking, to the multimillionaire Los Angeles real estate operators—or, more properly still, to the Los Angeles newspaper owners. It is not surprising that the Owens Valley natives tried to hit back. The bitterest of the war broke out after the aqueduct was finished and carrying water. Several times the conduits were dynamited by night riders in the valley who made no attempt to conceal their identity. In the face of this ruckus Los Angeles felt compelled to go whole hog and buy the entire Owens River Valley—towns and all. The ranchers whose places were not bought out in the first go-round were forced to sell at condemnation prices by the fact that the city of Los Angeles put in great pumps that drained the water from under their land.

By the time of the Hoover Dam on the Colorado (1930), the principle had been established that the best way to store water in arid areas such as Southern California was as ground water, building up the water tables. This was done with surplus water from the aqueduct from the Colorado River, and again the San Fernando Valley was chosen. Again incredible fortunes were made by the same millionaires or their sons, who now sold the land at country estate values, and lush estates indeed they were and are.

Not only ground-water storage but ground-water irrigation has progressed through the years. It is good practice because it eliminates a large part of the senseless evaporation and seepage losses that have made irrigators more reckless with water than drunken sailors with beer. This technique of an artificial

water table requires a subterranean barrier layer at which percolation stops or a permanently high natural water table on
which an additional table can be built. Among the places where
subirrigation is well practiced are: the Sacramento-San Joaquin
Delta in Southern California; the Everglades of southern Florida; the San Luis Valley in Colorado; the Egin Bench in southern Idaho; smaller scattered sections in Kansas and Nebraska,
and in organic soils of the Great Lakes States of Michigan, Indiana, Minnesota and Ohio, where the practice is known as
"controlled drainage."

Ground water is our most massive heritage. Our total
ground-water reservoirs amount to far more than the combined
capacity of all surface reservoirs and lakes, including the Great
Lakes. Ground-water reservoirs in order to be efficient should
be pumped down—but not too far down—so that there is room
for recharging by rain. A very shallow water table, because of
the danger of waterlogging, is worse than a deep one. Water
will not remain docile under a piece of property until the owner
is ready to use it. Thus conservation is not automatically
achieved by letting it be.

The rate of recharge of ground waters by rain or from rivers should balance the rate of pumping off. Unfortunately this
is seldom the case. A ground-water reservoir of over 6,700
square miles area in the South High Plains of Texas is estimated
to hold five times as much water as Lake Mead (formed by
Hoover Dam) but its annual rate of recharge is less than half
of one percent of the annual inflow to Lake Mead.

Aside from irrigation, the municipalities of the country receive 25 percent of their total domestic supply from the water
table. Of large cities, however, only Houston, San Antonio and
Memphis have depended almost entirely on ground water.
Ground-water reservoirs are perfect for avoiding evaporation
losses but they cannot be pumped fast enough to handle giant
peak loads in cities. The biggest peak load a town or city ever
faces is the water needed for fire fighting. This determines the

size of its mains, at least in cities less than half a million in population. The United States is not only a water hog, it is a firebug. Our city fire losses are four times as large per capita as those of Great Britain or Continental Europe.

We have seen that the federal government through the brilliant presidency of Theodore Roosevelt expressed the country's basic support of a magical complex of actions in regard to water, known generically as "conservation." We have also quoted a senator of the Grand Old Party of the East in 1902 in his fearful growls about "burgeoning bureaucracy."

Burgeon it did. In the bibliography there is a nearly complete list of twenty-four federal agencies and commissions concerned with water.

IN ADDITION, the Federal Power Commission is, of course, concerned with water power. The National Science Foundation has spread its wings over research on weather modification, and the Soil Conservation Survey has a special study going on now. Between the time this was written and the date of printing, further agencies may have been hatched.

One notes immediately the fact that various bureaus and services in different departments of the Administration are staring at the same problems. Often this is from wildly different angles. This diversity has become most apparent in water pollution and especially in farm drainage. As we shall discuss later, the soil conservation people of the Department of Agriculture are all for everybody draining his farm, while the wildlife people in the Department of the Interior insist that somebody must leave some potholes and ponds for the wild ducks. Perhaps such diametrically opposed postures are useful, maybe even necessary. Somebody has to stand up for ducks. More discouraging is the fact that the superstructure has grown so massive and clumsy that it often cannot pull itself together and move; it simply stares—or debates.

On December 8, 1908, in a special message to Congress,

President Roosevelt said: "These needs [of river improvement] should be met without further dilly-dallying. . . . The time for playing with our waterways is past. The country demands results."

Fifty-seven years later the dilly-dallying is still going on. It is true that we have a Hoover Dam, a Grand Coulee, and scores of other impressive constructions. But during the same time we have almost hopelessly polluted our rivers, we continue to have disastrous floods, we continue to have desperate water shortages. Is it true that the U.S. federal government is and should be a Lord of our Modern Waters? If so, what could be done to make all the tentacles move in coordination, like an octopus opening an abalone?

This question has troubled all U.S. Presidents since Theodore Roosevelt and the Presidents' answer has always been to appoint an *Advisory Committee*. This is almost a reflex. One typical "Advisory Committee of Water Resources Policy" deliberated in 1956. It did not come up with any proposal to reorganize or to lop off any of the 25 government agencies then dealing with water resources. Instead, it offered an elaborate intermeshing of reviewing committees and an independent "Board of Review for Water Resources." In effect, this recommends some high-paying jobs for criticism of proposals by mixed committees. However, being a committee itself, it showed a touching and almost religious faith that administrative committees can get things done—a faith completely unjustified by the history of either governmental affairs or private business.

As we examine special facets of our water habits and needs we shall keep a watchful eye on the underlying power struggles going on, from the county agent wearily slogging around in his 1954 Chevrolet up to the glossy secretaries of federal departments.

The river belongs to the Nation,
The levee, they say, to the State;
The Government runs navigation,
The commonwealth, though, pays the freight.
Now, here is the problem that's heavy—
Please, which is the right or the wrong—
When water runs over the levee,
To whom does the river belong?
—MALLOCH, *Uncle Sam's River*

Stolen waters are sweet.
—PROVERBS 9:17

6 WATER *for* LAWYERS

IN THE arid countries of antiquity water rights predated land rights, but in the well-rained countries of Western Europe there was more interest in the ownership of land. Any equity in the water of a river depended on the land being on the bank of a river. In Western Europe the "doctrine of appropriation," which made irrigation possible in the Western United States and which allows a water user whose land may be far from the river to acquire an equity in the water, would have been horrifying to Englishmen and Frenchmen, and in fact it still is.

The various doctrines of water and their interpretation in the courts have provided a bonanza for American lawyers. Because of the pragmatic instinct of jurists to twist the old body of common law to fit new situations, such as large-scale irrigation projects in Arizona rather than trout fishing in the squire's brook in Sussex, water law in this country has become very complex. It varies from state to state, and usually the state with the least water has the most complicated water laws.

In the "humid" Eastern areas of the country (humid being defined as more than 30 inches average rainfall per year) the common law of England, involving the doctrine of riparian rights, became well established. But even this doctrine is not as old as it may seem. It was brought to the Atlantic seaboard by two American jurists, Story and Keat, who took it from French Civil law. The "common law of water courses" is thus not the ancient result of English law but is a French doctrine (and a relatively modern one at that) received into English law only under the influence of American jurists. The riparian doctrine became law not only in the East but in several of the Western states that adopted the common law of England before irrigation came upon the scene. And the doctrine had become a part of Texas water law even earlier, by reason of its application to grants of land made by the government of Mexico and of the Republic of Texas, in accordance with the principles inherited from the civil law of Rome.

In common law the owner has the right to have a stream flow by or through his land undiminished in quantity and unpolluted in quality, with one exception: any riparian owner may take what he needs for his so-called "riparian uses," i.e., domestic and household purposes and the watering of animals. In one of the more ancient rules of common law, however, the surface water is regarded as a "common enemy." The owner may fend it off as he pleases, even though he may injure the lands of his neighbors. In common law streams may not be diverted from one watershed to another.

As actually interpreted in the Eastern States, ownership of riparian property is sacred and confers the right to do nothing about the water. The owner can sit and watch it run out to sea; he can let it flood his farm if that is his pleasure. He is not legally bound to do anything constructive about the water as long as he holds his land.

It was when the newfangled notion of irrigation, which was

foreign to Europe and to the Atlantic States, became important that the riparian doctrine was strained. A large diversion to irrigation upstream obviously does not leave the stream flow "undiminished in quantity" and very often it also returns downstream by percolation polluted with silt or salt. The additional doctrine of "reasonable use" came into play. But what constitutes "reasonable use"? The courts say it depends. Because the question of reasonable use is one of *fact*, which a jury must decide, the irrigator in states using the common-law or riparian-rights doctrines, must go to court to get the answer. This is costly and the jury decisions have been wildly inconsistent, often depending on the jurors' personal opinion of the litigant, who is usually their neighbor.

Another defect of the common law became evident when it was applied to ground water. The early jurists did not realize that the ground water moves. In some common-law states one landowner may pump his own well so as to drain off the ground water of his neighbor and the neighbor has no recourse. Here also resort has been had to "reasonable use" but again a jury decision in court is required. The rule of reasonable use in this case is really an exception to the strict rule of absolute ownership to everything "on or above the lands upward to the heavens and everything in and under the lands downward to the center of the earth."

Well-defined subterranean streams also are subject to riparian rights.

Two specific historical adventures simultaneously knocked holes in the riparian-rights or common-law doctrine as applied in the new West. One was the Mormon occupation of Utah and the other the California gold rush.

Brigham Young said: "No man has a right to waste one drop of water that another man can turn into bread." The principle was laid down that water belongs to the people and no man can gain title to more than he can use in a beneficial manner.

In a way, the Mormons were echoing the Mohammedan religious feeling for water, also engendered in arid lands. Mohammed saw water as an object of religious charity. Free access to water was the right of every Moslem community. The Koran reads: "No one can refuse surplus water without sinning against Allah and against Man." The Mormons simply proceeded to take the water out of streams and apply it to irrigation. For fifty years there were no water laws in Utah. Every case was handled by the local community.

In California the miners helped themselves to the waters as well as the minerals in the public domain. They developed a system of water titles fashioned after their improvised system of land titles. Each claim, whether to gold or water, was based on prior appropriation. By definition a water right became a right only to the use of water, not a right to a body of water. *"Qui prior est in tempore, potier est in jure"* was not just a rule of law but a way of life in the West. Phrased another way, it is the right to the use of water by appropriation. Miners often would pipe water across canyons and down hillsides. They upheld their right to such water against claims of owners of land abutting on the streams.

There was a peculiarity in the California situation, however, that later made for bad trouble. The mining area was public domain ceded by Mexico to the United States by the Treaty of Guadalupe Hidalgo in 1849, the year gold was discovered. The miners were actually trespassers, but the federal government acquiesced silently. When the California legislature met in its first session in 1850, to everyone's dumbfounderment, it adopted the common law of England. But to appease the miners, the Supreme Court held that, since the true owner of the soil and riparian rights, the government, was not in court, there was applied the common-law principle that property rights could be had in mere *possession* and *use*. The occupant, being a trespasser, could not assert riparian right against the true owner

—the government. His claim of riparian right versus later appropriators was good only so long as he held his mining claim.

Thus California, before the days of irrigation in that state, rocked along on a cockeyed mixture of riparian and appropriation water law. The appropriation doctrine in the meantime was recognized in several states. Recognition by Congress in 1866 of the doctrine of appropriation was restricted to public lands and to water rights accrued under state law.

By the end of the century irrigation had become the focus of the water law of the West. In 1894 Congress passed the Carey Act to allow irrigation of public lands with private capital. The appropriation doctrine was recognized directly or indirectly in all 17 Western States and Territories, including Texas. Since Colorado was the first to reject outright the claims based on ownership of land next to streams, the pure and undefiled appropriation system is often called the "Colorado doctrine" and is applied in Montana, Idaho, Wyoming, Nevada, Utah, Arizona and New Mexico. The schizophrenic mixture of appropriation-riparian system is often called the "California" doctrine and is used also in Oregon, Washington, North Dakota, South Dakota, Nebraska, Kansas, Oklahoma and Texas. This is where the lawyers thrive. Some state supreme courts had to go through extraordinary acrobatics. The Arizona Supreme Court claimed that the common-law or riparian doctrine had never existed in the territory even while it was part of the Mexican state of Sonora. the New Mexico court went even further and maintained that solely the right of appropriation had existed in the Republic of Mexico—a sort of rewriting of history in the interests of Big Brother.

The height of judicial somersaulting was reached in Montana when irrigation began to be important. In 1921, after having rendered over 90 decisions on water over 50 years, not plainly in favor of appropriation, the court decided in a case of riparian versus appropriative rights that all its previous decisions were mere *dicta* (not pertinent to the present decision). In effect, it started again from scratch and held that the doctrines of riparian rights had never been recognized by the legislature or the courts. Hence no riparian rights had ever vested in Montana. Here again we have a curiously American pragmatism. What we don't want in history never happened.

In Oregon one can claim water on both riparian or appropriation grounds, but anybody trying it on the former doctrine is looked upon as a city slicker from the East and juries seldom favor him. Riparian right is a ghost of an ancient legislature.

At the present time in the dual-system states riparian owners have no vested right to the waste of water. This was not true in English common law, is not true in theory in the Eastern States, and was not always true in California.

Perhaps the most important practical difference between the water laws in the Western States and those in the East, however, are those involved in ground water or so-called "percolating" water. In some of the Eastern States the farmer with the deepest well and the most powerful pump may monopolize the local water supply and the others have no recourse. In the West such behavior would result in a lynching. In order to make the lynching legal, so the speak, the rule of *correlative rights* has been developed in which the owner of overlying land is allowed only a reasonable share of the available supply of ground water, with apportionment in case of shortage. Curiously, this does not hold in appropriation of surface water. When there is no more water left in the stream than enough to satisfy the earliest priority, the holder of that right is entitled to the whole stream. This has made for some ugly tensions in time of drought.

Pumping ground water is still nonetheless a lawyer-haunted activity in the West and the laws differ from state to state. "Priorities" may have to be shown and there is nothing a law-

yer likes better than to chase down priorities in yellowed pages
at $300 a day.

In the arid West states as well as private parties are always
going to court over water. In the preceding chapter we mentioned the avid thirst of Southern California which impelled it
first to depopulate the Owens River Valley, then to latch on to
most of the Colorado River. By the compact of 1922, drawn up
by commissioners representing the Colorado Basin states, an
agreement was reached on diversion of the river's waters. California agreed to limit itself to 4.4 million acre-feet. This compact
went into effect when Congress passed the Boulder Canyon
Project Act, despite protests and court challenges in Arizona.
Later, in the Hoover administration, Arizona took it on the chin
when Secretary of the Interior Ray Lyman Wilbur, a Californian
like the President, signed a contract with California which allowed the state 5.3 million acre-feet. The decision was justified
in a rather mystical way by a special interpretation of the "law
of the river clause" in the compact and the act. Nobody paid
much attention and the Great Depression ensued. Arizona, a
David fighting a Goliath, did not forgive or forget.

In 1954 a special master was appointed by the Supreme
Court to recommend a solution to the interminable California-
Arizona dispute. After conducting 340 hearings and compiling
25,000 pages of testimony, the special master upheld Arizona's
claim that California was illegally exceeding its Colorado water
entitlement. In 1963 the Supreme Court upheld the special master's recommendation on the California-Arizona allotment issue
but rejected his suggestion for prorata allocation of water during
years of shortages. Instead the Court ruled that in dry years
authority for allocation be vested in the Secretary of the Interior.

Now that Arizona has won and is proposing to use the water
in its ambitious Central Arizona project to make Phoenix, so they
say, a rival of Los Angeles, the Southern Californians have failed

to go into the expected state of convulsive shock. This is because they have sold the bonds for the North-South Project, which will bring water from the rampant Northern California rivers. Now the shoe is on the other foot. The Secretary of the Interior is now an Arizonan—Stewart Udall—and his proposition (the Southwest Water Development Program) is to take water out of *Northern California* watersheds to fatten up the Colorado for the benefit of Arizona. Coming right on the heels of the Supreme Court's action in cutting California's Colorado River allotment by a million acre-feet, this proposal was like asking someone to kiss you after you had pasted him one in the mouth. Governor Pat Brown of California immediately rejected the proposal.

A more appetizing approach for Californians is for the Colorado Basin states to gang up on the Northwest and divert water from the gigantic Columbia (which normally has a flow ten times that of the Colorado). A specific proposal has been blueprinted by F. Z. Pirkey, a retired planning engineer for the California Department of Water Resources. At a cost of $11 billion, Pirkey would extract 12.9 million acre-feet yearly from the Columbia at the Dalles Dam in Oregon, lift it 500 feet over the mountains with *atomic power* and carry it 1,200 miles to Hoover Dam on the lower Colorado with a branch feeding water through Northern California into (guess where!) Southern California. This amount would nearly double the present water supply in the Pacific Southwest. An alternative plan would be to divert part of the Snake River to the Colorado. Still another suggests tapping the Yellowstone River in Wyoming and Montana.

The Northwestern States do not want their water resources to be pies to be cut up at the pleasure of Arizona and California. Governor Hatfield of Oregon says people should come to where there is water, not vice versa. However, Oregon with only five congressmen glumly agrees that *some* diversion of the Columbia is probably in the cards and Idaho is similarly philosophical about the Snake. All the Northwestern States are hard at work on studies of their own "ultimate needs" in water.

The Southwesterners claim that the Columbia each year discharges about 170 million acre-feet into the ocean. The cost of diverting 10 to 15 million acre-feet from this river would, they insist, be less than that of diverting 1 to 2 million acre-feet from the Northern California rivers, such as the Eel, the Trinity and the Mad.

The water struggle is not confined to the West. Since the northeastern drought started in 1961 there has been renewed urgency about the question of the Delaware River and who can take how much of its waters. Since the blood does not heat up so much on the Atlantic seaboard as in the purely hydraulic states of the Southwest, this has been a rather decorous disagreement.

The dispute which ultimately resulted in the compact goes back to 1925, when New York City first considered tapping the headwaters of the Delaware. Since the Delaware extends from New York City's Catskill Mountains to Wilmington, Delaware, 200 miles south, forming the boundary between Pennsylvania and New Jersey, the city tried to negotiate its rights to the river water with downstream states. When the talks failed, New York moved on its own to tap the river in 1928, touching off a battle in the United States Supreme Court.

The Court's 1931 decision was suspiciously like a kiss for the appropriation doctrine applied to states rather than to private parties. The smell of the Colorado sagebrush was in it. It ruled that a state's rights to shared waters depend on its needs and not simply on the length of its riverbanks. It awarded New York 400 million gallons a day but, at Pennsylvania's insistence, declared that the award was not perpetual—it was subject to the development of more pressing needs.

After various additional amendments and clarification by

the Supreme Court, the twin hurricanes of 1955 so devastated
the regions of the upper Delaware Basin that all the riparian
states were jarred into teamwork. The compact was formed by
laws enacted both in Congress and the state legislatures and
was signed in 1961. It created a commission to develop long-
range water plans and to allocate water among the states. Most
significantly it gave the commission the power to declare an
emergency and to change water allotments.

The emergency was declared in July, 1965. Because of the
reduced flow in the Delaware, the Philadelphia water supply
was threatened by salt creeping up the river. New York City,
which draws about one third of its water supply from the
Delaware headwaters, was asked to part with some of its
reservoir water, which it did and with surprising grace considering its own miserable drought situation.

New York is justly critical, however, of recent Congressional
water resources legislation which bars the Federal Water Council
or any Basin Commissions from so much as studying the feasi-
bility of transferring water between adjacent river basins. (This
restriction was added at the insistence of Columbia River Basin
users to discourage diversion of water to the Southwest.) New
York is developing a water recovery project on the Hudson designed to merge with aqueducts carrying water from the Delaware. The recent Congressional bill would, theoretically at least,
have blocked New York from designing such a marriage of different waters.

On a smaller scale but echoing the aqueous bellicosity of the
arid West, Kansas filed a Supreme Court suit after the Arkansas
River Compact had failed to decide a dispute on a dam which
the Colorado Game, Fish and Parks Department built with the
Compact Administration's approval. (This compact had all the
authority that a spiderweb holds over a woodland cattle path.)
The dam is on Clay Creek, four miles southeast of Lamar, Colorado. Nobody knows how much water is involved, especially

since the early summer flood of 1965 made the question somewhat like arguing about a teacup full of bourbon lost overboard at sea. However, it is the mode and not the fact that is of interest. When anybody picks a fight with Colorado, he is asking for it. At last account Kansas had decided to forget about it.

Of more interest to the pollution problem is the Great Lakes diversion controversy. This also has been a lawyers' festival, not only for lawyers with shingles but for the lawyers who are congressmen. In 1930 the Supreme Court had permitted Chicago to pump its water supply from Lake Michigan and to discharge sewage through the Illinois River into the Mississippi River system. The states of Wisconsin, Minnesota, Ohio, Pennsylvania, Michigan and New York maintained in various petitions that this decision should be reversed, on the grounds that Chicago was lowering the level of the Great Lakes. They succeeded in progressively cutting down the withdrawals of Chicago from 11,500 cubic feet per second of water to 1,500 cubic feet. In 1963 the states mentioned decided that they would rather put up with Chicago's sewage (which is more highly treated than that of any other large city in the country) than low lake levels, so they petitioned that Chicago discharge its treated sewage back into Lake Michigan rather than into the Mississippi. Chicago is in the embarrassing position of claiming that this would involve a water pollution hazard of the first magnitude. In effect, the sister states are demanding that Chicago drink its own sewage; that it pollute all its pitifully few beaches in order that navigation levels be kept up along with Niagara Falls hydroelectric power peaks.

This question is still pending. It represents indeed the crux of the modern pollution problem. Can a city re-use its own water? As we shall see later, the application of modern concepts of nuclear heating to water purification may make this the only ultimate answer not only to Chicago's dilemma but to that of many large cities throughout the world.

It was crawlin' an' it stunk,
But of all the drinks I've drunk,
I'm gratefullest to one from Gunga Din.
—KIPLING, *Gunga Din*

The thirsty earth soaks up the rain,
And drinks, and gapes for drink again . . .
—ABRAHAM COWLEY

7 WATER FAMINE

DROUGHT IN modern times is not simply a lack of water. It is a lack of foresight. The short-cycle drought that has irritated the Northeastern United States since 1961 is only in part a result of low rainfall. New York City, for example, has a great river running by it which it cannot use as a water supply because the river is fantastically polluted. The Northeast has inadequate reservoirs, undersized transmission lines, antiquated treatment plants and poorly planned distribution.

Geologists, however, have deduced long-cycle periods of low and high rainfall which have had dramatic effects on the earlier natives of the North American continent. The close of the Pleistocene epoch 15,000 years ago in the New World saw Clovis man (a hunter of mammoths, horses, camels and giant bison) roaming over a Southwest that was cool and wet. Some 12,000 years ago a profound climatic change dried up the Southwest and reduced the rainfall over the entire continent. The climax of this period of high temperatures and dryness was reached in the years from 4000 to 2500 B.C.—the so-called "Altothermal age."

Again there took place a long cool cycle and, even though

the rainfall increased, the ancient agriculturists were apparently not ready for the change. There is evidence that the farmers were at first embarrassed by the short growing season—especially in the uplands where they had migrated during the millennium and a half of dry, warm weather. However, reaction to the cooler climate was prompt and the great agricultural complex of corn, beans and squash became established and was continued into the Christian era. This period had its short cycles, as do we, of drought and flood years, but on the whole it was a temperate and creative climate. The period A.D. 700 to 1200 saw the culmination of a thousand years of prosperous village life in the Southwest. But then the famine came again. Frantic attempts were made by those people to manage water by check dams, floodwater diversion and irrigation ditches. Corn was abandoned as a staple crop. A terrible drought on the Great Plains lasting from 1439 to 1468 is reflected in Nebraska tree rings and at about that time villages along the desiccated streams of the Great Plains were abandoned.

The arroyos, or dry washes, of the Southwest, which began to form about 1880 may have been partly due to overgrazing after the arrival of white men, but climate was the more important reason. Grass was driven out by mesquite. The water table dropped. Different kinds of fish took over the skinny streams. The Southwest is still in this long-cycle drought.

Who is to say that water famines of this kind which have lasted in Arizona, New Mexico, Southern California, Nevada, Utah and southwestern Colorado since about the time of the Norman conquest of England cannot descend upon the Northeast or the whole country? The meteorologists cannot say because they can find no explanation of the long cycles. There has always been vague talk of sunspots but obviously we do not know how the sunspots were behaving in the years before Galileo when the sun was a big hot god and in the firmaments of the night there was only a paper moon.

The climatologists cannot pin down even the basic reasons

for the *short*-cycle droughts nor can they predict them. Dr. Vincent Schaefer of the Atmospheric Research Center in Albany believes that air pollution is an important cause of drought. He reasons that dust particles from sources of pollution absorb the moisture that would normally fall as rain. Since Schaefer is the scientist who, when he was with General Electric Company, invented cloud seeding to induce artificial rain, his opinions are not to be regarded as frivolous. He calls air pollution the "sewer in the sky." Another theory is connected with the behavior of the Gulf Stream. There is no doubt that the stream influences weather. The warm water it carries across the Atlantic has long been recognized as the main reason why Northwestern Europe has a far milder climate than other regions in the same latitude. But there has recently been discovered a peculiar cold patch of water locked at sea just off the Middle Atlantic States. It is nearly 10° F. colder than the water usually found between the shore and the Gulf Stream. Some meteorologists think that this cool water pool may be the clue to the four-year drought in the East and the floods in the Midwest. It could cause an almost constant offshore low-pressure area, which in turn could affect the weather of the whole continent.

However, the most widely accepted explanation of the five-year rainfall shortage in New England, New York, New Jersey, Pennsylvania, much of Maryland, northern Virginia and the Great Lakes area is the shift of the "jet stream," the high-speed wind which moves from west to east in the earth's upper atmosphere and upon which high-flying jet airplanes can ride with profit. Normally the jet stream comes in from Alaska, sweeps in a southward loop across North America, then heads northeast and out to sea. In the summer the southern border of the loop normally is in Southern Canada and in the winter it drops to northern Florida.

But for the past few years the jet stream hasn't been migrating; it's been skulking stagnant deep in Canada. Thus the cold air which normally meets the warm air in most parts of the United States to bring rain is colliding elsewhere. So we get warm weather but no rain. There is no very persuasive theory of how the jet stream got into this bad habit. Again vague resort must be had to our sunspots. We are going through what is mellifluously termed by scientists the "Years of the Quiet Sun." Sunspots and bursts of hot active particle radiation are few and far between, which is good news for astronauts but is tough for water drinkers and car washers, people who like to take long showers and sprinkle front lawns, fountain-side philosophers, players in back-yard swimming and wading pools and recreational water reservoirs. Although people in New York and Massachusetts have got the most mileage in the form of squawks and screams and newspaper publicity, they are not the ones who have actually suffered the most. In the northern Great Plains, farms in Nebraska were forced in 1964 to sell off a good part of their cattle herds because of feed shortages. Many of the animals came down with "dust pneumonia."

The low level in the Great Lakes, just twelve years after a crisis over excessively high water levels, led to light cargoes of limestone and iron ore in order to clear the bottom of the St. Mary's River (between Lake Superior and the lower lakes) and the St. Clair River (between Lake Huron and Lake Erie). Of all these great waters Lake Erie has been the most affected and Lake Superior the least, since outflow through the St. Mary's River is controlled. In general, 1965 lake levels are the lowest they've been since measuring began 104 years ago.

Barge traffic has been affected on parts of the Mississippi, particularly north of St. Louis, which has had several drought years. There are huge dams on the upper Missouri impounding enough water to run the Missouri and Mississippi rivers at navigable levels for four years even if it never rains again. Bargemen have pleaded for the dam gates to be kept open longer. But their interests and those of industries needing water

along the river run smack up against the politically muscular
agricultural, flood-control and hydroelectric interests upriver.

Texas has suffered. In rangelands where in 1900 the grass
grew stirrup-high, 75 percent of the turf had died clear to the
roots in 1964. Dallas entered a 6-year drought starting in 1957.
They were selling drinking water there at 50 cents a carton.
Emergency water was pumped from the Red River. This was so
salty that it corroded water heaters and pipes. Automobile radiators were replaced at four times the normal rate.

In the summer of 1965 rain soaked the lower Great Plains
(Kansas particularly) but an unexpected rain shortage burned
the Northwest.

Pumping of water from Florida's Lake Okeechobee into the
Everglades National Park is now considered necessary to keep
the park alive. Park rangers have had to feed alligators by
hand and the area echoes with explosions as drilling teams try
to reach the falling water level.

Drought is a broad word. The 1961-1965 water famine in the
Northeast is the worst since 1800. The fact that New Yorkers
find it necessary to ask the waiter for a glass of water and that
neat Scotch has displaced Scotch and water on the drinking
man's diet is very distressing, of course, but it is not quite as
serious as the fact that the Delaware River estuary has gone so
low that salt water has begun to seep in and to contaminate
permanently Philadelphia's supply of fresh water. It is not as
serious as the fact that the water tables have been falling and
the shallower wells have dried up. Most serious of all is the
evidence of a flabbergasting lack of vision and common sense
on the part of the New York government. When New York City
reached out to grab a big part of the Delaware River watershed,
after the celebrated 1949-1950 shortage, it was complacently
announced that this would handle the city's water supply problems at least until the year 2000. A pumping station on the
Hudson five miles above Beacon, New York, and well up from

the salt-water and city pollution stretch, was actually built in 1950 but never used and, in fact, was dismantled.

The helpless day-to-day wringing-of-the-hands posture in New York in the recent few years contrasts in a sorry way with the foresight shown in the 1880's. The present immense Forest Preserve, which is the biggest park in the United States, one eighth of the total area of the state, was set aside because of fears of a drought eighty years ago, and indeed this action can be said to have launched the whole national conservation movement. The federal government followed by setting aside the national forests modeled on the New York State preserve. Thus, in a sense, the wonderful chain of national forests and wilderness areas (186 million acres) dates back to the 1881 drought that dried up Canada Creek and the Mohawk River.

One of the obvious partial remedies in New York is better policing of water. The city needs universal metering. Leaky faucets are a surprisingly fast way to waste water. For example, a leak the size of a pencil lead amounts to a water loss of about 1,500 gallons a day. New York needs better maintenance on leaky mains that are forever bursting. Sooner or later it will have to use the Hudson, which has never furnished drinking water for modern New York. The city actually consumes, day in and day out, a volume of water equal to more than half the Hudson's flow past the gauging station near Albany. (Curiously enough, the best detailed picture of New York's water crisis is in a book of fiction by Charles Einstein, *The Day New York Went Dry*.) The most reliable long-term solution for New York and all coastal cities which face cyclical water famines is large-scale desalting of sea water, a subject which we shall discuss in a later chapter. It is noteworthy that the Southern California cities, San Diego and Los Angeles, which are located in semi-desert, have been more aggressive in planning along this line than those of the Eastern seaboard. The planning has been accelerated by the fact that the area is in the twentieth year of a bone-dry cycle. Furthermore, they are in much better shape for the present and the immediate future than the cities of the so-called humid East. Under construction for the use of Southern California is the great North-South or Feather River project that will bring water in 444-mile aqueducts from the wild, wet watersheds of northern California.

It is significant, from the point of view of global climatology, that recent years have been drought years in many parts of the world. Things are tough all over. A 4-year water famine has reached the verge of tragedy in parts of South Africa, particularly Bechuanaland. In many areas this has resulted in starvation. People are too weak to walk. In the countryside surrounding Gaberones, the capital, the land looks like hide that has been flayed until the pelt has been worn away. Four tribesmen were sentenced to death by the high court for the ritual slaying of a 6-year-old boy in the belief that human sacrifice would end the drought.

The worst drought in sixty years has afflicted Korea. The Han River just barely flows but it has been narrowed by widening stretches of sand and stinking mud along its banks. Smaller rivers have been reduced to feeble streams or have dried up. Planted fields that should remain flooded for fifty days are desiccated and the rice stalks are drooping.

Calcutta has had a dry hot spell which has evaporated natural sources of water. People walk miles daily for a small jugful.

Tokyo nearly canceled the Olympic Games in the fall of 1964 because of a continuing water shortage. The water supply in three reservoirs was down to a little over 5 million tons. Normally they stock up to 200 million tons. The city normally uses nearly 2 million tons daily. One of the reasons for Tokyo's shortage is a system of old mains, many of them shattered by bombs during World War II. About 20 percent of the water pumped into the city's 5,000-mile water main system leaks out.

Hong Kong has had to rely on occasional typhoons and emergency pipelines from Red China to save it from disaster. During one recent drought the U.S. Navy supplied drinking water to the city from sea-water distillation units installed aboard the great aircraft carriers. The original Hong Kong water system was unique in relying on a series of reservoirs fed solely by rain water. This is indeed dangerous practice for a city of 4 million people. The ultimate dependence of Hong Kong on water from Red China may indeed constitute the essential economic lever to justify Communist take-over of the city. No coastal city in the world would welcome so heartily a break-through in the technology of desalting ocean water.

In Spain the rain has not been falling mainly on the plain. On the plain of La Mancha in the summer of 1965 the innkeeper could not offer you water but would give you wine. Or if you had bottled water, he would trade you two bottles of wine for one of water. There is, of course, a great drought-proof tradition involved here. Professor Henry Eyring, the illustrious chemist, who happens also to be a Mormon, once arrived in Brussels tired from a long flight and asked the welcoming party for a glass of water. Consternation ensued. Eyring maintains that in the whole city nobody had ever drunk a glass of water before.

This hydrophobic tradition used to exist in the United States and there is a famous Navy story (possibly a bit apocryphal) about the *Constitution* ("Old Ironsides"), which makes one sigh for a lost robustness.

On the 23rd of August, 1779, the USS *Constitution*, carrying its regular cargo, set sail from Boston with 475 officers and men, 48,600 gallons of fresh water, 7,400 cannon shot, 11,600 pounds of black powder, and 79,000 gallons of rum. Her mission was to destroy and harass English shipping.

Making Jamaica on the 6th of October, she took on 826 pounds of flour and 68,300 gallons of rum. Then she headed for the Azores. Arriving there on the 12th of November, she provisioned with 550 pounds of beef and 64,300 gallons of Portuguese wine.

On the 18th of November she set sail for England. In the ensuing days she defeated five British men-of-war, captured and scuttled 12 English merchantmen, salvaging only the rum.

On the 27th of January her powder and shot were exhausted. Unarmed, she made a night raid up the Firth of Tay. Her landing party captured a whisky distillery and transferred 40,000 gallons aboard. Then she headed for home.

The USS *Constitution* arrived at Boston on the 20th of February, 1780, with no cannon, no shot, no food, no powder, no rum, no whisky, and 48,600 gallons of stagnant water.

To rule the mountain is to rule the rivers.

—ANCIENT CHINESE PROVERB

Great floods have flown from simple sources.

—SHAKESPEARE, *All's Well that Ends Well*

8 FLOODS

THE EXASPERATING THING ABOUT floods is that they so often occur in some places in the country at a time when other places are simultaneously suffering drought. In 1964-1965, the wicked northern Mississippi inundation, the boisterous floods in Northern California and Oregon and the Colorado-Kansas floods occurred against a background of dramatic water shortage in the Northeast. Thirty years ago during the water famine of the Great Depression, two of the worst floods of history visited the Susquehanna and the Ohio River basins.

The amount of water wasted in floods is astronomical. During the disaster of the spring of 1965 in Northern California, the Eel River alone in one 24-hour period poured enough water into the ocean to have taken care of the entire needs of the people of the city of Los Angeles for three years. Such lavish injustices on the part of nature emphasize the point that our national problem on water supply is not one of water shortage but of poor apportionment of water in both place and time.

For drought and floodwaters not only present dolorous contrasts during the same period in different parts of the country but continued drought can give rise to floods in the same places when the rains, long solicited by prayer, finally arrive in downpours.

This is a familiar scenario in Southern California. The chaparral of the foothills and the low mountains is burnt to a crisp by a prolonged drought. Fires are then started, often by neurotics or by submorons flicking cigarette butts into the tinder. Suddenly, come winter a torrent of rain decides to fall. The water rolls down the bare hillsides like three dozen Johnstown floods. Cars with drowned occupants are found buried in mud or wrapped around live-oak trees. The bodies of drowned babies are pulled out of storm sewers and even from coastal bays 30 miles from the sites where the water and the people had their fatal collisions.

Nearly 2,400 years ago Plato said: "There are mountains, in Attica which can now keep nothing but bees, but which were clothed not so very long ago with fine trees. . . . The annual supply of rainfall was not lost, as it is at present, through being allowed to flow over a denuded surface to the sea, but was received by the country in all its abundance—stored in impervious potter's earth—and so was able to discharge the drainage of the heights into the hollows in the form of springs and rivers."

When rain falls at the rate of 30 inches in 12 hours, as it did in Pennsylvania in 1942, something's got to give. Practically all of such a rain is wasted in runoff. Few realize the tremendous mechanical force of a downpour. The dead weight of one inch of water on an acre of land is over 110 tons. When rain falls at 2 inches an hour, the drops are expending energy at the rate of 250 horsepower per acre. This is theoretically enough to lift a 7-inch layer of topsoil to a height of 3 feet 86 times during an hourlong storm. The energy of the falling drops is up to 100,000 times that of the rain in the form of runoff. Thus so-called "splash erosion" of soil is much more serious than is usually regarded. More attention has been given to "scour erosion" caused by flowing water.

Any rain consists of drops of many different sizes with more large drops being contained in harder rains. The drops are

viciously large in a summer thunderstorm and may turn to hail.
This takes place when raindrops are falling through turbulent
layers of air, alternately warm and cold. A hailstone has been
on a crazy journey to earth. Before attaining perhaps the
majestic Texas size of a baseball, its life as a raindrop has been
a series of ups and downs, tossed on wild updrafts, plummeting
through atmospheric "holes," and finally reaching sufficient
weight and dignity in the form of ice to slam the earth. Without wind, large raindrops will hit the ground at a speed of
about 30 feet per second. In the presence of wind, their speed
may be much greater.

One of the exceedingly unhelpful things that big fast raindrops do is to compact the surface soil. Although part of the
soil is scattered by the impact, some of it is also hammered
flat. The effect is virtually to waterproof the surface during the
first few minutes of a hard rain. Thus as much as 95 to 98 percent of the water, even on sands and sandy loams, is lost in the
runoff.

Because of the double-barreled effect of rain in eroding and
hammering as it falls and in carrying splashed soil away in
runoff sheets or rills, two different types of cover crops are
needed to retard flooding. The selection of such vegetation is
at the very heart of common-sense land management in the
flood control of watersheds. One needs crops that act as millions
of tiny umbrellas to cushion the soil against rain pounding.
Practically complete elimination of soil compaction requires
only 2,000 pounds per acre of short sod grasses, 3,500 pounds
of bunch grass but as much as 6,000 pounds of tall crops and
weeds.

For putting a stop to runoff from higher land, densely
packed stems are needed rather than umbrellas. For this mode
of flood control there are almost unlimited varieties of cover
crops which the soil conservationist can choose from. Bermuda
grass is justly popular because it can not only be densely grown

but has a deep stubborn root system and can be wilted in dry hot spells as brown as clay without dying out.

All the crop cover that a soil can grow is not enough to stop floods if the rains are hard enough. In true "cloudbursts" the water moves across land and vegetation, houses and cattle, like a tidal wave. By the most intensive cover-cropping, a 1-inch per hour runoff can be reduced to half an inch, but a peak runoff of 3 inches per hour would still be reduced by only half an inch, and what is left is still a flood. For big rivers big dams are needed. This brings in the Bureau of Reclamation or the Army Corps of Engineers. But even the single farmer himself or small associations of farmers in flood-prone areas can do a big part of the job. In addition to cover crops the farmers can put in small dams in gullies (as that extraordinary man, Patrick Henry, said, "He is the greatest patriot who stops the most gullies"). The closer the conservation work is to the man who owns the farm the more realistic the benefits. When ferocious floods engulfed eastern Nebraska in 1949 and 1950 a heartening sequel was the formation of the Salt Wahoo Watershed Association—a group essentially of farmers—which could stand as a model of watershed associations throughout the country.

The Watershed Protection and Flood Prevention Act, unlike the earlier Flood Control Act of 1936, shifted initiative to the people themselves. Financial help for watershed improvement could be applied for, provided the watershed was no bigger than 250,000 acres. A watershed association can handle this without hollering for the invocation of clanking and ponderous federal machinery which eventually puts the Corps of Engineers to work moving dirt. Upstream water-flow blocking and channel stabilization can be done without massive federal butting in. At this stage of flood prevention the Soil Conservation Service is the appropriate Big Brother and should be an adviser rather than a Santa Claus.

Consider the ways the farmer can get help from his government in water management. There are so many avenues of aid, federal and state, that he is a smart farmer who even understands them all.

First, in every agricultural county in the United States there is a county agent. He is supposed to know about everything, including water and the latest gossip, and provides a good shoulder to cry upon.

The Internal Revenue Code gives the farmer a break on taxes. Expenditures for soil and water conservation may be treated as deductions from gross income.

Four out of five farms and ranches in the United States are in "soil conservation districts" which are locally organized and locally managed subdivisions of the states. They are assisted by specialists of the Department of Agriculture.

Through the Agricultural Program Service, landowners and farm operators can obtain financial aid up to 50 percent of the cost of applying soil and water conservation to their individual farms. This program is run by the County Agricultural Stabilization and Conservation Committee, of which there is one in every farm county of the country.

A landowner can obtain long-term, low-interest loans from (or guaranteed by) the Farm Home Administration for his out-of-pocket costs for soil and water conservation and water facilities.

As decided in 1965 by a U.S. Circuit Court of Appeals, irrigation farmers in the southern High Plains of Texas and New Mexico are entitled to a water depletion allowance for income tax purposes. This is where the irrigation water comes from wells on the farmers' property. It seems doubtful that this decision could stand up, since it goes back to the old juridical error that ground water is motionless and part of the property right. However, those Supreme Court jurists who are indignant about the petroleum depletion allowance and feel that the farmer needs every fringe benefit will doubtless make this decision national in scope.

Under a new federal law passed in 1965 farmers can even

collect money on crops destroyed by floods on acreage which the farmer had promised to leave unplanted under the acreage reduction and price support rules.

The situation is not so clear in disaster loans. One weakness in the help from Big Brother is in the provision of relief after a flood disaster. Farmers can obtain loans for conventional building purposes from the FHA for 33 years at 4 percent interest. However, when his farm has suddenly washed out from under him, the best terms he can get are 20 years at 3 percent. The interest is smaller but the payments are bigger because of the shorter amortization time. Inconsistencies as wild as these are very common in the immense rat's nest of farm-help legislation that Congress has built up since Teddy Roosevelt's time.

Insurance payoffs under the Food Insurance Act of 1951 are conditioned upon prior "flood zoning," a complicated gimmick which few farmers pretend to understand.

The trouble is that people forget about floods and Congress becomes noisy only after a flood has made the headlines or become photogenic enough to show television shots of houses drifting downstream with pigs and chickens on the roofs. Examining the Congressional appropriations of the past few years, we see that after the floods in New England there followed a flurry of new studies, *ad hoc* committees and water-control funds. The great Pacific Coast floods inspired a fever of appropriations. When trouble seemed to be building up in the upper Mississippi in the winter of 1965, one congressman proposed to a Wisconsin delegation that the surest way to get action was to arrange for a modest flood. They arranged a flood but it was not modest.

It is important to note that simply getting a flood-prevention law through Congress does not mean that anything at all will be done. Public Law 516 of the 81st Congress included authorization for flood control in the South Platte Basin in Colorado. Such work might have prevented or at least have gentled the worst flood in Colorado history in that basin in the spring of 1965, which was followed immediately by the flooding in southeastern Colorado and western Kansas of the Arkansas River. The floods were attributed to strange atmospheric conditions. Two high-pressure systems near the Great Lakes and two low-pressure systems in the South combined to pull vast quantities of moisture-loaded air from the Gulf of Mexico over the Rocky Mountains where the clash between warm and cold air produced deluges of rain plus some tornadoes.

But before this happened, no specific Congressional appropriations had been requested and not a single bag of Portland cement had been moved. Now, in a post-mortem period, both river basins are swarming with Congressional subcommittees and *ad hoc* investigators.

A case history of the "forgotten floods" is the story of the Red River Valley of the North, mainly in North Dakota and Minnesota. Severe flooding in this basin took place regularly in the 1880's and 1890's. Then there were flood-free years including the long drought of the 1930's. What drainage improvements had been put in were totally neglected. A new generation had grown up which knew only water shortage. Newcomers arrived in the dry thirties and most of them considered that soil-conservation practices designed to guard against flooding were a waste of money.

Roads were built with no drainage, not even allowance for passage of water from one side of the road to the other. Road ditches had no outlets. The farmers sometimes placed fills across ditches to make the field operations easier. Requests were even made to have the Civilian Conservation Corps build dams in ditches to alleviate the drought.

Then the rains came. Bad floods tore the farms to pieces in 1943, 1944, 1948, and 1950. The farm crop damage in the North Dakota part of the basin alone in 1943 was over $60 million, which is pretty big for this poor state.

Overnight 14 soil conservation districts were organized in North Dakota and 4 in Minnesota. It was found that North Dakota had on its books a weird law limiting the expenditures on any drainage project to $100. This had to be kicked out before anybody could do anything. At the present time the issue of drainage is a peculiarly bitter one in North Dakota but since it relates to ducks rather than floods we shall reserve discussion.

In truly monstrous floods, such as those of the Columbia River Basin in 1948 and the Kansas River in 1951, watershed improvements are not enough. Very large expensive dams must be built. Such floods may be caused by a single short storm if the storm travels in such a way that the swollen tributaries hit the main river at about the same time. In general, however, big floods mean long storms. The Columbia River disaster had everything a big flood needs: abnormally heavy rainfall during the preceding nine months, abnormally heavy snowfall in the mountains, then the sudden arrival of very hot weather in the entire watershed on May 17 along with dozens of thunderstorms and very heavy rains all during May. More than 40 lives were lost, along with part of the city of Portland; 61,000 were made homeless. Property damage alone (not including agricultural crops) was over $200 million.

The Kansas River flood in 1951 was still more damaging, chiefly because of very heavy farm losses. The total cost was nearly $1 billion and 250,000 people were driven from their homes. The rains had begun falling steadily in April, continued high through June, which was the wettest month of 65 years of Kansas weather history, and culminated in cloudbursts between July 9 and July 16.

It had been the 1936 flood in the upper Ohio Basin, its highest on record, which inspired the passage of the original Flood Control Act. The concept of multipurpose river basin development has emerged since those days and as a result the 1936 act had been amended thirteen times. One of the things the Flood

Control Act did was to bring the Department of Agriculture definitely into the spotlight. The Soil Conservation Service was charged with carrying the flag for upstream programs connected with land treatment, water-flow checking and construction of gullydikes. Congress likes to pass laws on water. The Watershed and Flood Protection Act of 1954 echoed the 1936 act, stating more specifically the role of the Department of Agriculture.

However, of over 250 authorized local flood projects in the Ohio Basin, only 62 have been completed.

This lag is true also of Corps of Engineers projects. For example, Congress long ago authorized 13 dams above Pittsburgh. Only 8 have been put into operation. In fact, some of those authorized will never be built because the Pennsylvania Turnpike now stands in the way.

From the standpoint of money, a distinction used to be drawn between flood prevention and flood control. The individual states were supposed to spend money for prevention, while the federal government built the big dams. However, this dainty categorization loses meaning in view of all the ways that farmers, alone or in gangs, can get their hands into Uncle Sam's pocket whenever the word "water" is used as an open-sesame. One of these ways is to have vote-hungry opposition congressmen in a presidential election year. Thus the 1956 amendment of the Watershed and Flood Protection Act provides in theory at least for 100 percent federal payment of the costs of flood prevention. This was passed over Eisenhower's veto. A sort of Gresham's law ("bad money displaces good money") is at work on federal financial policies concerning water. The tendency is for higher standards of repayment by state, local and private beneficiaries to be replaced by lower standards.

One of the modifications of the 1936 Flood Control Act came in 1944 following the Missouri River flood of 1943 when all land adjacent to the river from South Dakota down through Iowa, Nebraska and Missouri was inundated. Six large dams were built, which effectively stopped flooding in the Missouri River Basin. However, there resulted artificial-lake formation covering a million acres. Now the Dakotans want their land back in the form of reclaimed and irrigated acreage elsewhere. This absurd proposal again belongs to the Kingdom of Pork and will be discussed later in that context.

In spite of all that has been done in the way of flood control since the days of the Great Depression, we continue to have a total annual flood bill averaging over $1 billion on public works, much of which is on flood control, but like some gargantuan King Canute we cannot seem to make the waters behave.

It should be noted that the losses mentioned do not include damage from hurricanes, which of course have killed more people than river floods (the record being 5,000 drowned in the Galveston hurricane of 1900). This is a subject outside the purview of this book.

In spite of the fact that we appear to be swimming against an ever-stronger current, flood control has generally paid out. It is possible with a somewhat lenient pencil to arrive at the estimate that, since the general flood-control program of the Corps of Engineers was started thirty years ago, savings of $2 have resulted from every dollar invested. As we shall see in the chapter "Pork Is Soluble in Water," this is not going to be true of many present grandiose "multipurpose" river projects.

> . . . a tree planted by the waters,
> and that spreadeth out her roots by the river,
> and shall not see when heat cometh,
> but her leaf shall be green;
> and shall not be careful in the year of the drought,
> neither shall cease from yielding fruit.
>
> —JEREMIAH, 17:8

9 TREES and OTHER WATER HOGS

THE WAY plants drink water, although much more complex than our simple gulping, is usually very inefficient in terms of the amount of water required to keep a plant in business. Plants have the excuse that they require supplemental nutrients (nitrates, phosphorus, potassium, etc.) which are water-soluble. Not having mouths and fangs, they cannot obtain these nutrients by gnawing on solids (except for certain exotic insect-eating varieties). Nevertheless, the water consumption by such prodigal vegetation as alfalfa and wheat is scandalous from a chemical engineering point of view and it is possible that one of the great scientific breakthroughs of the future will be to breed food crops which are more efficient hydraulic engines.

For every pound of dry matter in the plant there are from 5 to 10 pounds of water, depending on the amount of woody material. But for each pound of dry matter produced the average land plant must absorb several hundred pounds of water. The difference between the 5 or 10 pounds and the several hundred pounds represents water lost by *transpiration*. This water evaporates from the leaves and is lost to the atmosphere. By contrast, an aquatic plant has to absorb only the water required for its growth.

The average grain plant such as wheat goes about its search for water underground in a most elaborate and greedy manner. A single wheat plant will set forth a root system as much as 35 miles in total combined length. Many millions of root hairs will increase the surface of this already large water-absorbing network by ten times or more. In a development scheme of great subtlety the plant internally modifies itself to transport the water it finds. Special, greatly elongated cells begin to form in the roots, the stems and the leaves. After these cells have grown, the protoplasts degenerate and disappear, leaving a long hollow tube or "tracheid" as a conduit of low resistance to the movement of water. The end walls of the cells in many plant species are digested away as the plant matures, and resistance to flow is further reduced. These units are called "vessels." Vessels and tracheids are the cells that remain alive to form the xylem tissue, or wood. The xylem affords a continuous system of hollow tubes from near the tip of the root, through the root and stem and into the leaf. Here it is part of the familiar leaf-vein network.

All plants make some attempt to conserve water, otherwise it would pass through them in a sort of automatic, short circuit-wicking system and the plant would constitute a combination pump and vaporizer. The engineering challenge that the plant has to meet is to conserve water without excluding air, since the carbon dioxide and oxygen of the air must be absorbed by the leaves in the all-important primary business of the plant— photosynthesis and respiration. The former results in the formation of carbohydrate tissues and the latter oxidizes some of these tissues in order to obtain energy for living. This is essentially the way animals use oxygen.

The way plants manage to conserve water is a marvel of hydraulic finesse. The pores, or stomata, of a leaf, through which a plant breathes and also sweats, are associated with so-called "guard cells." The pore or stomata is actually the space between these guard cells. If the guard cells are fully turgid with water, they protrude from the surface and the stomata are open to the fullest extent. Water loss by transpiration can proceed rapidly. As the guard cells lose turgor, because of loss of water, they relax and approach each other, closing the stomata. Water loss through the pores is thus stopped. Most plants are further proofed against water loss by the presence of a waxy cuticle or skin on the leaves and stem. With older, woody stems, when the growth in diameter results in rupture of the cuticle, water loss is controlled by a most extraordinary emergency mechanism (a sort of self-applied "Medicare" for old trees)—the development of layers of cork cells.

The variation in water demands of different plants, indicating the difference in the refinement of the internal conservation mechanisms, is very wide. Among food crops alone, millet needs 300 pounds of water to produce a pound of dry matter. Alfalfa needs 1,000 pounds. Root systems vary enormously in size and aggressiveness. In the San Joaquin Valley of California grapevines will send roots down as deep as 40 feet, to the bottom of the water table. In the same soil potato plants will venture down only 2 feet. A tree with almost frighteningly strong and irresistible roots is the eucalyptus, imported before the twentieth century to California from Australia. Sewerage engineers have an endless struggle to keep the roots of this tree out of clay sewer pipes. Sensing the water, they will insinuate themselves into the joints, penetrating inches of asphaltic or coal-tar mastic used as pipe-joint compound. These eucalyptus roots think nothing of heaving up sidewalks and uptilting shacks and small foundationless homes. If they were not so tall, beautiful and aromatic they would be chopped down as insolent pests.

As long as a plant or tree yields food or possesses extraordinary personal charm, one can forgive it for being a water hog. This is not true of a large number of water wastrels called "phreatophytes" (well plants). In the 17 Western States alone these plants waste 20 to 25 million acre-feet of water per year. They occupy about 15 million acres. They do not belong to any one family but all have the ability of sending down roots to the water table. Among the worst are salt cedars, willows, cottonwoods, juniper, salt grass, greasewood, baccharis and mesquite. All occur in valley bottoms and along streams. (Alfalfa is a phreatophyte, from the standpoint of root habits and water hogging but, being an important fodder crop, it is babied rather than cursed.)

Along the Rio Grande Valley in New Mexico, the high consumption of water by salt cedars is the big reason why New Mexico has had trouble in delivering water to the Elephant Butte Reservoir, as required by the Rio Grande Compact with Mexico. The juniper, a small evergreen tree, has sopped up some 14.6 billion gallons of usable rain annually in the north-central Arizona area, where there are more than 7 million acres supporting this water thief.

The transpiration of water by such plants is greater than the evaporation from bare soil and occurs at much greater depths. The ground-water level in some places falls during the day and rises at night with clocklike regularity on account of the tremendous transpiration flow.

Because of the deep, strong root system of these plants it is almost impossible to get rid of them by conventional means. In the Safford Valley of Arizona they tried getting rid of salt cedars by burning and uprooting with heavy equipment. The disturbance of the soil stimulated the remaining roots to greater activity. They went looking for the water table and the net result was that by the end of the next growing season there were more new salt cedars six feet high grouped sneeringly around some holes in the ground, transpiring like mad.

The best answer, although an expensive one, is the use of herbicidal sprays, such as "2,4-D." Willows are mowed in the fall and the regrowth is sprayed the following spring. But the salt cedar not only can take a lot of spray without flinching but appears to develop resistance to the poison. At least seven applications of 2,4-D are necessary to make the salt cedar say "uncle." This technique is dangerous from the standpoint of water pollution.

If one tries very hard, some redeeming virtue can be discerned in the phreatophytes. Their roots are so matted that they act like sieves and therefore screen heavy sediment particles out of streams or moving ground water. It has been suggested that vegetation with complex root structures would be useful when planted above the heads of water reservoirs to help check the sedimentation before it reaches the main storage basin. This would prolong the life of reservoirs. However, the plants selected would not be our rough friends, the willows or salt cedars, but would be gentler phreatophytes such as the wild rose, the sand cherry, the hackberry and the Russian olive.

The worst hazard connected with the vampire-type phreatophytes is that much of the water they suck is from the water table. It is important to understand that they do not simply dry up the surface soil. Soils differ greatly in their capacity to hold water. The "field capacity" of a soil is the moisture content to which each layer must be raised before water can drain through it. Ordinary plants, whose roots deal only with surface soil, can dry the land only to the "wilting point." This is the moisture content at which the molecular force holding water to the soil particles is equal to the maximum water-absorbing force of the plant roots. Just as clay soils can hold more water at field capacity than sands, the wilting point of a clay is higher than that of a sand. But the phreatophytes do not wilt as long as their roots are in the water table and the texture of the soil affects them only in so far as it limits the rate at which their roots can push down to the ground water.

There is a great deal about the mechanics of water absorption by plant roots that we do not understand. When a root hair absorbs moisture from a particle of soil, water must move over the surface of the soil particle. Yet the rate of movement of water in soils holding less than their field capacity, observed microscopically, is negligible. Some essential part of the mystery eludes us. It is almost as if the roots had a water-pulling force over and beyond the molecular force of absorption. The mystery arises only in the case of ordinary plants watered by unsaturated surface soil, since in the water table the soil is saturated. A lot of research is needed to understand how much water in the surface soil is actually available to root plants.

Research has already demonstrated that the time of irrigation in the growth stage of the plant is important. Thus corn needs the most water between early tasseling and the silking stage. This is one of the advantages of irrigation compared to dry farming. The water can be supplied when it is needed most.

Trees never grow tall in climates where the air is dry and strong winds blow during the growing season. The rate of transpiration is too great (the wind removes water vapor from the leaves and the loss of water is accelerated). This is the same effect that people sense when their sweat evaporates in a breeze. When dense forests are thinned out by fire, insects or cutting, the remaining trees are exposed to excessive transpiration. Trees thus suddenly exposed to more wind and heat will decline in vigor, look haggard and old, and often the tops will die back for several feet.

Trees need less rain in cool regions. Parts of the tropics with 40 inches of rain a year are treeless. The ponderosa pine needs 20 inches or more in the mountains of New Mexico but 15 inches is enough in Montana. The spruce and fir forests of Saskatchewan receive no more rain or snow than the grass-covered plains of North Dakota, but the summer heat is less.

The dependability of the rain is important for trees. In moving westward the settlers found the great forests of the Eastern States giving way to grass in Illinois, although the annual rainfall averaged the same. (This Eastern dependability has been somewhat shaken during the years 1961-1965.) The extreme droughts of 1913 and 1931-1934 killed many trees on the margin of the prairie and the forest boundary was pushed back. Winter rather than summer rain is what trees want. Thirty inches of rain, mostly in the winter, is enough for the Douglas fir forests of southwestern Oregon. But the same amount falling mostly in summer produces only grasses in Iowa.

Interspersed with the broad-leaved deciduous forests of the humid East and Southeast are forests of pine—for example, the great Southern pinery which occupies the coastal plain from New Jersey to East Texas. Because of the lack of fertility of the sandy coastal-plain soils, the pines have been able to hold this large region even though it is in a climate that favors the broadleaf deciduous trees. The pines, like most immigrants, are tougher than the effete natives.

All the giant trees, with the exception of the eucalyptus, grow where there is plenty of winter rain and summer fog: the redwoods, the Douglas fir, the Port Orford cedar, the western hemlock, the Sitka spruce. Shelter belts and windbreaks will grow in the naturally treeless Great Plains only if special wind- and drought-resistant species are chosen. After a search all over the world, the Siberian elm and the Russian olive were planted on countless Kansas and Nebraska farms. They are as common as the native cottonwood, hackberry and juniper. Needless to say, they also are water hogs. The farmer gives up some water for some wind protection.

There has been a good deal of controversy between the foresters, on the one side, and the farmers and lumber merchants, on the other side, as to just how useful trees are in a watershed. A great deal more snow than rain can be held by trees. In the Rocky Mountains of Colorado snow accumulation on the ground was increased by the equivalent of two inches of water by removal of all merchantable timber from a forest of lodgepole pine. In this particular case no soil erosion took place because the summer rains were light and the winter storms brought only snow. In this particular situation, trees interfere with the water-storage function of mountain snow, since the rate of evaporation from scattered snow or snow clinging to needles, leaves or branches is much higher than when it is packed on the ground. Coniferous trees will retain snow against even a moderate wind. This is one disadvantage of evergreens. In the same area aspens, which lose their leaves in the winter, intercept hardly any snow.

On the other hand, evergreen forests hold down the evaporation from the snowpack. The trees shade the snow, catching sunlight and converting it to long-wave radiation, much of which goes back into the atmosphere. (The *albedo*, which is the ratio of light reflected from an unpolished surface to the light falling on it, is different for various forms of vegetation. Grass has an albedo of 0.26; pine forests 0.14.)

It has been found that snow water supplies may be increased by converting from conifer to hardwood forests. Certainly the hardwood forest would intercept less snow. A still unanswered question is whether a hardwood forest uses more water during the summer.

The tree controversy is not confined to snow. On the Coweta forest watershed in western North Carolina an interesting experiment was designed to find out how much water is used up by the trees in transpiration. All the trees and shrubs were cut down *but not removed*. Reducing the transpiration loss in this way increased the stream-flow rate by 65 percent the first year after cutting. Because there was no removal of logs or disturbance of roots, the increased amount of runoff did not give greater soil erosion. Flood peaks were unchanged.

Experiments such as this will show whether municipalities should follow the rather general practice of complete forestation of watersheds or use some kind of plant cover that will prevent erosion but use up less water.

The value of forest cover in reducing soil erosion and thus lowering flood danger depends greatly on the soil type. The porous glaciated sections in New England, the Lake States and the Pacific Northwest can hold large amounts of rain. The heavier clay soils of the northern Appalachia and southwestern Colorado are easily washed off. The "loess" soil near the Mississippi is easily eroded when the protective forest cover is removed because it is an unstable product of wind-blown material.

In Arizona, South Carolina and eastern Oregon needle frost occurs on the surface of soils not protected by forest cover. The effect is to create a fluffy layer which is carried off by the next rain.

One seldom appreciated fact is that some of the most valuable commercial forest stands in the West are the result of fire. Had it not been for the recurrence of fire in the forest of northern Idaho, the famous white pine would long ago have been replaced by the less valuable western red cedar, western hemlock and white fir. These trees tolerate a greater amount of shade. The fabulous Douglas fir of western Washington and Oregon similarly owes its abundance to fire, which gave it an advantage over the cedar and hemlock. Beyond this rather subtle ecological point, fire is still all bad. It is not so tragic in the Eastern hardwood forests where trees and shrubs will sprout from stumps or roots after a fire. But coniferous trees are killed by a hot fire. Burning exposes the soil not only to water erosion but to wind erosion and to deep penetration by the "concrete" type of frost in winter. And it still takes a century to grow a big tree.

An absurd myth, which still persists in many sections of the country, is that burning off grasslands helps the soil. What happens is that the burning process does release some plant nutrients, such as potash, in readily available form from the ashes of the grass. When leached into the soil by gentle rain or snow-melt, the soluble ash may promote a temporary lush growth. But the reduction in growth during the succeeding years explodes the myth. And in the meantime the soil goes through a period when rains that are not so gentle can carry off both nutrients and top soil.

It must be pointed out that the Plains Indians were great grass burners. They started grass fires to make the buffalo herds go in the direction they wanted. Some climatologists blame the Indians for the great extension of the prairies as a result of their hunting practices. On the other hand, the Forest Indians were better conservationists than Smokey the Bear. Huge forest fires were unknown in the forest primeval because the Indians started smaller, more frequent blazes and kept the big ones from breaking out. In the spring the old squaws began to look around for the little dry spots of headland or sunny valley and as fast as dry spots appeared, they would be burned. By this means the Indians always kept their forests open, pure and fruitful, and conflagrations were unknown.

(It has become fashionable to regard the Plains Indians as noble creatures whose pure way of life was defiled by the white man. Actually they were savages in an early stage of social evolution. If they had been better organized and if their population had been larger, they would have been the equivalent of the fifteenth-century Mongols, to whom they are racially related, in general destructiveness and in acts of abominable genocide. The age of Hitler has nothing to be proud about in its human animal but one must not forget that, with fewer engineering capabilities for mass killing, the Mongols are still far ahead of the batting percentage of any white gang. With a strong dictator, to bring in the Comanches and the Blackfeet, and with 50,000 good horses, the Sioux could have become a North American "golden horde.")

Cattle ranchers have their water problems. Ever since they trailed the first herds across the "mile-wide-and-inch-deep" rivers of the Great Plains on the way to Northern markets, Western stockmen have fought for dependable water supplies. Most

Western rangelands have enough water for cattle but not enough for grass to feed the cattle. One half of the water on Western ranges is wasted, either by runoff, too much evaporation, or the production of useless vegetation. How much grazing should be allowed? A rule of thumb for stockmen is "Take-half-and-leave-half," but this is seldom obeyed. The abnormal loss of moisture under skinny plant cover may change grasslands to shrub deserts in a few years. Overgrazed clay-loam soil will absorb only about 10 percent as much rain as well-grown pasturage.

Considering again the woodlands, how does one run a good forest? In my generation every boy wanted to be either a forester or an Al Capone. The girls in my generation, who were much more restless and corruptible than those of subsequent generations, did not want to be foresters' wives. Needless to say, few boys wound up as foresters. It is nevertheless an exacting and challenging job. It is not simple to see that the soil stays intact on a forest area while timber is being logged and forage is grazed. An intricate balance must be kept.

The dream of a forest watershed manager is to have enough drainage to support a productive stand of trees ranging from seedlings to fully grown timber. A complete and stabilized road system has been built in this dream forest. The removal of salable forest products from harvest cuttings and thinning takes place with a minimum soil disturbance and a minimum silting up of streams. The road system also allows intensive fire protection as well as access for fishing, hunting and camping. Near the mouth of this ideal forest watershed the stream may flow through a valley with irrigated farms, several small communities and a wood-using industry, consisting of two sawmills, a pulp mill and a furniture factory. All are dependent on the watershed for a regulated flow of clean water, sustained supply of wood products, a source of recreation. All the people look up to the forester. None of them smoke cigarettes.

The ideal doesn't exist. The forester is continually bothered, for example, by present-day trends in road construction. Wider roads and straighter roads, so trucks and cars can zoom through the forest, mean much greater land disturbance and hence added dangers from erosion. Speeded-up logging practices are another cause of erosion. The removal of logs by skidding (dragging the logs along the ground by tractors) makes a trough-like trail where floods can run. Usually the skid roads run up and down hill, funneling toward a loading point. They make ideal channels for urging on concentrated floods. Skidding is often done across quiet, well-established streams. This rips out the protective bank vegetation, leaving a mass of debris. This junk precariously dams the flow of high water until finally a washout carries large masses of it downstream, tearing out exposed banks. The process is repeated until a wide scour has replaced the original tranquil little stream bed. Logging can be most destructive in emergency salvage of dead timber, killed by disease, insect attack or fire. There is great incentive on the part of the logger to get the dead timber out before it decays. Precautions against soil damage are forgotten in the rush to salvage a few bucks' worth of decay-free timber.

Strip mining, right-of-way for power-line construction, camp ground development, clearing for ski areas—all these disturb the forest soil, in some cases so seriously that minor floods can be attributed to the gougings and bulldozings. Tractors should never be used on steep slopes or wet ground. Yet they nearly always are.

As logging progresses into steeper terrain, the problem of maintaining soil stability becomes even more serious. Some of the more rugged sections of the Rockies, Sierra Nevada and Cascade Ranges should not be logged at all by present methods. If the logging must go on, the best answer is radically new techniques such as the Wyssen skyline crane developed for mountains in Switzerland. This device suspends the logs in mid-air during much of their travel from stump to loading point. Skidding is eliminated.

All the considerations above involve common sense or extensions of common sense. We come now to discoveries so revolutionary in plant physiology that they may result in completely new agricultural practices. I refer to the scientific work on the water saturation of plants by dew, fog or mist, done mostly by Professor F. W. Went and his large group of associates at the California Institute of Technology and by Israeli plant physiologists such as Duvdevani. The question that Duvdevani answered was whether in a semiarid area, such as the coastal plains of Israel, dew could help plants grow. He found that squash and corn, when they received dew during the night, grew twice as fast as canopied plants receiving no dew.

The effect is not from wetting of the ground. *The leaves absorb the dew directly.* It can even be shown that the water thus absorbed can be extracted from the roots. Thus certain plants can completely reverse the direction of their water traffic —a profound discovery. Since growth in most plants occurs during the night, the water supply in the form of night dew is especially timely. It is also fortunate that the amount of dew is higher during the dry summers than in the wet winters. Even in the dry and hot Jordan Valley dew is a common phenomenon and occurs on nearly half the nights. In the Negev Desert it is still more frequent. Although the total amount of dew in Israel amounts to only about one inch per year, it appears that this could be a really Big Inch.

The ordinary dew gauges are inadequate. They have been shown by Went and others to measure only about 10 percent of the potential dew. Went estimates that in some places in the United States 20 percent of the total water supply can come from dew.

Dew does not form on cloudy nights, since the precipitation of dew on a plant involves a radiation effect. Nearly all sunlight absorbed by plants on the ground during the day is radiated as heat back to the atmosphere at night. If the atmosphere contains water (clouds), this reradiation is reduced. If the atmosphere is clear, however, the reradiation goes on at a high rate. The ground and the plants become cool enough, through loss of heat by reradiation, to reach the dewpoint of the surrounding air. Dew is then deposited and no further drop occurs in the temperature of the leaves.

Dust and haze also prevent reradiation. Smoggy areas have little dew. In a narrow smog-free coastal area of Southern California, however, there is enough dew to grow tomatoes, peppers, and beans in the summer without rain or irrigation.

Professor Went has also pointed out the peculiar and charming relationship between certain forest trees and fogs and mists. (Fogs and mists are simply low-hanging clouds in which the water droplets are so small that they do not settle on horizontal surfaces and thus do not register in a rain gauge.) Forests of giant redwoods stand on the northern coast of California in a narrow fog belt. They never range inland beyond this belt where fogs occur almost daily. Walking in a redwood forest during a fog, one will see the trees dripping, although in a nearby nonforested spot not a drop falls. *The redwoods are able to condense fog droplets to raindrops.* The same effect is observed in pine forests or under live oaks in the California foothills during autumn fogs.

It appears that the narrow surfaces of pine or redwood needles act as strainers or surface condensers for fog, especially where there is a gentle air movement.

Coastal fogs formed by moist air rising against coastal mountain ranges are ideal for condensation of fog on trees. It is noteworthy that redwood growth is phenomenal against the western mountain slopes but is much poorer against the eastern slopes, with the same amount of rain.

Fog must account for the strange growth habits noted in

Southwest Africa and the coast of Peru. In both locations mountains rise behind the coast and cause ocean fogs as the air rises against them. In each case a cold ocean current (the Benguella and the Humboldt) limits the total rainfall to one inch per year. The lowlands are desert but a shrub vegetation occurs in the fog belt. Parasite vegetation of the type normally found in rain forests occurs even on cactus; lichens and mosses cover the branches of shrubs.

Just north of San Diego there is a small area where the Torrey pine abounds. The trees are limited to the upper part of slopes facing the ocean where the fog hits. It is an otherwise very dry area. Similar phenomena are observed behind Oran in Algeria, except that the tree is the holly oak.

One can get an idea of the total amount of water that can be precipitated on the right trees by using a rain gauge over which a set of fine wires is placed. During a heavy storm in South Africa only two tenths of an inch fell in a regular rain meter but the special gauge collected 6 inches.

Practical advantage is being taken of dew and fog in watering olive trees in the water-poor Maghreb countries (Tunisia, Morocco, Algeria).

Went, in charge of the famous Earhart Plant Research Laboratory at Cal Tech, has found that the leaves of several chaparral plants can take up water vapor from the air at a relative humidity of 80 percent or even less. It is known that water vapor from the air is an important source of water for certain tropical orchids which hang from the branches of jungle trees.

The implications of these phenomena are immensely exciting. If plants can be developed as two-way water conduits, not only can transpiration losses be greatly reduced but one can visualize vaporized fertilizers, so that the root system becomes just a device to anchor the plant to the ground. One might even look ahead to generations of mobile plants, which have feet instead of roots. A science-fictionist with some degree of technical justification could portray a future plant organism that is simply a brainless blind animal with chlorophyll. It lives on wet air and sunlight with a sniff of ammonia, phosphate and potash. Its greatest hazard, having escaped from the back yard, would be getting run down by automobiles or strangled by smog.

The sea is in the broad, the narrow streets,
Ebbing and flowing; and the salt seaweed
Clings to the marble of her palaces.
                    —ROGERS, *Italy:Venice*

Plow with salt your fields;
And there no harvest grows.
                    —WHICHER, *Ave Caesar*

10 SILT *and* SALT

IN THE FIRST CHAPTER we agreed that the chief cause of ruin of
the ancient hydraulic civilizations of Mesopotamia was the silting up of the rivers and the irrigation canals. This is a long process from the viewpoint of human history but through geologic
time it has occurred without the help of man. During the
Paleozoic era about 60,000 cubic miles of mud, sand and gravel
were deposited in the great trough that constituted the Appalachian Valley of Virginia. This deposit is 8 to 10 miles thick in
places. If it were spread over the area of Virginia southeast of
the Blue Ridge, from which much of it was derived, it would
raise the level of the state to over 10,000 feet above sea level.

Processes that include the erosion of soil and its removal and
deposition somewhere else are lumped by reclamationists under
the general term "sedimentation." It is estimated that in the
United States only about one quarter of the materials eroded
from the land surface ever reach the ocean. The amount reaching the ocean, from all the rivers in the United States, is about
a billion tons per year.

This proportion tends to become less and less as the rivers

become dammed artificially. What now happens is that the artificial and natural reservoirs become filled with silt. Lakes are thus all temporary features of the landscape, with the possible exception of high mountain lakes such as Titicaca. Geologically speaking, lakes have a short life expectancy. They will eventually be filled up with dirt. This includes the Great Lakes.

The sediment yield of a watershed depends mostly on the size of the drainage area. The sediment yield of the Mississippi watershed above the delta is about 500 million tons a year. The lower Mississippi is confined between levees which are nearly continuous all the way down from Cairo, Illinois. Floods that formerly spread widely over the delta below Baton Rouge are now contained. Hence the present growth of the delta is in the direction of greater length and lesser width. Ultimately there will be a great peninsula there.

It is now predicted that 20 percent of the nation's 2,700 water-supply reservoirs will have a useful life of less than fifty years at the present rate of siltation. The silt from such reservoirs or from polluted streams must be settled out in ponds in order to use the water even for industrial purposes. This treatment can be expensive. The state of North Carolina found that where only half the watershed was forested and farming and forestry were sloppy, the cost of purifying municipal drinking water was $27 per million gallons (in the Asheville area). Where all the watershed was in virgin forest, as at High Point, the cost was less than a third of this.

Silting is usually blamed on the farmer and the logger, but the most recent villain is the real estate developer. In the clearing of vast acreages for urban housing projects the bulldozer is allowed to tear the soil to pieces. Trees are seldom preserved. A whole area is leveled and replanted later. This leaves large sections of raw ground open to heavy erosion for a critical year or two.

The sudden silting of rivers and reservoirs that results from an ambitious real estate project can assassinate a river. Aside from the fact that the river becomes a sort of brown molasses "too thick to navigate and too thin to cultivate," the silting has a murderous effect on water life and the ability of the river to assimilate organic waste. If not overloaded, every natural river can cleanse itself through the activity of the organisms living in it. This is often referred to as the "food chain." The bacteria use pollutants, such as sewage, as a source of food. Protozoa eat the bacteria and keep them in check. Green algae use as food the substances formed by the bacteria and in the process of photosynthesis the algae give back to the water some of the oxygen used by the bacteria. Insects and small fish feed on the algae and keep it in balance. Big fish eat little fish.

When over the period of development of a big riverside real estate project you run off great quantities of soil into the river you break the food chain at one vital link—the algae. The sunlight cannot penetrate the water deep enough to keep the algae alive and to keep the process of photosynthesis going. Aside from removing the food source of small fish, you take away a precious supply of oxygen. Without oxygen the aerobic bacteria can no longer digest organic pollutants. Thus the "assimilation" capacity of the river has been cut way down and the river begins another, alternative process of waste decomposition. It putrefies. We have a stinking river.

The Delaware is an example of a badly silted river—a very important one since it serves the greatest concentration of people and industry of any watershed in the United States.

Perhaps there is no more disgusting example of devastation of vegetation cover in the history of watersheds than the bleak story of the Delaware Basin. The early nineteenth-century inhabitants were nearly as voracious a breed as the present real estate developers. Even before the Revolution iron ore was discovered in the lower basin. Smelting furnaces needed charcoal, and tens of thousands of acres of woodland were stripped and

restripped for this purpose. In the 1800's sawmills along the
Delaware turned out 30 million board feet of lumber a year
from dense forests running to 100,000 board feet per acre. Timber was so plentiful that hemlocks were felled for the bark
alone for tanning and the wood was left to rot where it fell. Today less than one third of the forest areas in the basin have as
much as 1,500 board feet of saw timber per year.

The anthracite coal industry hacked down the forests most
viciously of all. Timber was regarded as unimportant in relation
to hard coal, and no one gave a thought to the value of forests
in watershed protection. By World War I the mines were using
50 million cubic feet of wood per year. Small timbers were
used as props and lagging in the mines. Thus second-growth
stands were recut repeatedly as soon as they reached usable
size. Accordingly the forest lands were destroyed in the interests of an industry that itself is now practically defunct, and
with the destruction of the forests came the beginning of destruction of the river itself.

Although hard-coal miners no longer cut adolescent trees,
the strip miners have left a swath of absolute soil destruction.
Once the coal is power-shoveled away, the land is totally useless. A strip-mined area is a worse eyesore than a giant automobile junk yard and a million times as unwholesome. The land is
left to be a continuous source of sediment and acid runoff water. Although present laws in Pennsylvania require the rehabilitation of strip-mined lands, the process of rehabilitation
lags far behind the process of land destruction. As Senator
Gaylord Nelson of Wisconsin observed, uncontrolled strip mining everywhere, including Kentucky, is going to leave an area
not fit for mice to live in.

A curious ecological event occurred in Pennsylvania with
the cutting of the forests. Brush took over and the original
dense woodlands became a vast feeding ground for deer. Pennsylvania had more deer than any other state in the Union. The

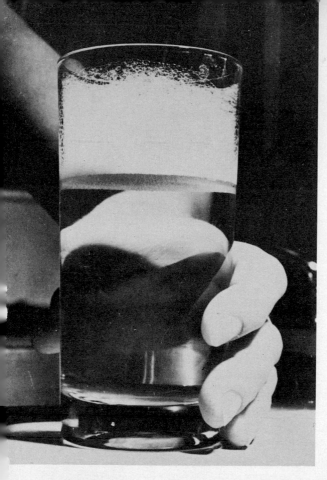

DEATH OF THE SWEET WATER:
Drinking water from the
public wells of Suffolk
County in New York —
with detergents added
from private cesspools
via ground seepage.
Wide World Photos

MONTGOMERY COUNTY,
PENNSYLVANIA:
A woodland stream with
detergent foam.
USDA Photo

STUBENSVILLE, OHIO: The Liberty Carton Company at Stubensville, Ohio, dumps its industrial waste into the Ohio River.

USDA-SCS Photos

DELAWARE: The wastes of three large industries and the sewage of an entire community are discharged into the Brandywine River through this open drain.

PATTERNS OF POLLUTION: Industrial waste from factories along the
banks of the James River in Virginia.   *Wide World Photos*

THE HUDSON RIVER: There are areas in this great and beautiful
river where the only forms of life that can subsist are sewage-eating
eels and worms. Here Rensselaer sewage enters the river beside
the wild flowers.   *New York State Dept. of Health*

CANEY RIVER NEAR DEWEY, OKLAHOMA: Salt, silt, and junk line the banks of this source of drinking water.
Junior Chamber of Commerce, Bartlesville, Oklahoma

At right, WESTCHESTER COUNTY, NEW YORK: A once beautiful woodland pool in one of the richest suburbs in the nation.
Wide World Photos

Sugarbeet wastes killed these fish in Ohio.
W. E. Seibel, County Fish & Game Association

Orange County, California: Severe sheet erosion on an almost level bean field — since corrected by basin-listing, broad-base terracing, and contour subsoiling.

The effects of uncontrolled terrace outlets.

INDUSTRIAL ACCIDENT: Governor Karl Rolvaag of Minnesota examines ducks killed by soybean oil and petroleum in the Mississippi Basin.

POLLUTED MARSHLAND: Two egrets among thousands of sea and marsh birds found killed by polluted waters in a single, local survey.

Wide World Photos

UNSAFE
FOR
SWIMMING
DEPARTMENT OF HEALTH

U.S. Dept. of Health, Education and Welfare

deer multiplied until there were so many that during a dry year thousands would die of starvation. They browsed the new growth so clean that future timber trees were chewed to death with the loss of shelter for other wildlife. And again the river suffered.

The silting of Pennsylvania rivers has not only been a pollution problem but has caused navigation problems. Thus, during the Civil War steamboats used to run between Harrisburg and Wilkes-Barre. Now you would have trouble running a canoe up there.

The Potomac River is very badly silted, to a large extent because of urban redevelopment upstream from Washington. The 2.5 million tons of silt carried down the river each year are enough to fill 6 million bathtubs full to the brim, but anybody desirous of taking a bath in Potomac mud ought to have his head examined. It is full of putrid wastes.

St. Louis has many water problems, but as a river port one of its worst is Mississippi mud. Since it is located on the inside curve of the river, the city's waterfront tends to accumulate huge amounts of silt as the river cuts its channel farther from the shore each year. The river is cutting an ever-deeper channel, one foot every decade, so that even in the best of times older docks can be left high and dry.

Silting and salting of water are connected in the sense that watershed vegetation cover can be killed by salt invasion, thus starting the fatal chain of soil erosion and sedimentation that silts up rivers and reservoirs. Water as salty as sea water not only is not absorbed by plant roots but can extract water from the roots. This is because of the effect known as "osmosis." In general, when a water-permeable membrane (such as the outer surface cells of a root) is placed between waters of different salt content, water will diffuse through the membrane in the direction of the water of greater salt concentration. This is the reason why salt spilled on the lawn will kill the grass.

In natural waters of low salt content sodium bicarbonate is the chief impurity. But in rivers of fairly high salt concentration, such as the Arkansas, the Colorado, the Gila, the Pecos and the Rio Grande sulfates and chlorides predominate. Selenium, lithium and fluorides are found in some waters and soil and may be stored in plant tissues. Selenium and fluoride have no effect on plant growth but of course affect animals. Up to 1 part per million fluoride protects teeth against cavities while more than that results in teeth-mottling. (The absolutely irrelevant fact that fluorine gas and hydrofluoric acid are violent poisons has been used by certain quite insane people to go into abominable fits about the fluoride-doping of municipal drinking water.) A fraction of a part per million of lithium in irrigation water is enough to injure citrus, avocados and grapes, although it does no harm to human beings. Lithium as an impurity in many wells in California has caused mottling of leaves, severe "burning," defoliation, and even the slow death of many citrus groves.

Boron at concentrations of over 3 parts per million is a poison for citrus and walnut trees in Southern California.

So-called "alkali" soils contain enough active sodium to interfere with the growth of most plant crops. "Black alkali" soils can be cured by a chemical reaction known as "ion-exchange" in which calcium from gypsum or from calcium chloride takes the place of the sodium, which is leached away by surface water before planting.

The Public Health Service has checked the sodium content of the drinking water in 3,000 communities for a specific reason: some heart patients rely on salt-free and low-sodium diets. Many doctors prescribe extra water intake to help flush the body clear. If excess sodium occurs in the water supply, the heart patient should use distilled or bottled water or (in Milwaukee and Cincinnati) stick to beer.

Saline waters in this country are defined as those having a salt content of over 1,000 parts per million. (Sea water normally runs 35,000 parts per million.) Many brine deposits, including those produced along with petroleum, are "connate"; that is, they were entrapped in ancient oil-containing sediments. The water is as old as the oil. Similar to connate waters but of later origin is the residual water often found in ground-water reservoirs of modern coastal areas. Most of these saline waters crept into the underground reservoirs when the land was flooded by high level seas of the ice age.

Another source of saline water is deep beneath the earth's crust where water is a normal constituent of rock solutions known as "magmas." Where the magma rises into the upper parts of the earth's crust it solidifies into rock such as granite and water is driven off. Such newly formed water is known as "juvenile." It may escape by seepage, by volcanoes, hot springs or geysers. But not all, or even most, of the hot springs or geysers consist of juvenile water. Most are of "meteoritic" (rain) origin. When such water comes into contact with hot igneous rocks it rises to the surface, as in the geysers at Yellowstone National Park. The mysterious medicinal virtues of hot springs and spas can be duplicated without paying $30 a day by mixing some salt in your own bath water at home.

In reference to salt water, it should be pointed out that a slow, world wide rise of the sea level is taking place. Our own records go back only to 1893, but since 1930 there has been a 6-inch increase along the Atlantic Coast. The reason is that the glaciers are melting faster than they are being renewed. (If all the glacial ice on land were to melt at once, the sea level over the planet would rise more than 100 feet.)

The Geological Survey has calculated that the contact line between salt water and fresh water in the New Jersey coastal water table is receding inland at rates of 1 to 4 miles a century, depending on the dip of the water table.

Salt water has seeped into the underground water supply in parts of California. The same is true of El Paso and the

Wellton-Mohawk reclamation area in Arizona. Operations in Arizona have caused trouble with Mexico. That country by 1944 treaty is guaranteed a million and a half acre-feet of Colorado River water each year. At the reclamation project the American farmers in 1961 were leaching so much salt into the Colorado that Mexico's share rose in salt content from 800 parts per million to more than 2,500. Mexico in the meantime had built a dam, dug irrigation canals, and rejuvenated the old desert lands around Mexicali. When the water became undrinkable and killed off the cotton, Mexico had a case against the United States in international law because of water pollution. The best solution now seems to be to divert the Wellton-Mohawk brine to the Gulf of California.

In the Salt River Valley, which includes Phoenix, there is a typical example of how irrigation can salt up a water basin. Both the stream flow and the ground-water flow bring water into the upper end of the valley and remove the outflow from the lower end. As the water makes its way down the valley, irrigators use it over and over. With each use the water becomes saltier. An excess of at least 350,000 tons of salt a year has been deposited in the valley.

It is now believed that salt water probably ruined the advanced Pima culture in central Arizona, which flourished between A.D. 1100 and 1300. Like far earlier hydraulic people, the Pimas had a tricky system of canals that carried Gila River water to 250,000 acres of cultivated fields. Because of the excessive use of irrigation in an area lacking natural subsoil drainage, the water table rose and the soil became waterlogged once again. The salt content of the ground water crept up and salt shriveled the roots of the crops. Lacking any bright hydraulic engineer who could show them how to lower the water table, the Pimas picked up their red terra-cotta gods and lovely pottery and abandoned the land. One can trace them straggling up to the sad mesas and meeting with fierce hunter tribes in the cooler uplands, where they were cut down, family by family, until they were only frail aromatic ghosts of a proud people, smelling of the sagebrush that they had despised.

There are other ways to bring salt in. Heavy pumping has lowered the water table of California ground-water basins bordering the ocean to below sea level. The most serious resultant invasions of salt water have been in the west and south basins of the Los Angeles plain, the Santa Clara Valley, and the mouth of the Salinas River Valley. Some trouble has been had on the Oxnard Plain in Ventura County and in several small valleys in San Diego County.

A remarkable experiment was carried out in Los Angeles County where, between Palos Verdes and Santa Monica, the Silverado water-bearing zone is open to the ocean for a stretch of 15 miles. Along the stretch fresh water or treated sewage water was injected to raise the water table above sea level and thus to create a "fresh-water dam."

Drainage of the Florida Everglades was started with a surge of civic energy in 1910 and nobody stopped to consider that this might have ruined Miami and other eastern Florida cities. Quickly the mucklands were so overdrained that the water table sank 5 feet at Miami and badly upset the equilibrium between salt and fresh water. Salt water began an implacable inland migration that cost the city two big fresh-water well fields (Spring Gardens and Coconut Grove) and thousands of private wells. Florida is now very cautious about drainage.

Salt-water encroachment in oil-producing states is a problem that is still with us. In the earlier days of wild, uncontrolled drilling the connate brines that came up the well bores with the oil were slopped all over the landscape and, particularly in Texas, caused very bad pollution. There were no laws to control this. Evaporation pits were tried for disposal of these brines when the various early booms calmed down, but this didn't work out, since heavy rains would wash the salt into streams.

Texas has over 500 widely scattered oil fields. Not only were private water wells ruined but the municipal water supplies of such cities as Beaumont, Longview and Graham were badly damaged. Along the Pecos River, on small tributary creeks draining oil fields, salt contents as high as 46,000 parts per million were recorded, which is saltier than the ocean.

In modern unitized oil fields, the large companies have resorted successfully to salt-water disposal wells. The brine is collected and pumped into deep earth, far below any water table. This works very well, but the oil people, as in any vast industry, include cheaters and quick-buckers. There are independent operators hidden in the thickets of rural Oklahoma and Texas who let the brine wander its way to the nearest stream or water well. The citizens have to get used to gagging on salty drinking water. When one talks to the waterworks manager of a small town in such an area, he is likely to change the subject. After all, in this town he is a poorly paid public servant, while the owner of sixteen stripper oil wells hooked together with rusty pumping linkages powered by a one-lung gasoline engine is a man of substance.

Although such practices are hard to pin down in the opaque jungles of county politics, it was not so long ago that the injection of oil-field brine from the booming Oklahoma City field and scandalously improper disposal of sewage wastes from Oklahoma City had so polluted the ground water along the North Canadian River that the city of Shawnee, 40 miles downstream, had to abandon its fine wells and develop a new water supply.

A state with a problem which it passes with alacrity downstream to Oklahoma is Kansas. Although the principal sources of salinity are natural salt springs and salt marshes, industrial and oil-field brines enrich the mixture. Salt marshes along Rattlesnake Creek have for years changed the Arkansas River from fresh to salty below Hutchinson, Kansas.

Oklahoma is proud of its dams, such as the Keystone, but the water impounded there is not fit to drink or to irrigate with. In addition to the salt it gets from Kansas, Oklahoma has its own salt springs and salt plains which contribute 10,000 tons of salt a day to the water of the artificial lake behind the Keystone Dam.

Michigan is in constant trouble. Saline waters underlie many of the river basins and occur as heavy brines everywhere at depth. These are the sources of supply that have made Michigan a leading commercial salt-producing state. The upward migration of saline water caused by hell-for-breakfast ground-water pumping has endangered the fresh-water supplies of such cities as Grand Rapids, Pontiac, Royal Oak, Flint, Kalamazoo, Lansing and Holland.

Mississippi has become a classical salt mess of polluted waters. Oil-field brines have been injected directly into fresh-water underground reservoirs. The danger of brine invasion has been insanely increased in coastal areas by allowing artesian wells to flow wide open to waste. This has lowered the underground pressure and profoundly disturbed the equilibrium between fresh and salt water. The curious primates of this state may have to be the first to learn to like salt water rather than branch water.

Aside from the threatened incursion of the ocean in all Northeastern seaboard rivers affected by the 1961-1965 drought, New Jersey has also managed to draw salt water into its ground reservoirs by overpumping. Dredging of the salty Passaic River turned out to be a dismal idea since, by removal of relatively impermeable sediment from the river bottom, it established direct hydraulic connection between the fouled-up river and the underlying table of sweet water.

New Mexico has followed the Michigan technique in salting up most of the water east of Roswell, where the land is underlain by salt deposits. Heavy irrigation pumping has induced a flow of salty water into the irrigated area. As in Michigan, the highest salt content occurs at the greatest depths.

As will be pointed out in the next-to-last chapter of this book, the desalting of brines represents the most rational way out of this growing dilemma. Although most of the research has been devoted to sea water, it is actually the less corrosive and lower salt-content brines of the inland regions that may best respond to treatment.

What do you say when the world is dying?
                    —NOYES, *Tales of the Mermaid Tavern*

And when they came to Marah, they could not drink the waters.
                    —EXODUS 15:23

11 POLLUTION IS GOOD BUSINESS

SINCE SEWAGE FROM body wastes has added a sort of homey, although occasionally treacherous, family odor to human history, we have discussed its ramifications in the second chapter. The smell of feces and urine and of dead bodies rotting was as familiar to all of ancient man as to twentieth-century armies, but modern man has introduced a new spectrum, a new line of merchandise, in water pollution. This consists of the by-products of industries situated on the banks of rivers or on the shores of lakes. Some water-using industries hover over streams and defecate, so to speak, directly into them. In this they resemble the innumerable privies perched over the flowing waters of the upper Mississippi and the Chattahoochee and the upper Potomac and any river stretch where poor farmers or sharecroppers meditatively sit and enjoy the modest pleasure of moving their bowels into the river.

The polluting industries are located near water for three very cogent reasons: the manufacturing plants use lots of water in the process; they must have a place to dispose of the dirty water that is not consumed in the process (a very large percentage); they can often save money by delivering their products by barge rather than by truck or railroad.

It must be emphasized that, unless the process in the plant is a very high-temperature one, industries (including electric power plants) do not consume much water in the absolute sense. They simply pollute it if only by adding heat to it. There is another more subtle sense in which they do consume water, in that they make it fit for only certain purposes. Industrially polluted water, for example, may no longer be fit for fish or to drink, to swim in, or even for other industries downstream for manufacturing processes. The water of a big industrial river, such as the Ohio, may be re-used a dozen times before it reaches its rendezvous with the Mississippi.

Modern processes use enormous volumes of water. It takes 18 barrels of water to refine a barrel of oil, 300 gallons to make a barrel of beer, 600 to 1,000 tons for each ton of coal burned in a steam-power plant, and 250 tons of water to produce a ton of paper. A large paper mill will need more water than a city of 50,000 people. Once again this is the water that the plant takes in, but usually it rejects to waste nearly as much. It is similar in this sense to a human being in his house. People who do not water their yards actually consume only the relatively small amount of water that they drink or receive in the form of food and even here a large fraction returns to the sewer. In this sense water is consumed only when it is evaporated or absorbed into soil, later to be transpired by plants. The scare figures on an over-all water shortage for the North American continent are thus confused. Water used or "borrowed" is mixed up in the bookkeeping with water consumed in the sense of evaporation. The shortage we have is one of *clean* water.

The kinds of industrial water pollution we suffer may be understood by looking at some rivers. We present two tables from the U.S. Public Health Service. The first table includes 26 rivers which are so badly polluted that the federal government is trying to do something about them. The second table names more rivers which are more or less dangerously polluted but with which the government has not had time or opportunity to start any action. These are all major cases. (The Public Health Service by law can act on its own in pollution emergencies involving two or more states but within one state it must await the invitation of the governor of that state.)

RIVERS WHICH THE FEDERAL GOVERNMENT IS TRYING TO CLEAN UP:

RIVERS — LOCATION	INDUSTRIES RESPONSIBLE
Androscoggin—N.H., Me.	Pulp and paper
Animas—Colo., N.M.	Chemicals, mines
Bear—Idaho, Wyo., Utah	Sugar, meat, and milk processing
Big Blue—Neb., Kan.	Nonindustrial
Blackstone and Ten Mile—Mass., R.I.	Textiles, metals
Calumet (Grand, Little) and Wolf Lake—Ind., Ill.	Steel, auto, rubber, oil
Colorado—Colo., Utah, Ariz., Nev., Calif., N.M., Wyo.	Uranium processing, agriculture
Columbia (Lower, Upper) and Puget Sound—Wash., Ore.	Pulp and paper
Connecticut—Mass., Conn.	Paper, chemicals, textiles, metals
Coosa—Ala., Ga.	Paper
Corney—Ark., La.	Oil wells
Detroit—Mich.	Auto, oil, chemical, rubber
Escambia—Ala., Fla.	Paper
Holston (North Fork)—Tenn., Va.	Chemicals
Mahoning—Ohio, Pa.	Steel
Menominee—Mich., Wis.	Paper, packaging
Merrimack-Nashua—N.H., Mass.	Textiles, paper
Mississippi (upper, lower)—Mo., Ill., Iowa, Minn., Wis., Ark., Tenn., Miss., La.	Oil refining, food processing, flour, power plants, sugar beet, chemicals, pesticides
Missouri—Mo., Kan., Neb., Iowa, S.D.	Stockyards, food processing, packing house, oil refining, soap and chemicals, auto, meat packing
Monongahela—W.Va., Pa., Md.	Coal mine drainage
Pearl—La., Miss.	Paper, chemicals
Platte (south and north)—Col., Neb., Wyo.	Sugar processing, packaging, oil, sugar-beet mills

142   *Death of the Sweet Waters*

RIVERS — LOCATION

Potomac—D.C., Md., Va.
Raritan Bay—N.Y., N.J.
Savannah—Ga., S.C.
Snake—Idaho, Wash.

INDUSTRIES RESPONSIBLE

Nonindustrial
Refineries, metals, chemicals
Paper, food processing
Paper

RIVERS WHICH ARE POLLUTED TO VARYING EXTENTS
BUT WHICH ESCAPED GOVERNMENT ACTION:

RIVERS — LOCATION	INDUSTRIES RESPONSIBLE
Allegheny—N.Y., Pa.	Mine drainage, oil refining, chemicals, food processing
Apalachicola—Ga., Fla.	Textiles, poultry packing
Arkansas (All reaches)—Colo., Kans., Okla., Ark.	Mining, metal processing (including uranium extraction), meat packing, food processing (including sugar beets), oil, natural gas, salt, agricultural runoff
Batten Kill—Vt., N.Y.	Pulp and paper
Beaver Brook—N.H., Mass.	Municipal primarily
Big Horn—Wyo., Mont.	Oil and gas, sulfur and uranium extraction, mining, sugar beets
Big Sandy—Ky., W.Va., Va.	Coal washing, acid mine drainage
Big Sioux—S.D., Iowa	Varied industries
Byram—Conn., N.Y.	Varied industries
Canadian—Okla., Tex., N.M.	Food processing, oil extraction, agricultural runoff
Catawba-Wateree—N.C., S.C.	Textiles, dyeing
Cedar—Iowa, Minn.	Food processing, slaughtering
Chattahoochee—Ala., Fla., Ga.	Textiles, poultry packing
Chesapeake Bay—Md., Del.	Varied industries and federal installations
Choctawhatchee—Ala., Fla.	Meat packing
Chowan—Va., N.C.	Pulp and paper
Delaware—N.Y., Pa., N.J., Del.	Slaughtering, dairy, chemicals, textiles, metal finishing, metallurgy, pulp and paper, petroleum, distilling
Deerfield—Vt., Mass.	Pulp and paper
Des Moines—Minn., Iowa, Mo.	Meat packing, dairy
Flint—Ga., Fla.	Chemicals, federal installations

RIVERS — LOCATION	INDUSTRIES RESPONSIBLE
French—Mass., Conn.	Textiles
French Broad—N.C., Tenn.	Tanning, textiles, pulp and paper
Grand—Iowa, Mo.	Varied industries
Hackensack—N.Y., N.J.	Varied industries
Hocking—Ohio, Pa.	Paper, gravel processing
Holston (South Fork)—Va., Tenn.	Small industries
Hoosic—Mass., Vt., N.Y.	Chemicals, paper, dairy, tanning
Housatonic—Mass., Conn.	Textiles, paper
Hudson and East—N.Y., N.J.	Varied industries
Indian Creek—Ind., Ky.	Municipal primarily
James—N.D., S.D.	Meat packing
Kanawha—W.Va., Ohio	Chemicals, coal and metal processing, acid mine drainage
Klamath—Ore., Calif.	Lumber, pulp and paper
Kootenai—Mont., Idaho	Lumber
Lehigh—Pa., N.J.	Oil, acid, chemicals, and varied organic industrial wastes
Leviathan Creek—Calif., Nev.	Copper mining
Little Blue—Neb., Kan.	Slaughtering
Little Tennessee—Ga., N.C.	Pulp and paper, textiles
Lost—Calif., Ore.	Pesticides from agricultural runoff
Marais Des Cygnes—Kan., Mo.	Few small industries
Maumee—Ind., Ohio	Chemicals, agricultural runoff
Mill—Mass., R.I.	Textiles, paper, metal plating
Montreal—Mich., Wis.	Iron mining
Mt. Hope Bay and (tributaries)—Mass., R.I.	Textiles, dyeing, bleaching, tanning
Muskingum—Ohio, W.Va.	Fiber products, paper, meat packing, pickle liquor, chemicals
New—N.C., Va., W.Va.	Food processing, chemicals, dyeing
Nishnabotna—Iowa, Mo.	Small industries
Nolichucky—N.C., Tenn.	Mining
Ochlockonee—Ga., Fla.	Mining, canneries
Ohio (All reaches)—Pa., Ohio, W.Va., Ky., Ind., Ill.	Metallurgy, petroleum, chemicals, and varied industries
Ouachita—Ark., La.	Oil, mining, pulp and paper
Palouse—Idaho, Wash.	Sawmills, agricultural runoff
Pawcatuck—R.I., Conn.	Textiles
Pecos—N.M., Tex.	Agricultural runoff
Pigeon—N.C., Tenn.	Pulp and paper
Picataqua—N.H., Me.	Textiles
Quinebung—Mass., Conn.	Paper, textiles

RIVERS — LOCATION	INDUSTRIES RESPONSIBLE
Red (All reaches)—Ark., Okla., Tex., La.	Oil refineries, oil fields, agricultural runoff
Red River of the North—N.D., Minn., S.D.	Sugar beet refining
Republican—(All reaches)—Neb., Kan.	Municipal primarily
Rio Grande—Tex., N.M.	Oil fields
Roanoke—Va., N.C.	Textiles
Rock—Wis., Ill.	Paper
Rock—Minn., Iowa	Municipal primarily
Sabine—Tex., La.	Agricultural runoff, chemicals, petroleum, food processing
Saco—N.H., Me.	Food processing, dyeing, paper, textiles, tanneries
St. Francis—Mo., Ark.	Slaughtering, food processing
St. Joseph—Ind., Mich.	Pulp and paper, meat packing, rubber
St. Louis—Wis., Minn.	Pulp and paper, meat packing, metal fabrication, railroad yards
St. Marys—Ga., Fla.	Pulp and paper
Spring—Mo., Kan.	Canneries, meat packing, dairy
Susquehanna (North Branch)—Pa., N.Y.	Dairy, food processing, metal fabrication, chemicals
Suwanee—Ga., Fla.	Chemicals
Lake Tahoe—Calif., Nev.	Municipal primarily
Tangipohoa—Miss., La.	Chemicals, sand and gravel
Tennessee—Ga., Tenn., Ala.	Dyeing, pickle liquor, chemicals, paper
Tombigbee—Miss., Ala.	Meat packing, dairy
Verdigris—Kan., Okla.	Oil fields
Wabash—Ill., Ind.	Fiber products, distilleries, paper, meat packing, chemicals, oil
Walloomsac—Vt., N.Y.	Paper
Warm Springs Run—W.Va., N.Y.	Sand and glass
Washita—Tex., Okla.	Oil fields, agricultural runoff
White—Ark., Mo.	Dairy, meat and poultry packing
White—Neb., S.D.	Municipal primarily
Withlacoochee—Ga., Fla.	Paper
Yadkin or Pee Dee—N.C., S.C.	Textiles
Yankee Creek—Ohio, Pa.	Iron and steel, metal plating
Yellowstone (Lower reaches)—Mont., N.D.	Oil refineries

In general, private industry is united to a man against federal regulation of water pollution. They prefer state control, if any. As it is now, each state has its own set of standards for water cleanliness, most of them very tolerant. (We have seen, for example, that the town of Red Wing, Minnesota, put in a modern sewage plant that made the effluent about three times as clean as would have been required by the Minnesota specification.) The fact that states along the same river basin may have quite widely varying standards makes it difficult for the Department of Health, Education, and Welfare to handle interstate pollution. This is the chief justification of the United States Senate version of the amended Water Pollution Bill which in 1965 called for setting up federal standards or guidelines. The reason for the clamor against this on the part of private water-using industries is easy to perceive. For many years the difference in water cleanliness standards between states has given industrialists a powerful club which they have not hesitated to use. They can threaten to move the plant downriver where the requirements are not so tough. Or they can threaten to move from a Northern state, grown more persnickety, to some Southern state, where one can dump anything short of straight cyanide into a stream.

Bad as the muncipal sewage problem is, that of industrial organic wastes is becoming worse. Five years ago, the Public Health Service reports, industrial plants were pouring out pollution at a rate equivalent to the domestic sewage from a 160 million population. By 1970 this organic waste from manufacturing and processing plants will equal the domestic sewage from the entire U.S. population of 210 million.

The favorite word of all industry in regard to rivers and lakes is "assimilation." The industrialists like to think of a river not in terms of the pleasure it can give or the fish it can support but in the amount of gunk it can "assimilate." This is a very elastic concept. To some it means that after assimilation a

river is in sufficiently liquid form that it can still be navigated
in a rowboat. To others it means that 10 miles upwind from the
river you cannot smell the dead fish. Our engineering schools
are still teaching, in sanitary engineering courses, that it is
proper to consider to the fullest possible extent the "assimilating
capability," as if this were some immutable virtue of the stream
like a pure heart. Assimilating capability depends on what you
put into the river. If you put in chemical wastes that kill off
the scavenging bacteria, the assimilating capability drops at
once to zero.

Heart-rending cries of anguish greeted the proposed phrase
in the 1965 pollution bill which reads that the waste water
from riparian plants should be rendered as "clean as possible."
It is contended that the phrase should be "as clean as economically possible."

A bible for the industrialists is the book by Richard B.
Engdahl and Frank C. Croxton, *Pollution: A Problem in Eco-
mics*, in which the key quote is as follows:

"To completely solve the problems involved, though it were
technically feasible at this time, would probably so increase the
cost of industrial operations as to endanger our ability to compete in world markets."

Let us examine this piece of bald-headed and bleary-eyed
sophistry. Our rivers have to be filthy so that we can compete
with *whom*? The West Germans, for example? The Ruhr River
Basin in Germany contains nearly half of that country's industrial capacity and only a skinny little stream flow. The annual low flow of the Ruhr and from smaller streams in the
basin combined is much punier than the lowest flow ever recorded in the Potomac. With such a small amount of water,
whatever its "assimilating capability," one would expect the
highly competitive West Germans to have on their hands a
smelly, septic, barely liquid waste ditch. The facts are that the
Ruhr River is clean enough to swim in, and to grow fish in, and
even to provide drinking water with only mild treatment.

The antipollution program that accomplished what to American eyes would appear to be an "uneconomical" miracle was carried out by the Ruhr Associations (*Genossenschaften*) or semigovernmental organizations. The gimmick they came up with was an extremely effective one. Instead of establishing treatment requirements, or effluent standards and trying to enforce them, the Ruhr Associations simply charge every town and every industrial plant a stiff levy proportional to the amount of pollution they deliver to the river. The effluent assay is based on the single measurement of "biochemical oxygen demand" (BOD), which is equivalent to the organic waste load in the water. The result has been that the Ruhr Basin has cleaned itself up. The water is used and re-used but is also treated and re-treated. In some cases, as at Essen, the solid waste is dried, included with the city's normal garbage, and used as fuel for a power plant.

To confess that American plants cannot do as well—that they would go broke in trying to do as well—is inadmissible. Nevertheless, our industries have had their way so long with most of the states and with local authorities that they are not about to give up their profitable superstition about rivers and lakes with rubbery assimilating capabilities. The common experience still is that when there is a conflict between recreational, agricultural and aesthetic use of water and industrial application, the latter wins out every time.

The more thoughtful industrialists, it must be said, are changing their viewpoints and a good deal of research on water disposal has been paid for with private funds and been translated into full-scale treating facilities, as we shall discuss a little later. In the meantime many of the big offending plants are located in municipalities where domestic sewage winds up raw in the watercourse and thus the companies have a reasonable "Why pick on us?" complaint. Industry spokesmen point out that sewage plants at Gary, Indiana, and Fort Chicago, Illinois, for example, have polluted Lake Michigan for years and it is

not fair to make industries in the area put in excessive pollution-control equipment to make up for it. The argument is that
even if all pollution were controlled on Lake Erie, it would take
over 25 years for the lake to return to a theoretical clean state—
and 500 years for Lake Michigan to return to the days when the
Indians used Chicago as a traffic circle for canoes.

Food-processing industries, especially the small operators,
are quite likely to take the line that if they are located in a
community that doesn't take care of its domestic sewage, including the unmentionable waste from mortuaries, why should
anyone worry about the offal from meat packing and dressing
chickens? In Troy, New York, the Hudson has been described as
a slimy cesspool where eels writhe and fight over chicken entrails. One of the few public hearings (which the U.S. Public
Health Service resorts to, if the conference stage of settling a
dispute fails) was held in 1958 to outargue the know-nothing
and do-nothing meat packers of Sioux City, Iowa, who continued dumping stinking offal into the Missouri River, thus con-
taminating the river waters of four states. Omaha meat packers surrendered more gracefully. Sugar-beet process wastes,
which smell worse than one would expect, polluted the whole
of the North Platte when delivered to the river in Wyoming.

Senator Gaylord Nelson of Wisconsin recalls that in his home
town with a population of 700, built over a lovely little lake,
the local creamery had always dumped all of its whey into the
lake, rendering the water useless for anything else. Everybody
in the village knew about it. But the creamery was the town's
biggest employer. Thus it eventually took the state water pollution commission to order the creamery to stop. The local citizens never let out a peep.

The canning industry is a large water user and the farmers
who sell their vegetables or fruit to the canneries are now
large pesticide users. It thus takes 50 gallons of water to wash a
case of canned fruit or vegetables where it took half that much
twenty years ago. The pesticide winds up in the river.

Edible vegetable oils can be as deadly to wildlife as petroleum oils. A famous proof of this occurred with the bursting of a tank holding several million gallons of soybean oil in Minnesota a few years ago. The oil rushed out, knocking over railroad cars, and got into the St. Croix River, which was frozen at the time. After the thaw, the oil took a ride through Wisconsin, where it killed thousands of ducks, damaged underground flora and fauna, and finally wound up on bathing beaches where it had to be scraped off. This was not a typical industrial pollution incident, since the oil spill represented pure loss to its owner, but he had built the tank on a hill without a catchall moat.

No industry has had more trouble and more violent public relations because of river pollution than the pulp and paper companies. There are about 3,000 such firms employing more than 600,000 people. United States production of paper and paperboard has more than doubled in the past two decades and is now about 40 million tons a year. The industry spokesmen make a big point of the fact that over this period a 50 percent reduction in pollution *per ton of paper produced* has been achieved. However, this is no great consolation to other water users, since they are concerned not with percentages but with amounts of gunk in the river—gunk per gallon.

What is the gunk? The worst pollution is so-called "sulfite liquor." This is spent cooking liquor containing the nonfibrous material removed from the wood chips during the cooking process. It is not toxic in the sense that it would poison an animal or infect a human being. It can be broken down by bacterial attack in the water, but this requires a large amount of oxygen. Thus the worst effect of paper- and pulp-mill wastes is to send the BOD soaring so high that fish and other water creatures are suffocated. This happens very quickly. Pollution of this kind is naturally most common in those river basins where the forest cover is of the type from which paper can be made. The northern coniferous trees were best suited to the sulfite process, hence plants using this device were mainly in the North. The

Columbia River has chronic sulfite-liquor pollution. In the past
fifteen years, however, the Kraft process, which will handle
southern pine, has resulted in the proliferation of paper mills
along the Chattahoochee, the Savannah and other Southern
rivers.

Senator Muskie of Maine still claims, apparently with some
degree of inverted pride that the Androscoggin River of his
native state is the worst polluted in the country. Years ago a
dam was built which trapped behind it the effluent from numerous pulp and paper mills. Even if there were no further pollution, he maintains that this trapped pollutant would make fish
life impossible for many years, perhaps forever.

The wastes from Kraft mills are alkaline rather than acid,
but the oxygen demand is just as great. One giant mill on the
Coosa River, which runs through Georgia and Alabama, pours
into the stream wastes equivalent in oxygen demand to untreated sewage from a city of 200,000 persons. It must be repeatedly underscored that such wastes, although not toxic or
dangerous in the sense that sewage and certain by-products of
the chemical industry are, has essentially the same end effect
since it robs the water of oxygen needed to assimilate the
more perilous gunk. We have seen that silt breaks the "chain of
food" in a river or lake because it makes the water opaque to
sunshine, thus killing microscopic plant life. Papermill waste
liquors break the chain at several links, since all the assimilation processes in fresh water, except putrefaction, require oxygen.

Textile factory wastes are somewhat similar in a broad
sense to those deriving from paper manufacture. The concentration of textile plants in the South over the past few decades
has put a new load on Southern rivers. One textile mill on the
Chattooga River in Georgia pours into it wastes equivalent in
BOD to the sewage of 112,000 people.

The processes of bleaching cotton, flax, hemp and jute produce a filthy waste containing fatty and oily crud washed from the raw fabric. Wool washings make a highly polluting waste consisting of an emulsion of dirt and bacteria in water, with soap and complex proteins as emulsifying agents.

Steel companies have been very busy in destroying rivers and, among all industries, have tended to be the least cooperative—in fact, the most belligerent. Pollution of the Mahoning River in Ohio and Pennsylvania by acid, lime, oil and grease discharged from steel plants has forced giving up this river entirely as a source of municipal water, hindered its use by other industries, and destroyed its value for recreation. The insolent refusal of three Youngstown steel companies to give effluent data to the Public Health Service has triggered a demand for a subpoena clause in the new federal pollution bill.

Three Indiana steel companies—U.S. Steel in Gary, and Youngstown Sheet and Tube, and Inland Steel in East Chicago are considered the chief sources of pollution in the Calumet River and the adjacent waters of Lake Michigan. The Acme Steel Company discharges raw sewage and unneutralized steel-pickling liquor (strong acid) into the Little Calumet River. The filth of the Calumet system of steel companies has affected the whole Chicago area. This may be permanent, since a lake is not like a river. The currents of Lake Michigan are so sluggish that the wastes do not disperse or float away. They just sit there in the water near the shore and fester. Health Service officials in Chicago detect a rather pathetic disinclination on the part of the citizens to talk about the matter. It is like tuberculosis in the old days—a subject which should not be discussed because superstition takes refuge in the irrational faith that if you don't talk about it it will somehow go away.

Petroleum oil and fuel have added to the hushed splendor of Lake Michigan's mixture of assorted crud. Although the production end of the petroleum business has in the main stopped percolating oil-well brine into fresh-water wells and streams, some of the giant refineries located near water have not been so scrupulous. Raritan Bay in New Jersey is guaranteed to smear any small boat up with oil after a few days. Even when expensive attempts are made to clean up refinery wastes, some of the extremely smelly chemicals, such as mercaptans and thiophenols, give any potable water which they contact a lingering odor of skunk. Oil chemicals are also responsible for unpleasant flavor in fish.

Pearl Harbor has a peculiar and sad oil-pollution problem. Petroleum fuel oil still oozes slowly up from the American warships sunk on December 7, 1941. An oil slick still forms above the USS *Arizona* Monument.

Heat has become the latest industrial polution worry. The temperature of the Mahoning River in Ohio (which has become something of a Ganges for pollution experts) at one time reached 140° F. and higher as it picked up steel-mill effluents near Youngstown. This forced local industries to slow down operations or actually to shut down entirely during periods of low flow.

Excessive heat does a lot of things to a river, some of which we do not yet understand. It kills fish. It accelerates chemical reactions, causing some wastes to be toxic which would have been harmless in cool water. It strips oxygen from the water and hence reduces the ability of scavenging bacteria to do their job. On the other hand, a modest amount of heating seems to make for good fishing. On Lake Erie and the Potomac and Delaware Rivers, at least in stretches where other pollutants are not too thick, fishing is best where power companies return their once-through cooling water. The warmer water apparently stimulates the growth of fish food.

The tightest regulations are Pennsylvania's, set up in 1960. Stream temperature may not be raised above 93° F. at any time. No new discharges may be made into a stream suitable for trout propagation if it will drive stream temperature above

58° F. These regulations have been under steady fire. They are claimed to be unrealistic, both from the standpoint of economics (costly for electric-power companies) and because many warm-water organisms thrive at temperatures higher than 93° F. The heat problem is serious for atomic energy installations, as in the Columbia and Savannah Rivers. It will become an important factor in the location of future atomic-power as well as conventional steam-power plants.

Modern industry, at least the giant corporations, has over the past few years begun to spend real money on prevention of water pollution. DuPont, which makes more (chemical) products in its far-flung plants than anybody else, accordingly has a wider diversity of waste materials to dispose of. In dealing with DuPont, federal government agencies are dealing with an entity almost as large and complex as the state of New York. Something of this company's style and resoluteness in tackling pollution problems can be perceived by a look at operations in the Charleston, West Virginia, region of the Kanawha River Valley. There are 12 chemical manufacturing plants, employing 25,000 people. DuPont's Belle Works alone resulted in over 300 sources of wastes feeding into about 3 billion gallons of cooling water per day, then into some 40 outfalls to the river.

In 1958, at DuPont's urging, nine individual firms joined with it in cooperating with the West Virginia Water Resources Division and the U.S. Geological Survey in a quantitative assay of a 62-mile stretch of the river. DuPont's laboratories analyzed over 1,500 samples each week for six weeks. As a result of this survey, goals of waste reduction were set up. The biological oxygen demand has been reduced in DuPont's own waste effluents by over 90 percent.

Most of the highly diluted DuPont wastes are directed to a large biological treatment plant, where selected bacteria destroy the organic chemicals. Foam suppressants are added; the temperature and acidity are kept at the optimum. In order to cope with the extreme swings of the river flow, huge tanks of 6 million gallon capacity are used to impound the wastes when the flow to the Kanawha dips as low as 800 cubic feet per second. The liquids are then released under state supervision during the winter when the runoffs may be as high as 100,000 cubic feet per second.

DuPont is quick to try out new gimmicks. In one of its plants on the Sabine River, it uses air cooling by giant fans rather than water. At the Victoria Plant in Texas four alligators are part of the conservation system. These are put on guard to repulse an invasion of nutria (small rodents) which were in the habit of sabotaging the pond walls and canal banks.

Like the oil industry, DuPont and other big chemical companies have dug mile-deep wells to dispose of salt water and other unmanageable pollutants. Some of them are successful; some are just expensive holes in the ground.

A common DuPont practice in most of its river plants is to conduct waste water to "passport ponds," where it is checked for pollutants before going back to the river.

It has been estimated that since 1963 the entire manufacturing industry has spent 4 percent of its annual $14 billion capital investment on pollution control. In many cases, such as detergents, the amount compares poorly with that spent on advertising, but it is much more than it was a decade ago.

One noteworthy trend has been the buddying up of municipalities and private companies. If the company is bigger than the town, the municipal sewage may be accommodated in the private waste-disposal system. Thus the three small towns of Lake and Westernport, Maryland, and Piedmont, West Virginia, on the upper Potomac, all send their raw sewage into the pollution-control system of the West Virginia Pulp and Paper Company. Conversely, when a river or lake city has a large, modern sewage system, it will often contract to handle waste effluents from chemical companies. The technology of treatment of sewage and of organic chemical wastes is virtually the same. Main

reliance is placed on bacteriological ("activated sludge") processes in both. As we shall see in a later chapter, this is not a
safe parallel across the board.

Cooperation of industry with state authorities reached its
height in the United States in the activities of the Ohio River
Valley Sanitation Commission (ORSANCO). When this body
was organized in 1948, with state and industry representatives
from Illinois, Indiana, Ohio, Pennsylvania, New York, Virginia,
West Virginia and Kentucky, the Ohio was the stinkingest river
in the land. It is hard to realize, but at that time sewage treating of any kind was available to only 1 percent of the population along the river's banks. Today treating facilities serve 97
percent. However, most of this is primary treatment only. A
good deal of progress has been made in dealing with industrial
wastes but on the whole the standards remain somewhat lenient. Furthermore, 15 percent of the industries on the river have
failed to meet even the gentle standards.

The paper manufacturers, being on the whole the worst
offenders, have formed a National Council for Stream Improvement. What can you do with pulp wastes? As early as 1943 the
Sulfite Pulp Manufacturers' Research League started growing
yeasts on waste sulfite liquor. Today nearly every sulfite plant
has a baby-brother yeast plant next to it. This is not enough,
however, to make much of a dent in the massive total.

The Kimberly-Clark Corporation has built in a Wisconsin
plant a 30 million gallon evaporating pond to store spent liquor
during the summer. When partly dried this material can be used
in place of asphalt for roadmaking. The company makes no
charge and pays part of the hauling. At the Niagara plant there
are not enough roads in the vicinity to get rid of the liquor
in this way. Here a soil-filtration system is used. Sandy, permeable soil is sprayed with the wet liquor, which is carried deep
into the soil by rains. When it joins the natural ground water it
has had the equivalent of a bacterial treatment for sewage.

Other companies, such as Weyerhaeuser, have experimented

with the use of dilute spent liquor for irrigation in the Pacific Northwest. Sprinklers are used. Unfortunately this is a very expensive way to irrigate, except for crops such as tobacco, and tobacco is not grown in the state of Washington.

For the chemical industry a new type of consultant has emerged—the professional limnologist (the fresh-water expert). Limnologists will offer services such as (1) exhaustive surveys of stream biology and chemistry before a new plant is built and (2) continuous monitoring of stream health after it starts operating. The consultant will advise as to which sorts of wastes can be tolerated by the stream and which cannot. The guiding principle of limnology is that in the water "diversity is stability." As long as each of the major types of aquatic life (bacteria, algae, protozoa, mollusks, insects, fish) is represented by a relatively large number of species, each doing its ecological job, the self-cleaning ability of the stream is preserved, whatever pollutant may be present. But when pollution begins to drive out or destroy species, leaving some of the jobs undone, the stream is hurt.

This is a new science only in the sense of being applied to chemical refuse. However, there are more unknowns than knowns. Chemicals can be experimentally synthesized and put into production much faster than limnologists can decide what effect they have on the animal kingdom (including human beings) or the plant kingdom. Often, as in the case of lead compounds from gasoline additives, it was after more than forty years of universal use before they were found unexpectedly to be dangerous.

What incentive should be offered private industry to do a real cleanup job? In Pennsylvania, the League of Women Voters supports the idea of tax relief. Another possibility is faster write-off for investments in pollution-abatement equipment. The Administration is also considering pollution penalties of the same type used by the Germans in the Ruhr Valley.

I know some poison I could drink;
I've often thought I'd taste it;
But Mother bought it for the sink,
And drinking it would waste it.
—EDNA ST. VINCENT MILLAY, *The Cheerful Abstainer*

Yon foaming flood seems motionless as ice;
Its dizzy turbulence eludes the eye.
—WORDSWORTH, *Address to Kilchurn Castle*

12 WHITE BEER

OF ALL THE KINDS OF water pollution none has caused so much fuss as synthetic detergents. This is because they can put on such a show. The thrill of unbelieving horror that buzzes down a housewife's back as she draws a glass of water from the tap and finds a beautiful beery head of foam on it can only be matched by her discovery of bugs on the bedroom wall. In Wisconsin people have been known to have heart attacks while strolling at dusk along a quiet stream and suddenly around a bend finding themselves face to face with a 90-foot-tall ectoplasm of suds. Such foam agglomerations have the eerie togetherness of a summer iceberg or a Thing-from-Outer-Space. They are the more frightening because they are often known by the observer to have materialized from water that has been through a drastic sewage treatment; thus size is combined with the awful aura of indestructibility.

The age of synthetic detergents began in the 1940's. By 1962 the essential ingredient, alkyl benzene sulfonate (ABS) was reaching the home market in the United States at the rate of over half a billion pounds per year as part of the total of 4 billion pounds of packaged detergent powder or liquid, which includes phosphate builders, extenders and other biologically inert material.

As we have seen in the chapter on sewage, organic wastes are decomposed by bacteria. A good sewage-treating plant of the activated sludge type simply accelerates the bacteria cleanup which would take place eventually in a normal river or lake. Some chemical compounds resist the attack of such bacteria, however, and ABS is one of them. The ABS molecule is rather like an octopus. It consists of a benzene sulfonate nucleus, representing the octopus's central body and brain, and long "side chains" of hydrocarbon alkyl groups, representing its tentacles. The nucleus likes water and the side chains prefer grease or dirt. This is why ABS is a detergent; its molecules congregate at the surface between water and dirt, dislodging and suspending the dirt particles. They also lower the surface tension of the water so that air readily mixes with it, giving stable foam.

Now, when the friendly scavenging bacteria start to eat up a molecule of ABS they start first to chew at the ends of the tentacles. They chew right down to the head until the molecule is no longer a detergent; it has lost its tentacles. It is said to have been "biodegraded." There is a catch in this process, however. Suppose the side chains have branches? This would roughly be comparable to tying single-loop knots in the tentacles of the octopus. The bacteria chew down until they get to the knot; then they give up. But what remains still has long enough side chains to act as a detergent and to cause water to foam. It is nonbiodegradable. Unfortunately the ABS of commerce until the summer of 1965 had side chains or knots. This was beause the most convenient way of forming side chains on benzene was by reacting with a cheap and hugely available petroleum by-product called "iso-butylene tetramer," which is highly branched.

By somewhat more costly processes, industry has learned to produce alkyl benzene sulfonates in which the side-chains are linear or unbranched. These are much more readily attacked by the type of bacteria that work in the presence of air (aerobic). The detergent industry promised a full switch by the end of 1965 with a consequent disappearance of river ectoplasm and white beer. The new material is designated "LAS," which stands for linear alkyl sulfonate.

Although the industry spent $150 million and made the full switch ahead of time by July, 1965, such a sweeping promise is not likely to be kept. The chief reason is that in the absence of air, the anaerobic putrefying bacteria do not seem to like the taste of LAS any more than they like ABS.

We have seen that in all cesspool or septic-tank sewage-disposal systems, common in rural and some suburban districts, the sewage treatment consists primarily of *anaerobic* digestion. Hence in such systems the overflow from septic tanks will still contain undamaged detergent. It can still be destroyed if the soil to which the overflow is released is well aerated and when tile drains are used. Otherwise it will enter the ground water of the area and in many cases will get into wells. The farmer or the suburbanite will still have his white beer. This has been experimentally demonstrated in certain parts of Long Island.

A still more ominous report on the possible effectiveness and sales durability of the new LAS detergents comes from a two-year field test in Suffolk County, New York. Some of the housewives polled in the study were unhappy with the performance of LAS, which they knew according to the test code number used as "two-dot." The women, who used two-dot for ten months, complained that their clothes became progressively more yellow-gray, despite regular use of bleach. Once they switched to conventional detergents, they said, the discoloration gradually disappeared. A report of this kind causes cold chills to vibrate through the heart of the soaper. He has several million dollars of laboratory data to prove that LAS is a dove or a white tornado or a knight in armor, but it is the ladies of all the Suffolk Counties in the country who are going to buy the stuff.

There is already talk of a "third generation" of synthetic detergents which combine the total biodegradability of ordinary soap with the hard-water tolerance of ABS.

Nevertheless, the wholesale change of signals in the United States from ABS to LAS has represented an industrial revolution of unprecedented speed and élan. It follows by a year a similar revolution brought about in West Germany by legal fiat. In an industry that spends such a fantastic proportion of its income on advertising, it is encouraging to find that it has money or energy left for anything constructive.

If we admit that the "second generation" of synthetic detergents now being marketed full blast is not going to cure all the renegade foam troubles, what harm, after all, does the foam do except to startle people or to injure their aesthetic sensibilities? This is a good question that was argued passionately by the soapers before the decision to take the great leap. It was even insisted that detergent pollution was a blessing in disguise. Foam in your glass of water told you when your water supply was polluted and you were alerted and thus something was done in time before you got typhoid fever. This laudable function is not appreciated by the bulk of people who are said to make up the backbone of the Nielsen TV ratings. Even the Indians of New Mexico suspect foamy water. In the pueblo of Isleta a few miles south of Albuquerque, the Indians refuse to irrigate on Wednesday because the Albuquerque housewife washes on Monday. Foamy water is regarded as bad medicine even for growing beans and squash.

The U.S. Public Health Service in its drinking water standard recommends a maximum of one half of a part per million of ABS or LAS. Admittedly this gives an enormous safety factor as far as any toxic effect is concerned. Even soapy dishwater or the drained water from automatic washing machines is hardly toxic in the sense that traces of lead or arsenic are poisonous. The toxicity of ABS detergents (such as Dreft, Tide, Joy, Vel, Dash, Duz, etc.) is roughly the same as that of ordinary soap in soft water, although much more toxic in hard water. A concentration of ABS or LAS as high as 1 to 2 parts per million will affect some sensitive fish. The sodium tripolyphosphate used as a "builder" in the household detergents will actually increase the biological activity of natural water. It is a plant nutrient or fertilizer.

A study by the German Ministry of Health showed that ABS in sewage disturbs the operation of mechanically equipped purification systems and septic tanks. In some river sections interference with the sluice mechanisms was claimed actually to impede navigation. The seriousness of the German problem was greater than that in the United States because of higher population density and especially from the fact that the Germans and Europeans in general do not use domestic water as profligately as we do. There is a higher detergent content in the water going to the sewer. A study of samples from 90 sewage plants by the Ruhrverband (one of several large water-resource associations in the North Rhine-Westphalia industrial area) showed that detergent concentrations from the treated water ran as high as 28 parts per million, with one quarter of them averaging over 10 parts per million. They were deluged with complaints from Holland about the conditions of the German rivers as they reached the Low Countries.

Perhaps the most serious aspect, however, was not toxicity but navigation. Occasionally the foam would billow over the whole river. At such times, the Germans could not enjoy water sports; they could not even put out search parties to rescue drowning people.

Representative Henry Reuss of Wisconsin reported that on a trip to Denmark, at Elsinore, where Prince Hamlet confronted the ghost of his murdered father on the rampart overlooking the sea, Reuss saw a gigantic white quivering mass coming down from the north. He found out later that this was not a Danish simulation of the paternal wraith but a mountain of detergent foam. Wisconsonites in general have evinced a peculiar animosity toward the detergents. While the now Senator Nelson was governor, the State Board of Health had found that the underground water supply in 64 out of the 73 counties was contaminated with detergents, and a state law was passed forbidding the sale of nonbiodegradable ABS formulations.

Before the industry-wide decision to switch to the octopus with unknotted tentacles, desperate attempts were made by companies (such as Standard Oil of California) with large equities in ABS raw material production to show how sewage plants could be operated to destroy ABS residues. Perhaps the most interesting method involved separating the foam at the sewage plant exit and recycling it back to the activated sludge stage. Since the foam contained most of the detergent, this gave the treating process two cracks at the undegraded ABS. For some not very well understood reason, this worked (in a pilot plant). Another technique for blasting the ABS is to use hydrogen peroxide as a treating agent. Unfortunately elaboration of the sewage systems by methods such as these introduces a degree of complexity that is not matched by the available supply of sanitary engineers. One of the most exasperating problems in our national waste-disposal network is trying to get competent men. The relatively simple plants we now have are often improperly operated. The pay has been astonishingly poor. However, in the planning, construction and maintenance of St. Louis's new $95 million system, young sanitary engineers with master's degrees are demanding over $15,000 a year. This is more than is received by a Ph.D. in electrical engineering from Cal Tech, hitherto the fanciest paid young men in the country.

The switch from ABS to LAS will fail to remove one fearsome cloud on the horizon which is usually discussed, if at all, behind closed doors in debugged conference rooms. This is the possibility that synthetic detergents and the partly degraded residues of them may cause stomach cancer.

Cancer is a long-time thing and exceedingly difficult to pin onto one chemical agent. However, Dr. W. C. Huepner of the National Cancer Institute of Bethesda, Maryland, has reported cancer in mice exposed to extracts from rivers containing various pollutants, including synthetic detergents or their residues. Although his conclusions are hotly disputed by industry-slanted oncologists (tumor specialists), there is a distressful plausibility about them. The reason is that any chemical with an "aromatic" nucleus, such as a benzene derivative, is a suspicious character as far as cancer is concerned. The Food and Drug Administration in its extraordinarily stringent regulations on food packaging allows "zero tolerance" on aromatic hydrocarbon in paper, paraffin wax, polyethylene plastic food wraps, etc. The Draconian nature of these regulations has, in fact, cost the producers of food-packaging materials very large sums of money in setting up delicate analytical procedures. Yet in drinking water, the U.S. Public Health Service has far from matched the stringency of the FDA. Many water sources regarded as legally potable contain traces of aromatic chemicals that are not removed by chlorination treatment. The variety of such compounds exceeds the chemist's imagination, since in the world of parts per million or parts per billion (which *is* the world of water pollution as well as air pollution), the versatility of our chemical garbage is inconceivably enormous.

We are at the stage of sophistication in water-pollution analysis that we went through in air pollution when we worried about measuring only carbon monoxide. We have triumphed when the BOD of our water reaches a certain low value, although this number simply tells how much oxygen the water will react with and nothing about the presence of noxious hydrocarbons, such as the aromatics, that often fail to oxidize at all.

Although industry hygienists and sanitary engineers will

loftily dismiss the stomach cancer scare, it is not to be dispelled by sneering. Until we have a much greater body of information that will comfort us we can regard this as a health hazard entirely as realistic as lung cancer from polluted air.

While economists such as Galbraith have characterized us as the "affluent society," the biological chemist and the limnologist might go for the term "effluent society." It is quite probable that affluence and effluence are very close kin.

The fishers also shall mourn, and all they that cast angle into the brooks shall lament, and they that spread nets upon the waters shall languish.

—ISAIAH 19:8

Has it never struck you that the trouts bite best on the Sabbath?
—BARRIE, *The Little Minister*

Mother, may I go out to swim?
Yes, my darling daughter:
Hang your clothes on a hickory limb
But don't go near the water.
—OLD FOLK SONG

13 WATER *for* FISH, FOWL *and* FUN

THERE ARE SOME 40 million Americans who fish unprofessionally but regularly and about 40 million more who would like to fish. There is perhaps no other activity that so caresses the essentially simple and honest heart of the American male. Fishing has a profound hold on our spirit and this is probably because the North American continent was good for fishing. Its streams and lakes have been places that fish liked. At one time there were 131 species of fish in the Ohio River. Perhaps the most plaintive cry of our times, from all kinds of men, rednecks, philosophers, clerks, salesmen, clergymen and farmers is, "What has happened to our fish?"

In the year 1964, according to the Public Health Department, 18.4 million fish were killed by water pollution. Industrial

pollution of lakes and streams was the cause of 12.7 million
fish kills. Municipal wastes killed about 4.1 million and farm
operations including crop spraying killed the rest. This is not
the whole story. Floods and drought, ascribable to our basic
failures in large-scale water management, have killed millions
more fish. And pollution has killed or stunted the growth or
made dangerously inedible uncountable numbers of oysters,
clams and shrimp.

It is perhaps the plight of fish that will light the fire of public indignation (at least of the male sex), a blaze that burns
away the paper towers of governmental nonchalance and lack
of virility in cleaning up our waters. A single small instance is
illuminating and one hopes it is typical. The Rifle River watershed in Michigan was once a fisherman's paradise of the type
immortalized by Ernest Hemingway in *Big Two-Hearted River.*
Because of very bad soil erosion, however, the fishing dropped
off. Rough fish drove out the trout. It was really the fault of the
farmers but they couldn't be sold on the notion that watershed
improvement to hold the soil was worth any effort. When somebody demonstrated to them, however, that their own fishing, in
which they delighted, could be saved, they promptly went to
work. Watershed reclamation was partly financed with funds
from the sale of fishing licenses. In a year or so the streams
had been cleaned up to a point where trout could see May
flies through the water. Thus a small piscine paradise was re-
gained.

Fish are more sensitive to the pollution of water than human
beings. This is not surprising in view of the fact that they live
in it. Fish breathe air, and water without oxygen will kill them
as quickly as air without oxygen will kill human beings. There
is even a further vicious parallel: fish can be killed by polluted
air. Fish and game agencies are now concerned about the
survival of fish in water where motorboats with underwater
exhausts are used and especially exhausts from the popular

two-cycle outboard engines which usually run high in carbon monoxide.

For aquatic life the quality of fresh water is best defined in terms of dissolved oxygen. In completely pure water this will be about 15 parts per million. High-quality aquatic life requires at least from 6 to 10 parts per million of oxygen. A minimum quality water to avoid large fish kills is 4 parts per million. This enables most fish to survive part of their life cycle. It is not enough for the complete life cycle of vigorous, nervous fish such as trout and bass. The anadromous fish, such as salmon and shad (those that spend most of their adulthood in salt water but come to fresh water to spawn) are particularly disturbed by polluted water. Unlike most fish, shad do not flex their gills. To live at all they must swim constantly with their mouths open, or lie gaping into a current. They cannot "hold their breath" even for a few tail strokes to get through suffocating clouds of nasty water. The spawning fish are very exacting about the condition of river bottoms. They will not lay eggs on bottoms that are covered with sludge and tin cans. The salmon especially likes smooth stones or clean, roe nurseries of immaculate gravel. If they cannot locate such spawning grounds they will abandon whole river systems. This is why there are no longer salmon on the rivers of the Atlantic Coast, even in Senator Muskie's native Maine.

It is of interest to examine the natural and unnatural history of certain key Eastern rivers. The Merrimack River, for instance, is haunted with perhaps the oldest and most hopeless pollution of any in the country. The river rises in the White Mountains of New Hampshire and flows south, down the center of New Hampshire into Massachusetts. At Lowell it turns east and flows through Lawrence, Haverhill and Newburyport to the Atlantic. In 1839, when Henry David Thoreau spent a week rowing down the Concord and up the Merrimack, the pollution of the lower Merrimack was already all too evident to a man of Thoreau's sensitivity. In the upper reaches above Lowell the river was still pleasant: cool, abounding (Thoreau reported) with fresh-water sunfish, perch, trout, dace, shiners, pickerel, horned pont, lamprey eels, suckers, and a very few salmon and shad. He mourned the impending destruction of fish:

"Perchance, after a few thousands of years, if the fishes will be patient, and pass their summers elsewhere, meanwhile, nature will have levelled the Billerica dam, and the Lowell factories, and the Grassground [Concord] River run clear again, to be explored by new migratory shoals. . . . One would like to know more of that race, now extinct, whose seines lie rotting in the garrets of their children, who openly professed the trade of fishermen, and even fed their townsmen creditably."

Thoreau would not like to row a boat on this obscene river today. For the entire Merrimack the average oxygen reading is below the level required by most species of fish. Below Lowell there is usually no oxygen at all in the water. Fish that manage to locate some oxygen to breathe commonly die of starvation, for the settling of odious waste solids covers the river bottoms, destroying the small plants and animals that fish feed on. The surviving fish of the Merrimack are predominantly the coarser types such as bullhead, shiners and suckers, who feel for their food rather than see it. Furthermore, their bodies are so saturated with oils, phenols and dyes that they are considered dangerous to eat.

The shellfish industry that used to flourish at the mouth of Merrimack is gone. The densities of pathogenic bacteria and viruses in the water are so high that shellfish taken from these waters, if eaten raw, can cause disease. The Massachusetts Department of Public Health closed the shellfish beds in 1926 and it is now even more septic.

The Delaware River in Pennsylvania used to be a sort of aqueous avenue for shad. It was after eating a fish taken from it that Alexander Wilson, the Philadelphia naturalist, in 1808 gave the species its Latin tag: *Alosa sapidissima* ("the tastiest"). Early English sailors had reported mysterious shad kills in Delaware Bay, which may have been due to tidal flushing of natural organic wastes from nearby swamps. This is one of the few instances of mass fish killing without man's intervention. When the Delaware sank into its modern chronic condition of pollution, shad nearly disappeared entirely. Since about 1900 this rather stodgy river had become a slowly swaying sewer so foul that ferryboats churned up enough hydrogen sulfide to peel the paint off shoreside buildings. Then in 1963 a still not fully explained phenomenon occurred: the shad came back. From mid-April to mid-May in 1963 their spawning run rivaled the record year of 1896, when 19,203,000 pounds were taken from the Delaware. But in the midst of this magnificent and inexplicable run the shad stopped coming and started dying. Delaware Bay was littered with the pale corpses of a shad kill as vast as the spawning run had been, mostly near-ripe roe fish. The responsibility had vaguely been assigned to the severe drought of 1963. This may be true, but drought without pollution is seldom fatal.

In the streams of the Midwest floods have been more dangerous to fish than droughts. The truth seems to be that drought simply brings out, like a photographic developing process, all the hidden threats of a dirty river. If you pour crud at a constant rate into a dwindling stream, the pollutants will naturally increase in concentration, the oxygen will disappear and fish will die. It is of some interest that the surprising early shad run of the spring of 1963 is now attributed by biologists to the workings of natural selection. The fish that ran up the Delaware earliest and produced fry that stayed there the latest may yet be the progenitors of a new race of shad that will come back for good, or so the biologists hope.

That rivers *can* be cleaned up to bring the fish back is proved by the fact that Pennsylvania's "clean-stream" program in a few years has returned the Schuylkill River to a reasonable image of what it was before the days of heavy industrial pollution. Game fish are thriving in the upstream pools. Ominously, however, river-front real estate has risen in value, and one can see on the horizon that most insidious of all fish murderers—the "subdivision developer."

Of other great Eastern rivers, the Hudson is scarcely worth mentioning in connection with fish. For ten miles south of Albany, there are no fish, only sludge worms, leeches, rattail maggots and the larvae of flies. The Hudson, for a fish, can only be described by an ichthyologist with the pen of Dante.

The once thriving Roanoke River of North Carolina is filled with dead rockfish, brim and bass floating by the thousands belly up. In Georgia once the shad ran up the rivers to the site of the present University of Georgia at Athens, some 75 miles northeast of Atlanta. It is a fact that this annual run of shad was one of the reasons for the choice of Athens as the place where the state would educate its young men and women. In those days fish were believed to be brain food and it was confidently expected that the student, stuffed with shad, would construct a greater, sweeter civilization. The shad are gone. Only a few puffy-eyed dissipated-looking catfish are left to feed the Ku Klux Klan. Oysters taken from many parts of the Savannah area are declared unfit to eat, and oyster bootlegging has given rise to numerous cases of viral hepatitis.

Fishing in the Midwest has suffered from both silting up and industrial pollution. Southern Wisconsin lost much of its stream trout fishing because of land clearing, overgrazing and poor farming habits. The Whitewater River in southeastern Minnesota once provided 50 miles of splendid trout water. In 1941 only 60 miles would support trout, just barely. Improved watershed management has increased this now to 80 miles.

The once clear, spring-fed streams of the Missouri Ozarks have gone through flood after flood following a century of imbecilic land abuse. Constant logging, burning of woodlands and heavy grazing paved the way for the torrents which scoured out plant and insect foods, scrambled up spawning beds and choked streams with sand and silt. The drought of 1951-1954 proved less damaging to fish than the periodic floods. The Spring Creek watershed in the Missouri National Forest is an example of a man-ravaged area which has been put to bed by the government foresters and allowed to rest between vitamin shots. The raising of skinny livestock had furnished a precarious living for the local people. Forage had been depleted by the repeated burning over in the maniacal belief that burning was necessary to produce grass. The ground was barren of leaves and litter; erosion had exposed the ugly chert stone, typical of Ozark soils, which looks like the half-buried skeletons of the giant famished animals of the past. Replanting, good fire prevention, control of grazing, leaving the leaves and branches on the ground to sponge up the runoff and to restore the soil fertility—all these made a fishland of Spring Creek once more. Even in 1954, following three years of drought, the river had enough water to support healthy game fish.

It is on the Pacific Coast that the most violent wars against fish destruction have been waged. Justice William O. Douglas, who for many years has been a sort of roving delegate in behalf of the bill of rights of the American Wilderness, tells of his experiments just after World War II near the mouth of the Willamette River at Portland, Oregon. He put some healthy rainbow trout in a cage and lowered them into the water. They died of suffocation immediately. Although this was mostly due to local sewage contamination, more continuous and robust pollution was provided by paper mills. In the Northwest the feud between commercial fishermen and industrial river polluters is as savage as the ancient enmity between cattlemen and farmers on the Great Plains. The fishermen of the lower Columbia have recently set forth a manifesto in behalf of their own bodies as well as the fish. They wanted, for example, a coliform standard for the river of 250, which is very low; it is swimming-pool quality, unheard of in a modern river. Their words were most passionate:

"This is our working environment. We are in this water; our hands are in this water; we have it on our face and arms; we eat and live in this water all day. Why should we not have the same protection from bacteria that someone going to play for a half hour in a swimming pool has?"

When this manifesto was presented to both the states of Oregon and Washington and to the U.S. Public Health Service, the government services were persuaded and the coliform standard of 250 was adopted. It remains to be seen whether it will be enforced.

The paper mills have started very earnest research on river fish. The Weyerhaeuser Company, for example, has set up a woodland water laboratory where scientists work with three artificial streams. They report optimistically that midge larvae (found in streams where pollution is present) are excellent food for trout. They have also experimented with adding sugar to streams.

When the paper manufacturers go to California they find things very rough indeed. Kimberly-Clark of Wisconsin could not resist the availability in Shasta County of enormous quantities of lumber mill trimmings, practically for free. However, California is very proud of the steelhead trout and salmon who use the upper reaches of the Sacramento River for spawning. The California Central Valley Regional Water Pollution Control Board established controls on mill effluents so rigid that the boys from the Badger State nearly fainted. The oxygen content, for example, must not be reduced as the result of discharges from mills into the river by more than one half of one part per million. Even more confining was the stipulation that no deposits of clay or fiber should accumulate on the spawning gravels. (In most Eastern rivers the bottom accumulations of waste pulp are too great to be removed even by dredging.) It must be said that Kimberly-Clark was very manful about the whole thing. They put in the most pollutionless paper mill in existence.

California has been busy studying what might be called "instant fish" as a weapon against mosquitoes. The state's mosquito population has exploded because of the 9 million acres under irrigation and especially in rice-growing areas, where the fields are flooded from May to September. Fields growing other crops may be flooded as many as ten times a season, producing a new mosquito hatch each time. The inch-long fish from Brazil and Argentina will be introduced first in the rice fields. They live about a year and their favorite food is mosquito larvae.

In cruel contrast to the California environment, the salmon fingerlings in Puget Sound have to pass through the Bellingham Harbor area where levels of pulp waste range up to 200 parts per million. Extreme toxicity to fingerlings was proved by suspending fish in live-boxes and noting that they were all suffocated in a few minutes. A stranger malady is a sort of thalidomide-type effect on the larvae of the Pacific oyster. Sulfite waste liquor concentrations less than those which rob the water of oxygen cause deformation of the embryo oysters. For the Port Angles-Everett area oyster larvae abnormalities reach as high as 50 percent.

The executive secretary of the Northwest Pulp and Paper Association in Seattle has announced that the mills "can do little now in terms of translating results into the capital equipment that may be required." The implication is that a choice must be made between the fishing and the paper industries. One of them evidently must abandon the Puget Sound scene and there is no sign that the pulpsters are about to bow out.

Although by far the most damage is done to fish simply by preventing them from breathing, there are a good many killings by specific poisons in polluted water. The Bureau of Commercial

Fisheries of the Department of the Interior finds that six weeks' exposure of minnows to 5, 8 and 10 parts per million of synthetic detergent stunts their growth. A more alarming report, because the critical concentrations are so much lower, is that synthetic detergents at 1/100 of a part per million reduce the rate of development of clam eggs, while 5/100 of a part per million retards the growth of oyster and clam larvae. A quarter of a part per million definitely kills these larvae. Fish food, such as May fly nymphs, are poisoned by small concentrations of synthetic detergent. Detergents have also been found to erode the taste buds and the sense of smell of certain fish, which affects their feeding efficiency. It also makes them less able to avoid certain industrial pollution zones. A spill of toxic sewage from the Dover Air Force Base in Louisiana killed 10,000 eels.

Fish appear to be easily poisoned by chlorinated organic compounds. During spring floods many city water supplies are more heavily chlorinated than usual in order to make the water safe for drinking. This always results in a wave of deaths in tropical fish in bowls replenished from the tap. These pets are delicate indicators and since there are nearly as many in the country as there are dogs and cats, a great hullabaloo arises when they start belly-up-ing from concentrations of chlorine compounds which, if somewhat unpleasant to the taste, are apparently harmless to human beings.

The worst source of specific fish poisons, however, is pesticides. In 1964 the Public Health Service announced that massive fish kills since 1960 on the lower Mississippi River had been traced to incredibly minute concentrations of such chlorine-containing pesticides as endrin, dieldrin, heptochlor, DDT and DDE. Although a great to-do has been caused about accidental spills of bulk quantities of such agricultural chemicals in the river, it appears that the long-term four-year fish kill has resulted from "business as usual" spraying by farmers on the lands drained by the river. Endrin was found in dead fish in concentrations up to 7 parts per million, although it could be detected in the water in no greater than the trace quantity of one tenth of a part per *billion*. All the known fish-poison pesticides have also been found in shrimp from the Gulf of Mexico and in the livers of big marine fish from which vitamins are concentrated for pharmaceutical use. Shrimp and liver-oil industries are definitely threatened by this kind of pollution.

Here we meet a schizoid situation on the part of the state and federal governments. Although it has been three years since the President's Science Advisory Committee issued its comprehensive study on the use of pesticides and more than four years after Rachel Carson stirred public concern with her prophecies of a silent spring, the role of government in regulating those dangerous substances is still a weak and confused one.

The Secretary of Agriculture, for example, is in a spot. He must stick up for the farmer. He finds it easy to imply that industrial wastes, not pesticide runoff from crops, was a main cause of the Mississippi fish kills, and if the pesticides killed any fish it was from the mistakes of the pesticide manufacturers, not the farmers. Industry is thus still to blame. Thus, we find the Department of Agriculture, the Department of Health, Education, and Welfare, and the Department of the Interior paralyzed on endless investigations and engaged in an interminable tug of war of both semantics and motivations.

One of the Department of the Interior's responsibilities is to see that wild animals and birds as well as fish do not entirely disappear from the country. Since the settlement of the 50 states, some 24 birds and 12 mammals native to the United States and Puerto Rico have become extinct. Examples are the passenger pigeon, heath hen, Carolina parakeet, spotted Hawaiian rail, eastern elk, Texas and California grizzly bear and the Badlands bighorn sheep. These animals are gone forever from the face of the earth.

Interdepartment tugging also is bringing an impasse in

another area of wildlife conservation—the wild duck. Here we are not so concerned with pollution as with mating habits. When wild ducks court, they are very bashful. They want privacy— some degree of isolation from other ducks of the same species. The ideal courting and mating area would consist of a large number of small separate ponds—one pond for each mating pair. In rearing broods their need becomes not so much privacy as sufficient depth for diving and emergent vegetation for the ducklings to take cover in. Permanent lakes are not good breeding or rearing spots, since they do not allow the ducks to indulge their honeymoon bashfulness and they are too wind-swept for ducklings to swim in.

The ideal nesting place for wild ducks is the "pothole" country of Saskatchewan, North Dakota, South Dakota and Minnesota. These prairie potholes are temporary deep ponds that meet all the duck specifications. The U.S. Fish and Wildlife Service has been shocked to discover that after World War II these water holes were being drained and that drainage operations were being subsidized by the Department of Agriculture. Very good ducklands were being turned into very poor farmlands. Originally the American part of the pothole country covered about 115,000 square miles and supported at least 15 million ducks a year. Today drainage has eliminated over half the area, and the duck population has nose-dived to less than 5 million.

Saskatchewan produces more ducks per acre of wetland than North Dakota because individual potholes are smaller. But this Canadian province threatens the ducks in another unforeseen way, the same way in which their lives are in peril in the Northern California wetlands. In Saskatchewan a large number of ducks are raised in a grain-growing region where harvesting methods make the grain available to the birds. Farmers will stand for a little crop depredation but not much. In California the wetlands have been so reduced by drainage that in years when breeding conditions result in heavy flights the birds turn to agricultural crops. When they arrive before the crops are harvested, the ducks feast on such luxuries as rice and lettuce (widgeon and pintail prefer such dainties). Canadians observe that ducks of several species have developed indeed a stubborn preference for cereal grains over natural aquatic foods. Today many of the public waterfowl-management areas contain uplands where cereal grains are grown especially for ducks.

Between one breeding season and the next wetlands are still essential for housing ducks, but in a different way. As the birds migrate south to set up winter quarters, they no longer need small ponds to pair in. This is the period of gathering in flocks. Large numbers of birds can be accommodated on relatively small stretches of water provided there is enough food.

An ugly social status note has crept into duck hunting. The trend now is for private individuals or clubs to buy up attractive ducklands. The number of guns is limited in order to improve the quality of the shooting. Thus the man of modest means is being muscled out of this sport.

If he can no longer fish nor hunt ducks, can the average man and his family at least find a safe place to swim other than the eye-smarting water of a public pool, asquirm with other people's kids? Very seldom, unless he is close to one of the two oceans and chooses a spot far enough from outfall sewers.

The tremendous growth of multi-purpose dam projects in this country has given the public the illusion that the artificial lakes formed all may function as monstrous, beautiful swimming holes. This is far from the truth. Many of them are silted up, contain rural sewage or are tainted with pesticides.

It was the habit of President John Quincy Adams and his family to swim in the Potomac near Washington. At the beginning of the twentieth century this would still have been imaginable, but today a person might just as safely dive off the Washington Monument. One has to travel about 20 miles straight out into Lake Erie from Cleveland to find water that is safe to

swim in. Erie County has no safe beach. Only about 10 miles
(2 percent) of the 402 miles of shoreline of Lakes Erie and
Ontario in New York State have been cleaned up for swimming.
The safest thing to do if you want to swim in one of the Great
Lakes is to cross over to the Canadian side. The south shore of
Lake Erie was first destroyed by sand and gravel companies,
which were allowed to operate on the shore until 1940. Federal
law put a stop to this, but by that time pollution had delivered
the *coup de grâce*. Toward Buffalo the water becomes unbe-
lievably filthy and Niagara Falls has been nicknamed the "toilet
bowl of America."

Only 35 miles of New York City's 575 miles of shoreline and
waterfront are fit for swimming—and even then toe bathing and
flirting are to be recommended.

In the dear days of "Meet me in St. Louis, Louie!" there used
to be long-distance swimming meets starting from St. Louis on
the Mississippi. No one would dare so much as to trail his foot
in the water today. If you try to steer a small motorboat across
the Mississippi near St. Louis, the chances are very good that
you will get chicken entrails hung up on your propeller.

In Georgia long stretches of the Coosa, the Savannah and
the Chattahoochee Rivers are listed as too septic for swimming.
In some states the water near the shores is obviously polluted
but the local authorities are too ignorant or too anxious for
tourist money to admit it. This is true of Biloxi, Mississippi, where
children splash and dig their toes gleefully in the black slime
under sewage outlets.

The mere fact that a swimming spot is located near a sewer
outlet does not necessarily rule it out. It depends on what kind
of sewage system is at work. In Mississippi it is usually a completely inadequate one. In California it may be safe to swim
in the straight sewer water or even drink it. The town of Santee
near San Diego is experimenting with water reclaimed from its
sewage by heavy chemical and soil filtration treatment. Fishing

and boating are allowed on the sewage lakes, but swimming is not, nor can the fish be eaten until further information becomes available. Virus organisms so far have not been isolated from treated sewage water entering or leaving the recreational lakes.

One of the big choices in the future is between two different kinds of *conservation*—a word of vast ambiguity invented by Gifford Pinchot in 1907. Shall we go on wiping out river stretches by damming them and making them into artificial lakes? If we do we must see that they do not become quickly polluted. (We know that ultimately they are bound to fill with silt.) Otherwise, even on a dollars and cents basis they won't pay out. Studies of the Rio Grande and San Juan Basin have shown that the recreational uses of water can contribute three times as fast as agriculture to the economy of the state. Arizona has the highest per capita motorboat ownership in the country. This recreational use will drop off very suddenly with the occurrence of a few water-borne epidemics or with low water levels and wide mud flats and dead fish during the summer season.

How about the recreational values that have been lost by creating the reservoir upstream and the skinny trickle downstream? Is boating the only form of recreation? In several cases where impoundments have been made within national forests, the Forest Service has required power companies to release not less than 50 second-feet during June to September. This means releasing water worth $2,770 a week for power. For a 10-mile stretch of good fishing stream it would mean 10,000 people a week at 28 cents a day, to break even. It is not unreasonable to suppose that that many people would fish the 10-mile stretch if only to get away from the noise of motorboats.

The mania for building hydroelectric dams on the part of the Corps of Engineers has reached an intolerable stage. Many of these cannot be justified economically on a realistic book-keeping basis for power production and, unless they can be plainly shown to be flood preventive in function, they represent river destruction rather than conservation. A big dam may look pretty to the Corps but to many people the height of recreation is to have a virgin river to look at rather than a river to turn away from. For example, for 180 twisting miles east of Fort Benton, Montana, the upper Missouri flows as it did more than a century and a half ago when Lewis and Clark made their historic way upstream in pirogue and keelboat. Now the Corps is recommending that this last upper stretch of the river that has so far escaped the dozens of dammings downstream be inundated behind a $243 million dam at Cow Creek to permit production of hydroelectric power. There is no justification for flood control.

Some recent evidence of sensibility can be derived from the Corps's Lieutenant General William Cassidy, who overruled a recommendation of the Corps Board of Rivers and Harbors for a West Valley power dam on the Eleven Point River in Arkansas. He said a simple flood-control dam could be built without interfering with plans to develop the Missouri section of the stream as a wild river.

These, along with many other river stretches that the Corps of Engineers has to dig for justification way out in left field (the obvious dams having been built), equally deserve the protection of the Wild Rivers Act.

Deep, dark and cold the current flows
Unto the sea where no wind blows
Seeking the land which no one knows.
                              —ELLIOTT, *Plaint*

. . . crucify the soul of man, attenuate our bodies, dry them, wither them,
shrivel them up like old apples, make them so many anatomies.
                              —BURTON, *Anatomy of Melancholy*

14 THE UNKNOWN

THERE ARE, as already mentioned, a large number of chemical
compounds in industrially polluted water which are allowed
"zero tolerance" by the Federal Food and Drug Administration
in commerical foods but which are not absolutely excluded by
law from drinking water. (Among them, incidentally, is strych-
nine.) There is a desert of knowledge and information about
the cumulative effects of traces of such chemicals taken over
a period of years. Cancer of the digestive tract is suspected in
some cases, but the data are not clear-cut. In spite of the enormous attention given through the years to water contamination
by disease-causing bacteria and viruses and the revolution that
the science of bacteriology caused in sewerage practice, we
probably know less about other nonliving poisons in water than
we know about poisons in the air.

Take the case of water polluted with radioactive wastes.
Although the fallout from atomic bomb tests has created a
highly exaggerated alertness to strontium 90 and iodine 131
in milk and food crops, we have higher degrees of radioactivity
to worry about in rivers polluted with the wastes from uranium

ore mills. The Animas River in New Mexico and Colorado was found in 1958, for example, to be running far above the tentative admissible levels of radioactivity because of discharges from the mills of the Vanadium Corporation of America. Actually we don't know what the levels meant in terms of long-term human health, but since the Animas is a tributary of the Colorado, the problem was referred to the U.S. Public Health Service as part of the pollution complex which threatens this giant river basin. Remedial action was taken but not until a fish kill had occurred, not on account of radioactivity but because of the presence of excessive amounts of water-soluble heavy metal in the stream at the same time.

Accidents, of course, have to be anticipated and the location of future commercial atomic power plants with respect to rivers must be done thoughtfully. So far there have been no serious discharges of "hot" stuff into the Savannah or the Columbia as the result of operations concerned with purifying materials for nuclear bomb production. Plutonium is not only radioactive and fissionable but perhaps the most toxic of all the elements. It is probably the constant realization of this fact that has resulted in such stiff precautions that none of it has got away.

Much more serious mishaps have occurred in connection with the standard poisons of the Borgias, including cyanide salts. A typical example is the dumping in October, 1964, of 70,000 gallons of cyanide solution into a tributary to the Verdigris River near Tulsa, Oklahoma, by the Douglas Aircraft Company. Luckily this stream is not a source of drinking water, but all animals and fish in the vicinity were killed. When the alarm went out, the U.S. Army Corps of Engineers opened the floodgates of Oologah Dam in order to dilute the cyanide from 9 parts per million to a reasonably safe concentration below a half part per million. Here is a case where it is indeed handy to have river flushing systems.

We have seen that pesticides kill fish. It remains to be seen whether, over a long period of time, they kill mammals, including man. The most ambitious study of this question has been started at Miami University in Florida with funds supplied mostly by the U.S. Public Health Service. It will go on for at least five years. At the time of going into the research project U.S. Public Health experts were of the opinion that the newer chlorine-containing insecticides, such as DDT, endrin, etc., are probably killing fewer people than the older ones, such as those containing arsenic, mercury, thallium, phosphorus, etc. Pesticides of all kinds are known to cause about 1 death per 1 million population. The introduction of new pesticides is believed not to have changed this figure, which has remained practically uniform the past twenty-five years. Perhaps deaths from the newer pesticides have merely offset deaths caused by the materials, such as arsenicals, which they have partly replaced. Nor is there anything remarkable in those cases of pesticide poisoning which do occur. They follow the same general pattern as poisoning caused by other chemicals, including higher prevalence among children.

There is a bad fallacy in the soothing paragraph above. It assumes that the new highly chlorinated pesticides, which kill fish and birds, would kill human beings in the same obvious and dramatic way in which cyanide or arsenic kills human beings. One pictures a scene in which the princess eats the fatal plum, from which endrin has not been washed, and dies in convulsions. This, of course, does not happen. What is more likely is that the princess drinks water containing a billionth of a part per million of endrin throughout her childhood and girlhood; she is afflicted with chronic liver trouble, which she attributes to her fondness for lemon meringue pie; she staggers through an unhealthy motherhood and dies at an earlier age than her sisters who moved away from the creek.

In fact, the Public Health Service reports that the ratio of nonfatal to fatal cases of pesticide poisoning is about 100 to 1 for the entire population. Many of the nonfatal cases are apparently so mild that they might not have been reported if they had not been covered by workmen's compensation. It is precisely the mild and chronic afflictions, however, that result in mean, nagging and substandard lives and early deaths. There is a vast void of knowledge about the realm of "just a little" poison. Perhaps more importantly than with pesticides, however, we have realized quite recently that we are living in the "just a little" realm in conection with *lead.*

How harmless and tabby that word looks and sounds in English! In Russian it is "svinetz"; in German "blei"; in French "plomb"; in Spanish "plomo." These are rather fearsome and ponderous-sounding words, as they should be, since the metal is a heavy, vile one with a record of poisonings back to pre-Christian Greece and Rome. Livia, wife of Augustus, the greatest poisoner of them all, used lead poisons frequently in her elaborate and fatal diets for various cousins, nephews, daughters-in-law and ex-husbands. Lead pipe for water had been warned against by Greek and Roman physicans. Lead burners, plumbers (the origin of the word is obvious), lead miners, makers of lead shot and of lead batteries, painters, tinsmiths, typographers, children who eat the woodwork or plaster from the walls of old homes in sections of endemic lead poisoning—throughout history thousands of poor devils have suffered from chronic or acute poisoning, which is also known as plumbism or saturnism. Cattle and especially calves have been poisoned, in pens that have been painted with white lead.

What we face today is the possibility of mass poisoning by lead, mostly from the use of "Ethyl" type gasoline containing lead alkyls as antiknock additives. But oddly we face it not so seriously as an *atmospheric* poison in automotive smog but as a *pollutant of water and of food crops.* This is what has suddenly come to be realized. We had been looking for it in the wrong place all the time.

Since the advent of antiknock gasoline in 1923 over 6 billion pounds of lead in the form of lead alkyls have been marketed and burned, mainly in the United States. The average cumulative contamination from lead of the Northern Hemisphere averages 10 milligrams of lead per square meter from gasoline burning alone. In the highly motorized areas such as the Los Angeles Basin the content of lead in the air, in the water, in the soil, in the vegetable crops is several hundred times higher than this average.

What has fooled us all along is the fact that lead from the burning of high-octane gasoline was regarded as a possible poison only in *air* pollution. From the start, elaborate tests were made which persuaded the Surgeon General of the United States, the Ministry of Health in Great Britain, and other august official bodies that as an air pollutant the lead in the exhaust was not dangerous enough to justify holding up approval on such a dazzling improvement in automobile performance. The Ethyl Corporation and other manufacturers of tetraethyl lead have repeated over and over again that the lead getting into the bodies of people by way of their lungs in even badly polluted city air is not as much as they get in the food they eat. An unintentionally prophetic statement! It was imagined that the food and water were harmlessly low in lead content, yet they turn out now in many cases to be dangerously high, and the reason is the fantastic accumulation of lead coming from automobile exhausts in irrigation water, in soil and in food plants.

This discovery is so new that not all the implications have been drawn. It is still part of the Unknown. The first scientific scoop was the obscurely published findings of two Canadian geologists, H. V. Warren and R. E. Delavault, reporting high lead contents in vegetation growing near highways. Later the U.S. Geological Survey found lead in amounts as high as 3,000 parts per million in the ash of water-washed grasses near Denver. Chow and his associates of the Scripps Institute of Oceanography have proved by isotope analysis that the unexpectedly high lead contents of snow in the Lassen Volcanic National Park, a river watershed, is due to lead from auto exhausts. C. C. Patterson has pointed out in the *Archives of Environmental Health* that lead has accumulated in surface waters of the Northern Hemisphere to a hazardous extent. Recent French analysis of the lead content of various common vegetable foods shows the great concentrating capabilities of certain plant organisms in storage of lead from the air or the soil. Just as a fish liver can multiply the concentration of chlorine-containing pesticides in the water by a factor of a million, plants can multiply the concentration of lead in water (or possibly in air) by similar tremendous factors. Thus the plant, although strangely unaffected by the lead, may poison the animal that eats it. Warren and Delavault in comparing high lead contents in soils and plants in Canada and England with health data have suggested a correlation with several human diseases, including multiple sclerosis.

The concentrating power of food plants in an environment containing some billion pounds of scattered lead has become the heart of the matter. We may grant, although with some reluctance, that lead in its usual form of the chloride-bromide salt, as it issues from an auto exhaust pipe, does not attain concentrations sufficiently high even on a smoggy day to cause chronic plumbism through the act of breathing. We shall have to await more refined and voluminous data on water, plant, and food analysis, along with medical surveys, to assure ourselves that we are not getting chronic plumbism through the act of eating. In the meantime we cannot overlook the following facts established by Dr. Patterson:

The average American ingests some 400 micrograms of lead per day in food, air and water. This ingestion of about 20 tons of lead per year on a national basis is grossly excessive compared to natural conditions.

Existing rates of lead absorption are about 30 times higher than absorption rates in a state of nature. This is primarily because of gasoline additives but also because of food-can solder, lead pesticides, and from the millions of tons of lead accumulated throughout past decades and stored as paints, alloys, piping, glazes and spent ammunition.

The lead concentration in our blood now averages about one quarter of a part per million, which is 100 times natural levels. The latest medical information points to a blood concentration of one half part per million as the threshold for "classical" lead poisoning.

Dr. Patterson defines the condition of modern urban Americans as one of "severe chronic lead *insult*."

LET US ANTICIPATE without pleasure what sort of symptoms we might expect and perhaps are now enjoying.

Chronic exposure to lead in any form usually goes through four well-defined stages and it is unimportant, as far as symptoms are concerned, whether the lead is introduced into the body by the lung, the stomach, or by covering the body with lead paint. (We make an exception of lead introduced by means of a bullet through the heart or brain.) Of the gentler ways of getting plumbism, eating lead is the quickest to kill.

The first stage of chronic poisoning, lasting from three to six months, brings loss of appetite, loss of weight, constipation, nearly continuous headache, and a peculiar disorder in hearings: One can hear low-frequency tones but hardly any tones of high frequency. Aside from a fall-off in musical appreciation, a man can seldom hear all his wife has to say, but she can hear him, particularly when snoring, loud and clear. There are also periods of great irritability and tremor of the right or working hand. In the case of children, arrested mental development becomes noticeable.

The second stage is one of adaptation. Suddenly the body

seems to have found a way to assimilate the heavy enemy molecules. There is a feeling that "I've got it licked." Unfortunately
this lasts only a few months.

During the third stage, lasting from one to ten years, the
digestive system begins slowly to fall to pieces. There is acute
pain in the abdomen. In the case of men, there is now marked
storage of lead in the testicles, which results not only in sterility
but in sexual impotence. Often the person afflicted with plumbism at this phase takes to alcohol, which increases his suscepti-
bility to the lead. Needless to say, by this time his marriage
along with his digestion has usually met with shipwreck.

During the fourth and final stage, which may drag on for
over ten years, the victim has not only lost his digestion, he has
lost most of his kidneys and his brain has become specifically
affected. He suffers both from nephritis and encephalitis. He
(or she) is now much more susceptible to other diseases, particularly cancer. Thus, unless urine and blood tests have been
carried out, the death certificates may contain no reference to
the real cause of his perishing. Toward the end (without cancer
or other painful direct symptoms) he will start talking inces-
santly, will undergo epileptic-type trances, will have hallucina-
tions, will vomit unceasingly and unproductively, will come up
with bloody scars on the skin and will die in a stupor.

If this person has been significant to anyone, perhaps to
the one doctor in a hundred thousand who is not satisfied with
the hasty, blunt clichés of terminal diagnosis, a post-mortem
will show lead deposits which will be highest in the liver, lesser
in the kidneys, pancreas, brain, heart, spleen and lungs, in that
order.

Lead is thus a stealthy but implacable killer. There is no
good therapy, although massive shots of vitamin B_6 are regarded as helpful. This fits in with the curious fact that a higher
level of lead in the blood is measured when the victim is exposed to sunlight. The well-known antirachitic effect of the sun

leads to increased lead absorption from the gut and into the blood.

It is ironical that we may now be in desperate confrontation with a pollutant that is as old as history and one which we have been warned patiently against by inquiring doctors as far back as Hippocrates. It is tempting to attribute some of the mass disorders of our day to incipient plumbism. Noting that extreme intellectual irritability is a warning flag, perhaps the Negro riots in Los Angeles of August, 1965, may have been due to a combination of chronic lead poisoning and smog sickness.

Pork and pearls are on the counter,
But no locust or wild honey.
——HELTON, *Come Back to Earth*

We must remember not to judge any public servant by any one act,
and especially should we beware of attacking the men who are merely
the occasions and not the causes of disaster.
——THEODORE ROOSEVELT

15 PORK IS SOLUBLE *in* WATER

WITH THE water pollution problem quivering before us like a
mangled giant on a stretcher, it is a very sad thing to see billions
of dollars being spent on water projects for purely political, almost frivolous, reasons. Although there has always been the
pork barrel, it has never been so big and so watery. And never
before has the mechanism of the pork machine been so smoothly
oiled and automatic. Such moderationists as Senators Paul
Douglas and William Proxmire have almost given up trying to
talk sense or shame into the heads of colleagues, crazed by the
smell of pork. But there are still some dissidents and one example is worth giving.

The popular multimillion-dollar porkchop is usually a new
dam to make a new irrigation reservoir. Representative Langer
of Minnesota, a brave man indeed, in June, 1965, raised a
lonely voice against the absurd, so-called "Garrison-diversion
project" on the Missouri River to cost $248 million. This is
strictly an agricultural deal designed to irrigate 250,000 acres
of mostly "class 3" land in North Dakota, the poorest land that
is considered to be irrigable. At $1,000 per acre this is expen-

sive farmland, especially as the production will simply add to the crop surplus. During the 1965 crop year the federal government was required to make payments in North Dakota of $35 million, in order *not* to produce wheat, feed grains or cut hay on soil bank land. This is to say nothing about wheat certificates, soil conservation payments, price supports, purchases of dairy products, beef and lamb, sugar beets, etc., etc., and the many other economy get-well projects.

What does this Garrison-diversion project (which is by no means unusual) mean on a single-farm basis? On a 320-acre farm, which is the maximum amount allowed under irrigation regulations to a man and wife, this would require spending $256,000. This is enough money to make a direct present to that farm operation of $8,000 a year for thirty years with the man and wife spending their entire time watching television and gulping beer. In fact, the government could save money by doing this, because at least it would not have to pay other farmers not to produce the same crops that would be raised on this hypothetical farm, which now takes on the colors of a diamond mine—without any diamonds.

Representative Langer further put his political life on the block by pointing out that by a coldly cynical gag agreement opponents were allowed only a total of one half hour to discuss the bill. "The reason, of course, is obvious," said Langer. "This is a pork-barrel bill and therefore not to be considered by this House on the basis of its merits or demerits, but rather to be enacted for the sake of expediency. It is the kind of bill where you are asked to look the other way."

There are scores of bills that have come out of the same barrel. The Frying Pan Water Diversion in Colorado ($170 million) is one of them. The project will divert water from the west-flowing Frying Pan Creek to the east-flowing Arkansas River via a 5½-mile tunnel through the Continental Divide. To make the project appear rosier, the Bureau of Reclamation doctored up its estimates of benefits and the bill finally passed in 1962. The project water is supposed to increase greatly the alfalfa crop of Colorado, which already has about a million acres of alfalfa in the soil bank that no one is allowed to cut. As we have seen, alfalfa is a notorious water hog. Furthermore, the same area is still washing the mud from its farm stoops following the Arkansas River flood in the spring of 1965.

Both the Army Corps of Engineers and the Bureau of Reclamation of the Department of the Interior have become increasingly stained with pork. With such noble achievements as the Panama Canal and Hoover Dam, respectively, behind them, both organizations have now reached such ponderous proportions that they have to go out and look for work to keep their overblown staffs busy. Their proposals become more and more marginal but they are still the darlings of the pork-barrel congressmen.

Although the Reclamation Bureau is restricted to projects involving irrigation in the 17 Western States, the Corps of Engineers can dream up anything anywhere. So sacred is its image that is is enshrined up there with Mother and the Boy Scouts. Let us take a closer look at this remarkable group which, although part of the Army, consists mostly of civilian engineers.

On June 16, 1775, the day before the Battle of Bunker Hill, the Continental Congress authorized the appointment of a chief engineer and two assistants for the Grand Army and in December, 1776, the raising of a corps of engineers. Most of them were French or Polish volunteers. They built the fortifications at West Point and the siegeworks at Yorktown. After being temporarily disbanded after the war, the Corps was reconstituted in 1802 and its first job was to establish and superintend a military academy—West Point. This they controlled until after the Civil War. For some time it was the only school in the country giving a course in civil engineering. The Corps may indeed be said to be the father of engineering in this country since it later had a hand in founding engineering departments at Harvard, Yale, Rensselaer and many other schools. The Corps's present mighty responsibilities stem from the General Survey Act in Congress of 1824 which authorized the President, with the Corps as his agent, to select routes and to draw up plans and estimates for the construction of roads and canals. General Robert E. Lee came from the Corps.

During World War II the Corps reached a peak strength of over 700,000 officers and men.

However, from such awesome and urgent constructions as the dams at Fort Peck, Garrison and Fort Randall on the Missouri River and the Bonneville and McNary Dams on the Columbia, the Corps has descended to consorting with pigs. They have warmly backed and helped in selling perhaps the champion of all pork-barrel schemes—the Arkansas River Navigation Project—and they are rooting themselves hoarse for the Rampart Dam in Alaska, perhaps an even lower order of pork.

The Arkansas River project represents a classic in brutal politics, since it not only proposes a fundamentally insane notion of sailing barges 516 miles from the Mississippi to the prairie town of Catoosa, Oklahoma, near Tulsa, but, because of the extreme fragility of the soil which forms the banks of the shallow Arkansas River, it will result in a huge additional load of silt pollution for both the Arkansas and the Mississippi. It is basically an anticonservation plan. It is now about 40 percent completed and its total cost will inevitably exceed the original estimate of $1.2 billion. This is more than either the Panama Canal or the St. Lawrence Seaway cost. The Ohio River project, which opened that great stream to barging, cost only $125 million.

The essential foolishness of the Arkansas River Basin program was pointed out in a book, *Big Dam Foolishness*, by Elmer T. Paterson, editorial writer for the Oklahoma City *Times* and *Daily Oklahoman*. (It is important to point out that Oklahoma City is in the central part of the state and Tulsa, its rival, is in the east. When later there was serious talk of extending the project 135 miles westward, the Oklahoma City papers changed their music from tuba raspberries to trumpet blaring, and it is hard now to find an unburned copy of Mr. Paterson's masterly denunciation.)

It is only just to the Corps of Engineers to note that a navigable Arkansas River was one of the hearty compulsions of the late, powerful Senator Robert Kerr, whose motto might have been "What is good for Oklahoma is good for the nation." He had already so skillfully played the strings of the yearly omnibus public works bill called Rivers and Harbors to wangle dams in Oklahoma that a trip around this half-arid state is known as the tour of "Kerr's lakes," and most of them, it must be said, are well worthwhile from the standpoint of flood prevention and recreation. (During the 1965 session of the World's Fair, Oklahoma rubbed salt in the wounds of drought-weary New Yorkers by transporting water to its exhibit and letting it gurgle lavishly over decorative stones.) Making a 9-foot deep navigable water highway with 18 locks (and 3 giant reservoirs to hold the water level) out of the muddy Arkansas, the miserable Verdigris and the puny White River, across one third of Oklahoma and across all of Arkansas, is something else again.

All such projects have to be justified to Congress on a so-called cost-benefit ratio; that is, the future benefits divided by the cost have to be more than unity. The Corps of Engineers made two highly suspectful estimates, in which they threw in everything conceivable, such as a future multimillion-dollar barge business in canned meats, exceeding by a factor of 12 the nation's *total* barge traffic in canned meat. They multiplied by an infinite factor Arkansas's canned fruit business—the factor is infinite because Arkansas does not have a canned fruit business or any expectation of one. They estimated huge barge shipments of Oklahoma coal, whereas Oklahoma coal *priced at the mine sites* cannot now compete with Kentucky coal delivered at points of consumption such as New Orleans and St. Louis. They threw in large crude-oil and petroleum product shipments, whereas such deliveries now tend almost wholly to be made by pipelines. When it became apparent to its nervous supporters that the highly doctored benefits-cost ratio was not going to look attractive on the usual 50-year life expectancy basis, Senator Kerr got the ground rules changed. The project was thenceforth to be considered on a 100-year life span, which afforded the opportunity for more robust imaginations to run wild.

The degree of wildness was shown in 1965 by the big hoopla about the so-called "Ozarka Program," in which it was proposed to gild the monstrous lily of the Arkansas River Navigation Project by getting federal money to build access roads to future recreation damsites in the states drained by the river. Red-faced men, such as the president of the Arkansas Basin Association, have said: "What we need to do is put a stop to so much of the damn griping" (about the pork barrel). This in translation means that, having failed to pass a $150 million road bond issue in the state of Arkansas, the red-faced men are after federal loot to build access roads.

A careful item-by-item critique of the Corps's fictional dollar benefits, even on the 100-year basis, led three economics professors (two from the University of Chicago and one from Oklahoma State University) to conclude that the Arkansas River navigation system would lose heavily year by year; that it would cost more to keep the channels dredged than would be netted by barge traffic; that if, as seems inevitable, the project is completed, it will be best to let it stand there unused. As a monument, it could be called the River of Pigs to memorialize another great defeat in American policy.

Alaska is a much bigger state than Oklahoma and has a thousand times as much water. It is only natural to expect water-

soluble pork to grow in giant size in our 49th state, and this
is what seems to be taking place. Under the bewitching caress
of the Corps of Engineers, the porcine cancer has taken form
in the Rampart Dam project, which would cost even more than
the Arkansas River Navigation scandal. This would back up
the Yukon River in east central Alaska to create an artificial
reservoir bigger than Lake Erie. In order to produce water
power for nonexistent and in the future still highly dubious
Alaskan industries, the project would (a) destroy the nesting
grounds of 2 million ducks and geese, (b) wipe out a substantial
proportion of Alaska's fur-bearing animals (beaver, mink,
muskrat, otter, martens), (c) bury the ancestral homes and
hunting grounds of the Venetie and Chalkyitsik Indians, (d)
seriously threaten the Yukon salmon run, (e) erase one of the
best moose ranges in existence, and (f) drown under a mean-
ingless blob of water one of the few rich authentic wildernesses
left on the continent.

The power-hungry Alaskan politicians and real-estate mag-
nates have only one exhausted cliché for all of this: "Are you
for ducks or for people?" An honest answer would be to vote
for ducks rather than *that* kind of people.

It is sometimes hard to tell whether in the Run for the Pork-
chops the Corps and the Reclamation Bureau are ahead of or
are simply joyously following the political swineherds. Sometimes they seem to be mostly ahead. In apparent violation of
the United States Code on lobbying with appropriated moneys,
the Bureau of Reclamation has printed a brochure on "Lake
Powell, the Jewel of the Colorado," a glossy, thinly disguised
boost for approval of the Bridge Canyon and Marble Canyon
Dams. Reclamation Commissioner Floyd E. Dominey dipped
his pen in purple (or maybe azure) ink and came up with the
following deathless prose:

"You have a front-row seat in the amphitheatre of infinity.
The bright blue sky deepens slowly to a velvet purple and the

stars are brilliant—glittering in that vast immensity above. Orange sandstone cliffs fade to dusky-red—then deepest black. The fire burns low [*What* fire?] reflected in the placid lake. There is peace. And a oneness with the world and God . . ."

The three final dots are for free but that is all that is free. The pork-studded upper Colorado project will cost $988 million. Most of the dams will be far upstream where the river flow is low and the cost of construction high. The $81 million Flaming Gorge Dam, for instance, will generate power at a cost higher than its selling price. As in North Dakota, the irrigation projects will bring into use unneeded land at costs out of all proportion to what the land can ever produce.

Both the Corps and the Reclamation Bureau have a fey power which is hard to define for the rest of us mortals. They can conjure up such billion-dollar sapphire-lidded dreams and guide them through a ritual which includes a series of local and national public hearings, the Bureau of the Budget and thence to Congress, waiting wet-lipped and lascivious.

It is a source of great irritation to the Corps, to the Bureau of Reclamation, and to the Congress that the biggest power dam in the world is in Bratsk, Siberia. The Angara River, which drains Lake Baikal toward the Arctic Ocean, is already generating more than a million kilowatts of power, which is only one third of the installed capacity. There are no users for the rest and it appears doubtful there ever will be. Thus the Bratsk is pork-brother to the proposed Rampart project, proving that Russia is getting more democratic all the time. Senator Jackson of Washington is insistent that 3.6 million kilowatts of additional capacity—a third powerhouse—be installed at Grand Coulee Dam, the chief reason evidently being that this "will return to the United States world leadership in the construction of large power plants."

The Bureau of Reclamation's bookkeeping has received a bilious going over from some Eastern congressmen, particularly

Representative Saylor of Pennsylvania. One of the Bureau's tricks is to leave out of its financial statements the costs incurred by other federal agencies in the generation and transmission of power. A typical example is the Missouri River Basin Power System, where power revenues of $34,043,011 and costs of only $21,920,083 are claimed, leaving what might appear to be a highly profitable net income of $12,122,928. However, these costs represent only the expenditures of the Bureau of Reclamation and not the major cost of production of power, most of which is generated by Corps of Engineers dams. When all appropriate costs are included, the $12 million-plus profit becomes an $8 million loss. It is evident that the Bureau is better at writing poetic prose for brochures than at bookkeeping.

In 1965 the first omnibus public works bill since 1962 was passed, but not without some astringent observations on the part of Senator Proxmire. He believes the benefit-cost ratios are highly unrealistic since the costs are mostly based on 2.5 percent interest over a period of 100 years, whereas the government borrows money for 15 years at 4 percent. The 100-year life assumed for a dam is plainly ridiculous since the dam would silt up solid before the end of 50 years.

Another gay technique of getting the benefit-cost ratio safely above unity is to pile into the benefit column absolutely imaginary numbers relating to intangibles, such as national defense, enhancement of local land values, and recreation. A classical case is the tattered old Tennessee-Tombigbee Waterway, a project which Senator Proxmire fears has by no means been laid to rest even now. In 1947 the Corps of Engineers had reported a benefit-cost ratio of 1.13; in other words, the annual benefits were claimed to be 1.13 times greater than annual costs. The House subcommittee found, once the gaseous intangibles had been eliminated, that the actual ratio was only 0.27. In other words, benefits were actually only 27 percent or less than one third of costs. Phony benefit items made the difference between fiction and reality.

In the 1965 pork bill over a quarter of a billion dollars is asked for seven reservoirs on the Grand River and its tributaries in Missouri and Iowa. The benefit-cost ratios are highly inflamed by adding the spice of intangibles, including recreation. Nobody rightly knows how to put the dollar sign on this. What is actually done is to make the dollar sign big enough to get the benefit-cost ratio over unity. This particular slab of pork is doubly revolting since the Department of Agriculture fears that some of the proposed reservoirs would have adverse effects on both flood prevention and watershed protection.

On the other hand, some projects too preposterous even for the Corps and the Bureau have been punched through by sheer pig-muscle, obstinacy and mutual masturbation on the part of congressmen. Ex-Representative Walter Judd of Minnesota used to brag about wheedling $30.3 million for the construction of dams, locks and 9-foot channels to hike the water over St. Anthony Falls in Minneapolis for a purpose which defies detection. After twenty-six years in the works, nobody seems to want it or to know what to do with it, and the Corps long pulled its skirts fastidiously away from it.

The Corps also disavowed responsibility for a strange lonely deep-water canal that now connects San Francisco Bay with Sacramento and which cost $41 million. Its psychotic justification was that the port of San Francisco was so crowded that relief fifty miles away was necessary. This, like the future Arkansas River, will carry little or no traffic, since San Francisco needs more and not less docking fees, and like a sort of forlorn, expensive ghost of a navigable river it will simply be there, but it will also require constant dredging to keep open a port nobody wants. This project was authorized just after World War II when California congressmen were beginning to feel their oats. They wanted to prove they were a big state.

It is dangerous, at least to the blood pressure of red-faced congressmen, to state the facts about the pork barrel. When *Life* magazine in 1963 exposed some of the more glaring aspects of water-soluble pork, the reaction in the Congress was much more explosive than it had been to the news of Pearl Harbor. It was seriously proposed in Congress that magazine mailing rates be stepped up. In other words, the whole magazine publishing business should be shot down in order to zero in on the Luce publications because of their realism. Here we encounter a form of evil. It amounts to a porcine conspiracy much more expensive than the Cosa Nostra.

It is difficult to see any constructive gestures in regard to the great problems, such as water pollution, come out of a Congress that is wedded to a sort of ingrained legislative pollution of its own.

The water pure that bids the thirsty live.
—UNDERWOOD, *I Shall Not Pass This Way Again*

Its waters, returning,
Back to their springs, like the rain, shall fill them full of refreshment:
That which the fountain sends forth returns again to the fountain.
—LONGFELLOW, *Evangeline*

16 HOW *to* MAKE SWEET WATER

THE AMOUNT OF water on earth is virtually constant, hence the problem of an ever-multiplying human race is to get it in usable form and to apportion it. If we could obtain rain where we need it or could even accurately predict where and when it would fall and in what amount we would have a hold on the planet. Eventually we know we are going to need the oceans both for water and for atomic power, but we are now faced with the question of whether it is best for local scarcities to desalt sea water or to impound and transport the huge reserves of fresh water going to waste in subarctic rivers. In the meantime the challenge of rain making has nagged us, especially over the past twenty years, and we are beginning to realize that one reason for our notable lack of real breakthroughs in this field is that we don't know enough about the weather, and specifically there are too many things about the process of rainfall that we don't understand.

Congress woke up to the fact in 1961 that every department of government was spending some money on weather studies and countless miscellaneous agencies had wet their fingers to probe the air. In 1964 the head of the Weather Bureau (located in the Department on Commerce and now changed in name rather horribly to the "Environmental Scientific Services Administration") was given another hat as "federal coordinator" with an independent staff under instructions to come up with a broad federal weather program which both Congress and the executive branch could understand. For the 1966 fiscal year, which started July 1, 1965, weather services by all agencies will require the labors of more than 20,000 people and the expenditure of $238 million. Among the unsung heroes in the story of weather, not counted in this total, are some 10,000 unpaid public spirited citizens who make daily reports with nonrecording rain gauges in the United States, an average of three to each county in the nation.

From the nonrecording rain gauge to the weather satellites, such as Tiros and Nimbus, costing $30 million a year to operate, there is a gap in technology of some three thousand years, yet we cannot say we now understand the weather. The satellites have encouraged us, however. One of the surprises from their photographs has been the sharpness and clarity of organization of the earth's cloud systems. The satellites can by spectroscopic measurement determine at any time and place the vertical distribution of water vapor in the atmosphere. This is new knowledge; now we must find out what to do with it.

Actually the weather satellites overwhelm us with data. The problem now is one of more rapid digestion and interpretation of the signals with which they flood the ground stations. Information is measured in "bits"—a technical term for a single piece of data. In order to construct a complete weather map of the Northern Hemisphere, we need about 10,000 bits. But one cloud photograph from a Tiros contains 10 million bits and the 8 Tiros satellites have produced nearly 500,000 pictures in the past five years. Future satellites now being designed may generate 10 *billion* bits a day.

The satellites can only tell us about wind structures in so

far as these affect cloud movements. In order to know more about the winds at high altitudes it is now planned to step up enormously our launchings of weather balloons. Thousands will be floated up to constant levels and observation of their movements by ground radar or by satellites will reveal wind directions and strengths. Although these will be so light that they will not endanger aircraft, doubtless we will have a hundred flying-saucer scares a year, where now we have half a dozen.

Throughout the history of meteorology there have been almost frantic attempts to correlate cycles of rain and drought with something else—sunspots, for example. This has not worked out. Correlations are tricky. It has actually been shown that weather cycles will correlate, for example, better with the proportion of two-headed calves born in a given year than with sunspots.

The most recent and persuasive correlation of rainfall with anything at all is with meteors. The Australian physicist E. G. Bowen has shown a close connection between the earth's passage through meteor swarms and the whole terrestrial rainfall pattern some thirty days later. An especially good correlation in both hemispheres is with periodic meteor swarms such as the Perseids in August, the Giacobinids in October, and the Bielids in early December. The 30-day lag is the estimated time for meteors to be slowed up from their terminal velocity, to be ground down to fine dust particles by heat and to fall under gravity to the rain-generating altitudes. The dust spirals down in diminishing orbits most of which are in the plane of the ecliptic (the plane of the earth's orbit around the sun). This may explain why the aspect of the moon seems to have some connection with cycles of excessive rainfall, since the orbit of the moon around the earth is close to the ecliptic; the moon's gravitation may modulate the amount of dust reaching the earth.

The meteoritic dust theory of rain cycles fits in well with what we know not only about rain formation but of the seeding method of getting clouds to disgorge rain. It was in the early 1930's that a Norwegian meteorologist, Tor Bergeron, discovered one of the two ways that nature makes rain. Most clouds do not form rain because the droplets of water are too small to fall. Their diameters average about eight ten-thousandths of an inch, while they need to be at least ten times that size to get a one-way ticket to the ground. The droplets in common clouds grow only very slowly by condensation alone. They often stay liquid even when the temperature is 40 below zero. They have the habit, in other words, of "supercooling." However, Tor Bergeron observed that when some ice crystals are formed in a cloud of supercooled water droplets, the crystals, unlike the droplets, grow very rapidly and at the expense of the droplets. When they are big enough they drop as snow or ice, melting to rain if they hit warmer air on the way down. The crystallization of supercooled water as ice can be immensely accelerated by the presence of dust.

At one time it was thought that all rain was produced by the Bergeron process; in other words, the clouds had to consist of ice before the particles could get big enough to fall to earth. Yet in the tropics small cumulus clouds (white "cauliflower" type) often produce heavy showers, even though their tops never reach subfreezing altitudes. It thus appears that under certain conditions large raindrops can form without the freezing cycle. It is believed that the reason for this is that above the oceans large drops of spray are formed around salt particles. For causing tropical rainstorms, a seeding method involving simply table salt might suffice. On the other hand, we are not interested in fomenting tropical storms. On the contrary, we are interested in putting a stop to them.

In 1946 Vincent Schaefer of the General Electric Company, working along lines suggested by the Nobel Prize-winning Irving Langmuir of the same company, set his mind to rain making, assuming the Bergeron theory. His experiments consisted simply of dumping dry ice (solid carbon dioxide) out of an airplane into clouds. In this way a sudden cold shock triggered off the crystallization process. This is still the best way to disperse very low clouds (fog) and is used by commercial airports, such as those in the Pacific Northwest, which are frequently socked in.

Lately Bernard Vonnegut, also of General Electric, discovered that crystals of silver iodide, added to supercooled clouds, even at mild degrees of supercooling, will start to precipitate ice crystals. The effectiveness of this compound is ascribed to its crystalline similarity to ice. Most of the rain makers (there are eight commercial "weather modification" companies listed in the *Bulletins of the American Meteorological Society*) have used silver iodide ever since, generating it usually on the ground in burning acetone so that it is wafted upward as a smoke, aimed at a rain cloud. There is complete lack of scientific agreement as to whether any rain has ever been made in this manner. If apparently successful, the skeptics can always say that it would have rained anyway. However, in places in New England increases of rainfall in the neighborhood of 10 to 20 percent above normal have been pretty well documented from year to year.

By the early 1950's the cloud-seeding furor had pretty well subsided but the Departments of Health, Education, and Welfare, Agriculture and Defense were still supporting research. The Weather Bureau would have nothing to do with it, because of the prejudices of its then chief, Francis W. Reichelderfer, who seemed to consider cloud seeding experiments beneath his dignity or perhaps as insults to God. More recently the Department of the Interior has backed cloud-seeding research in connection with drought-ridden river basins, such as the Colorado, where so-called "orthographic" storms might be exploited. (Orthographic cloud systems are found in areas where mountains in the path of moisture-laden air force the air to rise and cool.) This is of great interest to the Western bloc of congressmen.

Some promising results have been suggested, although seeding cannot be held responsible for the 1965 floods in Colorado.

One result of the cloud-seeding activities that came after 1946 was that five states passed laws proclaiming their sovereignty over their rain clouds. They did not want the neighboring states stealing their rain by some hook or crook. Moreover, in West Virginia an "anti-Rainmaker" bill narrowly missed passing in 1965. This was supported by the state's eastern Panhandle farmers who protested that rain clouds had actually been dispersed by dropping silver iodide in them, thereby preventing, rather than inducing, rain. Washington, Oregon, eastern Colorado and western Colorado have seen similar disputes.

Cloud seeding is only a $1 million a year business but it can be expected to grow. New compounds, such as special clays, are believed to be more efficient and much cheaper than silver iodide, and the large U.S. rocket industry will sooner or later be inspired to get into the action.

What must be emphasized, however, is that one must have clouds to seed. Where there is no water in the air, one cannot summon it up, like a genie. Generally only about 1 percent of a cloud ever falls naturally as rain. Seeding may increase this yield to 2 percent. But 2 percent of zero is still zero.

Another revival of enthusiasm for weather control is associated with the desire to fight hail and hurricanes. Italians and South Africans have for some time had good luck with shooting pyrotechnic rockets to reduce the fall of crop-damaging hail. In 1959 alone more than 100,000 rockets were shot off for this purpose in northern Italy.

The use of silver iodide or dry ice as a means of quenching the "eye" of a tropical hurricane would on the face of it seem to be like defending oneself with a needle against a mad elephant, since the energy in storms of this type is enormous. In a single day a medium-sized hurricane releases as much power through water vapor condensation as the simultaneous explosion of four hundred 20-megaton hydrogen bombs or enough to destroy 400,000 Hiroshimas. The theory is that if condensation can be speeded up in the "eye" by silver iodide, the wind speed will be reduced. The energy will be dispersed over a much larger area and less damage will be done.

The first experiment, "Project Cirrus," in 1947, involved dumping 80 pounds of dry ice in the eye of a hurricane. The only remarkable effect (undoubtedly pure coincidence) was that the hurricane immediately veered off its path and hit the state of Georgia, inflicting a good deal of damage.

It was in a somewhat gingerly fashion, therefore, that two seeding experiments (Project Storm-fury) were carried out jointly by the Navy and the Weather Bureau during hurricane Beulah on August 23-24, 1963. For the first ten minutes or so after seeding the hurricane clouds grew upward an additional 10,000 to 20,000 feet. Then they expanded horizontally, more than doubling their original diameter. The storm was not dispersed, however. The proponents of hurricane pricking are in a stage of reappraisal, where they wonder whether they want to promote condensation in the hurricane's eye or to retard it. No foolproof method is known to prevent such nucleation, although the Air Force uses a classified method of preventing the formation of "con trails" behind airplane engine exhausts, which might be useful.

Tropical storms and in fact all rainstorms are nature's way of desalting sea water. The great water cycle of evaporation from the oceans, leaving the salt behind—rain, runoff to rivers, with huge intermediate losses to the air by evaporation from the soil, from bodies of fresh water, and by transpiration of plants— has turned out to be a most untidy way to run a planet covered with three billion human beings, whose demands for sweet water is insatiable. We usually get too much or too little at the wrong time. This is a fault of nature which we can forgive in view of the fact that among the Sun's children, our good blue-green planet is uniquely endowed with theoretically inexhaustible stores of both water and deuterium oxide ("heavy water") which nuclear physicists perceive as the source of limitless power needs of the future of the race. But it is our own fault that we waste such appalling amounts of fresh water, chiefly by evaporation from irrigation canals and reservoirs.

Over the past several years an unexpected strategy developed by chemists shows promise for cutting down these evaporation losses. This is to add to the water traces of harmless "Surfactant" compounds such as the higher alcohols which form molecular layers on the surface of quiet lakes or ditches and reduce the rate of evaporation by forming a micro-thin barrier through which the water molecules find it hard to escape. This does not work so well in large wind-swept bodies of water, since the waves break the surface film. The technique has shown promise in Australia and in the Southwest in certain large-scale experiments. Improvements in chemically anchoring the film, so that it is less easily ruptured, are being studied. The cost of the chemicals is still the discouraging feature, since everything connected with irrigation must be cheap.

Here we meet face to face with an economic dilemma of the highest, hairiest visage. Most of the present costs of water, especially as made available to the irrigation farmer, are wholly deceptive. Such a farmer claims he will be ruined if water costs him more than 1 cent per 1,000 gallons. He usually gets it at that price but it is a gift from the taxpayers pure and simple. The farmer pays nothing on the amortizations of large dams and reservoir construction, no small part of the expenditures for which consists in locating the impoundments or the conduits at such levels that gravity rather than pumps delivers the water to his crops.

Having the 1-cent water, the farmer proceeds to waste it in leaking ditches and in excessive irrigation runs. If we continue to evaluate irrigation water at the absurd and mythical price of 1 cent per 1,000 gallons, no method of desalting of sea water or even of large-scale transportation of water such as the North American Water and Power Alliance (NAWAPA) concept for bringing the excess water of the northwestern rivers of the continent to 33 states of the Union, to Mexico and to Canada, would be worth considering for irrigation uses. Pumping charges would lick it. We are up against social and political barbed wire packed with high voltage which may fence us in against considering any great continental water enterprises.

Critics of the desalinization program of the federal government have been quick to point out that, even if water were available from the oceans at prices lower than coastal cities now pay for water from other sources, it would still cost 10 to 15 times too much for the Utah or Arizona farmer. The importance of this point is heightened by the fact that, among large water users, it is only the irrigating farmer that actually *consumes* the water. Industry and municipalities borrow the water and dirty it, but they do not consume it to any really significant extent. One can easily conceive of water-purification systems operating on sewage water that would put an end to the water shortage for industry and municipalities. Here the major problem is pollution—a scarcity of *clean* water. It is the farmer, who cannot recover the water from his transpiring plants or his evaporating soil, who would in the long run benefit from desalinization of sea water on a gigantic scale, but it is precisely the farmer who cannot afford such desalted water.

Before we decide whether such vast projects as combination nuclear electric power and desalinization of the sea and NAWAPA should be pursued with full vigor we are going to have to take a more realistic look at agricultural water prices or, alternatively, to concede that we are going to saddle the city taxpayer with the most colossal load of farm benefits ever conceived. Since the city taxpayer is already making good the difference between 1 cent per 1,000 gallons of water to the irrigator and a realistic cost of five or ten times this, he may hesitate to make it a multiple of thirty or forty. In the meantime, however, as security against local droughts and as a substitute for much more stringent antipollution measures, the city man is interested in desalinization.

What is the status of this technology?

Not long ago a housewife wrote to the Office of Saline Water to tell them she had noticed that the water that condensed on the lid of a pan while she was cooking was not salty. Why not use her discovery to solve the nation's water problems? she asked. This is precisely the most popular method of desalting— by distillation or evaporation, where the overhead steam is condensed and the salt bottoms are left behind as a by-product. The housewife had not invented this process but the Office of Saline Water thanked her anyway.

Evaporation from the oceans is, of course, nature's way of providing salt-free water but it is not the oldest way for living creatures to desalt water from the sea. Sea gulls and other birds of the ocean have a mysterious process that is so poorly understood that discussion of it is prudently omitted in all popular books on birds. Sea gulls can sometimes be caught in the act of what can only be described as "Guzzling." The salt water is shaken in their bills and some of it drizzles away and is discarded: this is found to be concentrated brine. The gull is evidently equipped with a highly portable selective membrane system which enables it to separate the salt. Man has been able to perform the same membrane process only at high pressures ("reverse osmosis").

In general, for large installations, some form of distillation seems to be the answer and where power can be sold and mineral by-products can find a market, the heat of the distillation may best be provided by atomic fission. For smaller plants, operating on water of lower salt content than sea water, the *electrodialysis* process, in which salt is forced out of brackish water electrically through plastic membranes, is moving ahead fast and competes with the reverse-osmosis technique, in which a separating membrane is also used but high pressure instead of electricity is the motive force.

President Johnson, in justifying the research and development money he wants spent by the Office of Saline Water in the Department of the Interior ($29 million in fiscal 1966) has said we need new ideas. There is no paucity of them. The OSW now screens about four hundred proposals a year. The following is a partial list of approaches to desalting:

Flash evaporation (in which water near the boiling point is suddenly released to lower pressures, "flashing" off and condensing the steam as pure water).

Multiple-effect evaporation (in which at various stages of evaporation heat is partly supplied by condensing the steam in coils around a subsequent stage. Thus the heat normally lost to cooling water is conserved).

Vapor-compression distillation (in which heat economy is increased by recompressing steam and condensing it in the heating section of the evaporator itself. A variation of this, named after the noted water scientist Kenneth Hickman, pretreats the water to eliminate surface films which reduce the evaporation rate).

Electrodialysis (developed by Ionics, Inc., and used in about 120 plants throughout the world, mainly owned by oil companies in the Middle East, American and foreign resorts, soft drink bottling firms abroad and military bases).

Separation at critical pressures (near the temperature and pressure where normal water can no longer be completely condensed to a liquid, the salt remains with the liquid phase. Economies are possible since the large heat of evaporation need not be added).

Low-temperature difference method (in which distillation is achieved by cooling rather than heating. The difference between warm surface water of the oceans and the cooler deep water is used as the driving force. The University of California is following up on French work at Abidjan off the coast of West Africa).

Submerged combustion of natural gas (in which gas is burned under salt water, the heat being directly transferred for evaporation).

Use of solar energy (focusing the heat rays of the sun is a feasible way of obtaining heat to evaporate salt water, and improvements in the large capital investment costs have been made by the University of California and Battelle Memorial Institute).

Formation of hydrates (in which liquefied petroleum gas hydrocarbons under high pressure form water-containing but water-insoluble salt-free compounds, which are then decomposed under lower pressure to yield pure water).

Fractional crystallization (in which salt-free ice is crystallized from the brine).

Reverse osmosis (in which salt-free water molecules diffuse through thin oil layers or synthetic membranes under pressure).
None of these, even with considerable refinement, seems capable of making potable water at less than $1 per 1,000 gallons. City water in the United States now averages from 10 to 35 cents per 1,000 gallons. However, there are communities in this country and abroad that would think the dollar price a bargain. At least 1,000 towns in the United States have to use water containing up to 1 percent salt. Sea water contains 3.5 percent salt. The human kidney can secrete no more than 2 percent salt. Greater concentrations lead to dehydration and collapse as the body tries to wash out the excess salt.

Coalinga, California, used to import fresh water in tank cars at $7 a gallon. Now it uses the electrodialysis process to produce drinking and cooking water for $1 a gallon and uses the local brackish water for all other purposes. Buckeye, Arizona, and Port Mansfield, Texas, use the same process for all their water requirements. San Diego got a sample part of its water requirements from the Interior Department's million-gallon-a-day flash distillation plant until it was moved to Guantanamo Bay when Castro cut off the water supply. In Florida there are 26 municipal water supplies which provide water containing between 1,000 and 3,000 parts per million of salt. Another 28 such supplies serve subdivisions and trailer parks. In South Dakota there are 152 sources of water—60 percent of those in the state—that have salt contents between 1,000 and 3,000 parts and three others that range from 3,000 to 10,000 parts per million. Iowa is nearly as bad.

Home desalting units are now under development and have excited the real-estate developers, since in some parts of Florida and the Southwest lack of potable water has prevented both real-estate development and industrial growth. Hence the demand is increasing for saline water demineralizing devices which are within the price range of individuals for use in homes, beach cottages, boats and ranches. Such gadgets should be no bigger than a refrigerator or a washing machine and might well consist of a step beyond the common ion-exchange home water softeners used in so many areas of the country today. Here again electrodialysis holds the inside track, since the electric power needed is nearly always available.

Although all the processes mentioned and more besides are being studied at a research-spending level, two dramatic changes in our ways of thinking about water desalinization have suddenly changed the pace and direction of development. One is the favorable on-paper economics of very large combined nuclear-energy-desalting plants. The second (and perhaps more important) is the concept of applying such a process to reclaim mixtures of sewage water and sea water or of sewage water alone. The latter is such a powerful idea that it may eventually prove to be the billion dollar broom that sweeps away the water pollution problem of big, coastal, river and lake cities. The horsepower contained in the notion is proved by the tremendous counterattacks it has stimulated in the coal industry, which fears that this may dislodge coal from its last, precious stronghold as a fuel in electric power plants. The National Coal Association, the National Coal Policy Conference, and the United Mine Workers write passionate letters to the President, claiming with eloquence and bitterness that the nuclear processes involve government subsidies in the form of artificially low prices for nuclear fuels; they may blow up New York City, and even if they are successful, they would put five men out of work for every man they put in a job, since production of heat from coal provides about five times as many jobs as the production of the same amount of heat from nuclear fuel. In this last point they are undoubtedly right and indeed it is probably the strongest economical justification for nuclear processes. If it were not for their manpower savings, one would be somewhat suspicious of the correctness of estimated power costs from nuclear plants, since the Atomic Energy Commission makes it very hard indeed to find out just what nuclear fuels do cost at so much per pound. Some utility companies, such as Consolidated Edison Company, which has operated a nuclear power plant at Indian Point, just below Peekskill, New York, maintain that the burning of uranium costs 22 cents a million British Thermal Units of heat energy produced while by comparison coal costs 29 cents, fuel oils 33 cents and gas over 40 cents. The Con Ed people think that uranium will be under the 20-cent mark in a few years.

This is for electric power. The dramatic aspect of these numbers applied to water treatment has come out in the recent proposal of the Bechtel Corporation for a 150-million-gallon-per-day desalting operation for the Metropolitan Water District of Southern California. If electric power is produced at the same time from part of the steam evolved by nuclear heating and this power is sold at 4 mills per kilowatt-hour, a going rate in the area, Bechtel shows that the cost of water can be as low as

22 cents per 1,000 gallons. To match the 150 million gallons of water, 1,800 megawatts of power would be distributed, which is enough for a city of two million population and is considerably more than the hydroelectric power yielded at Hoover Dam.

A week after the Bechtel study contract was signed, San Diego had an earthquake. Evidently to quell superstitious fears of earth tremors releasing a mushroom cloud, Bechtel recommended that the desalinization electric power plant be located on an artificial island offshore from Sunset Beach.

The Bechtel prospectus has naturally been under the closest scrutiny by its enemies as well as its friends. There seems every likelihood that it will go through and that by the middle 1970's Southern California will have fresh water from the sea in enough volume to supply a city of 750,000—about one sixth of the Los Angeles population. This would be fifty times larger than the biggest present desalting operation, which is located in the Caribbean island of Aruba and is run by Shell Oil Company. There is some doubt that the water from the Feather River Valley in Northern California, which will start flowing southward in the 1970's, will cost any less, since over 400 miles of transportation are involved and pumping costs are usually estimated at 10 cents per 1,000 gallons per 100 miles. This water has to be pumped over the Tehachapi mountains, which separate Northern from Southern California. The Atomic Energy Commission has agreed to help California build a nuclear power plant to do this pumping job more cheaply.

In the meantime the state of New York, rendered unbearably restless by its awful pollution troubles and a long drought, decided to sign up with American Machine and Foundry Company for a small nuclear plant at Riverhead, on the northeast shore of Long Island, to turn out a million gallons of water a day (enough for the needs of 10,000 rural people) as well as 2,500 Kilowatts of electricity per hour and up to 500,000 curies of cobalt 60 isotope a year. The latter is a new idea and may show some by-product profit for plants of this size, since cobalt 60 is in demand the world over for miniature power packages and for scientific use. For much larger plants the by-products could be minerals from the sea, including chlorine, sodium, magnesium, calcium, potassium, bromine, boron, and even silver and gold. Phosphate fertilizers could be produced, as shown by W. R. Grace and Company, by pretreatment of sea water with phosphoric acid. This would also reduce the scaling up of evaporators with magnesium and calcium salts.

When the combination nuclear plants are applied to mixtures of sewage water and sea water, a distillation residue of considerable complexity will result. Some decomposition of organic material might take place, with the possibility of creating an air-pollution nuisance. However, the use of standard chemical absorbers and auxiliary treatment of the overhead water would probably still make the total cost of producing clean water from such a witches' brew reasonable in comparison with the present tortuous and clumsy methods of sewage handling. The greatest virtue of such total treatment is that it would eliminate the hideously complicated murk of thousands of trace chemical pollutants which we suspect will otherwise haunt the lives of those living in our river and lake cities from now on. The use of the nuclear process would also eliminate a large fraction of air pollution which now comes from the burning of coal or fuel oil for electric power production.

Desalting of sea water involves an embarrassing problem that has not been entirely solved: What do you do with all the salt obtained as a by-product? The amounts of sodium chloride would be so huge in plants designed to furnish drinking water to a large city that they could not possibly find a market. The only answer seems to be to pump the hot concentrated brine back into the ocean, hoping that it will disperse fast enough so that it does not build up in the processing cycle and does not unduly pollute the continental-shelf marine habitat, the most productive part of the ocean as far as salt-water fish are concerned. Probably there is more danger to the fish from the by-product heat than from excess salt. These questions need to be answered to be sure that we are not simply translating one form of water pollution into another.

In the application of nuclear energy to desalting, we are not alone. The Russians at Savchenko on the Caspian Sea have decided to take the salt out of the Caspian water with a nuclear plant, rather than to pipe Volga River water a distance of 500 miles. The situation is rather similar to the Southern California cases of Feather River water or Pacific sea-water desalting, except that the Caspian contains only half the salt content of the ocean.

In 1964 the United States and the U.S.S.R. embarked on a rather loose, informal cooperation in desalinization which started out with exchange of visiting research teams. The Russian team, before November, 1964, admitted that they were going to use a so-called "fast-breeding" nuclear reactor which can burn either enriched uranium of plutonium while working up to the point where it breeds its own fuel. Both fuels, but the plutonium particularly, have military use and sharing it with the military has been something of an issue in the Soviet Union. When the Soviet fast-reactor experts were asked what fuel would be used in the proposed Caspian reactor, they answered frankly: "That depends on the outcome of your election." One can suppose, since recent events in Vietnam, that very little plutonium will be diverted to the city of Savchenko.

In our race with the Russians in desalting, there is some doubt whether both nations are using the same set of ground rules. Questioning of the Russian engineers as to the cost of a present Soviet 1.5-million-gallon-a-day conventional desalting plant brought only blank stares. The Soviet plant was built with no attention to economics. Fancy stainless steel and titanium were used throughout the plant. They seemed to have the attitude "We built it; it works; who cares about the cost?"

But in considering grand programs, such as a series of half-a-billion-gallon-per-day desalting plants and comparing that with the colossal movement of waters, such as involved in the NAWAPA project, we need not only to take note of costs but to construct a new philosophy of costs. The NAWAPA concept was proposed by the Ralph M. Parsons Company and has been introduced to the Senate Public Works Committee by Senator Frank E. Moss of Utah. The enormous amount of water going to waste into the sea from Alaska, Canada and the Northwestern United States would be collected and stored in an intercontinental system of reservoirs at relatively high elevations. By means of a reservoir-canal-river system the water would then be redistributed throughout the continent (Canada, the United States and Mexico), generating power as it descends into the sea. NAWAPA could provide 36 trillion gallons per year, enough to irrigate 40 million acres of land in the Western States (more than is now being irrigated) and yield 100 million kilowatts of electric power, equivalent to 75 Hoover Dams. It would bring the Great Lakes back to their normal level, increase the output of Niagara Falls and open up a navigable canal from the St. Lawrence River to the Pacific Ocean.

It would cost about $100 billion and take twenty years to complete.

Senator Moss has somewhat tremulously come to the conclusion that such a colossus is probably as necessary as was the Louisiana Purchase but he has intimated that there is no agency or department or group of men in the government with the intellectual stature to evaluate it truly.

This is a profound and distressing deduction. We shall examine its implications in the next and final chapter.

Far better it is to dare mighty things, to win glorious triumphs, even though checkered by failure, than to take rank with those poor spirits who neither enjoy much nor suffer much, because they live in the gray twilight that knows not victory nor defeat.

—THEODORE ROOSEVELT

Water has sunk more grievances than wine
And will continue to. Turn the water on;
Stick your hand in the stream; water will run
And kiss it like a dog, or it will shake
It like a friend.

—MERRILL MOORE

17 WHO WILL DO *the* JOB?

THE NAWAPA (North American Water and Power Alliance) is by far the biggest public works project ever considered. However, it contains internal defects that should give us pause in which to reflect on our whole continental philosophy of water. NAWAPA would double our irrigation water supply, but do we want more irrigated land? It would create a "Northwest Passage," but what good is that? It would give Mexico the equivalent of an Aswan dam, but are we in the business of growing Mexican cotton? It would make the Great Lakes deeper, but is that a good way to solve the sickening pollution of Lake Erie and Lake Michigan?

In a sense, NAWAPA is another agricultural pork barrel, although it would be for the farmers of three countries, rather than for the farmers of one or two states. It is based on the erroneous premise that we have a basic water shortage in most of North America. As emphasized several times in this book we have only a shortage of *clean water*. Building a big dam and a reservoir for flushing purposes is one way to try to clean up a river. (The Army Corps of Engineers proposed it for the Potomac.)

Thus, from the standpoint of pollution control, NAWAPA is the largest toilet bowl tank ever proposed. But this is a very inefficient and very expensive way to cope with pollution. It would not help, for example, in one of our most critical poison-water dilemmas: how to remove trace quantities of dangerous organic chemical wastes. There is another defect in this method of getting more clean water: storage dams represent essentially an irreversible action committed upon a river. The river is tied in chains. If you decide later you must treat the river water instead of diluting it, you have already built your monument of concrete and are paying the interest on it. Acreage has been inundated.

For several decades the storage-dam concept has been fiercely defended by the sacred cliché that "electricity makes low cost water possible." This is certainly true where the electric power source is reasonably close to a large market for power, as would be the case of nuclear desalting plants in coastal cities. It is beginning to be not only a tired but a false cliché, as the easy hydroelectric damsites are used up. It costs a good deal of money to transport electric power. The claim of the Reclamation Bureau that the taxpayers are reimbursed (except for costs that are written off against nonreimbursable aspects such as flood control or recreation) by profits on power has been disputed by modern economists. There is some funny bookkeeping. As we have seen, Reclamation pays a low interest, well below the government's rate on new bond issues.

Three percent per year of the $100 billion NAWAPA scheme, however, would go a long way toward curing the pollution problem in this country by installing proper sewage and industrial waste-treating facilities.

Unless we have made up our minds that we are going to feed the whole hungry world for free, any proposal for creating new irrigated lands is nonsensical on the face of it as long as we are paying farmers not to grow crops. The chances are very good indeed that without any more irrigation projects we could not only feed the United States of the year 2000 but would still have an over-all excess of water. In spite of local scares, the best available data show that our ground water at shallow depths exceeds the annual runoff of all our rivers by 34 times and we have probably an equal amount in deep ground storage.

Recent experiments carried out by the Department of Agriculture show the dismal fallacy of present overirrigation practices. A lot of extra water may bring only a little extra crop yield. Tests in Nebraska, for example, showed that irrigated bean plants could get along with remarkably little water through the growing season and still yield abundant crops provided they got plenty of water during the period of flowering and fruiting. There is a consensus among experts that over-all irrigation efficiency could be increased by at least 50 percent. This does not take into account the inevitable improvements in applied agricultural science, assuming that the farmer will do his homework and listen to what he is told. Perhaps the most inviting and productive research is in growing food crops that do not waste such enormous amounts of water by transpiration.

Since roughly ten times as much water is withdrawn for irrigation in the Southwest as for all other purposes combined, even a 10 percent improvement in the efficiency of using water to produce food or cotton would release large quantities for household, commercial and industrial uses.

There is thus a great wave of urgency in the direction of making the problem of water pollution our first in priority. How do we stand on this? Who is going to do it?

In seeking answers to these questions, we need first to apologize to the Congress. In our chapter on pork, we have left a picture of complete impotence and even evil. But Congress, like all groups of men, has its angels as well as its serpents. In the wild and roistering field of water pollution, there are probably no two more knowledgeable men in the country, counting all scientific as well as practical elements of know-how, than Senator Edmund Muskie of Maine and Representative John Blatnik of Minnesota.

Senator Muskie knows the problem as ex-governor of his native state and he knows it down to the last dollar asked in gasps for a sewer pipe. For example, in his own town of Waterville, a local sewer district was established; it issued revenue bonds, completely rebuilt the city sewers, cleaned up the tributary streams, but found it had no money left for sewage treatment. It was up against the authorized debt limit. The device of forming districts or "authorities" of several communities to evade the debt limit was invented by a Waterville lawyer, and the idea spread over the country, but this did not help lonely Waterville. Allegheny County in Pennsylvania contracted a $100 million sewage-treating system to service 125 communities, created the Allegheny County Sanitary Authority, issued revenue bonds, and every three months the homeowner gets a bill prorated on his water bill, but this was not for the ten thousands of forlorn Watervilles in the country.

Edmund Muskie understands the terrifying rocky stubbornness of New England, which would rather decay in its own puke than spend money. He knows the story of the Merrimack River, probably the dirtiest stretch of water in the history of the world. But the political history of the Merrimack is even more soiled. While the Merrimack's pollution has been bemoaned for eighty years, not one town on the main stem of the River has treated its sewage.

The Merrimack psychosis is the reason we need the surgery of federal action. Until 1945 the Massachusetts Department of Public Health had no enforcement powers and could only make pallid recommendation to the legislature on the last day of its session when everybody was drunk. But even the present control law has no teeth nor any "carrot" in the way of grants. It is a depressed area and those textile industries that had not fled to the South let it be known that sewer rates would break their crooked, straining backs. Bonds for sewage-treatment issues were defeated by incredible margins: 5 to 1 in Haverhill and over 7 to 1 in Lowell. Even the U.S. Public Health Service got itself involved in a scandal when it was revealed that one of its officials had promised the Massachusetts authorities that federal enforcement would not be initiated. In 1963, when Governor Endicott Peabody requested federal help, the Public Health Service was refused data by the Massachusetts Department of Public Health. The latter would not name any industrial polluters. In a public hearing an official of the state public health service became so insulting to the federal representatives that the meeting ended in a sort of confused Irish donnybrook. A basic trouble is that the people are not willing to pay a reasonable price for fresh water. The people have a vague notion that water should be free —like air. Local water boards won't charge higher prices to pay off water or sewage treatment because, as the citizens along the Merrimack have shown at the polls, the members of the water boards would promptly lose their jobs.

The Public Health Service had even less luck in New Jersey in the sordid case of Raritan Bay. Here the details of the failure to act appear to have been hushed up, but such hearties as Representative John Dingell of Michigan have pointed out that every federal agency involved showed dereliction: the Public Health Service, because contamination causing infected shellfish was being put in the bay; the Coast Guard, because they failed to restrict pumping of oil into the bay waters; and even the Corps of Engineers, because the Flood Control Act of 1899 gives them responsibility to take action when dangerous substances were being inserted into water. No attempt was made, according to Dingell, to control even the pumping of sewage from federal installations into this gray lagoon.

(In the New York Harbor area, of course, almost any seemingly wild abnormality in the way of pollution control is totally expected. The Interstate Stanitation Commission gave its opinion that the Raritan Bay waters in 1961 were very healthful—good for fishing and bathing—just swell. At that time, off the Perth Amboy public beach, bathing was unusually pleasant because of the warm sewer effluent, rising in a boil less than 200 feet off the tidal mark, spurting fresh human turds. A few miles away Tottenville on Staten Island dumped its raw sewage and at South Beach each year there was enacted a little drama. The city health department regularly would warn the people not to swim there. The city park department just as regularly would then come along, open up the beach and staff it with lifeguards.)

The Arthur Kill has been preposterously claimed by the Interstate Commissioners to be immaculate as far as Raritan Bay is concerned. Humble Oil Company, American Cyanimid and General Aniline and Film have been dumping organic wastes from Arthur Kill into the bay for decades and a period of 8½ years of foot-dragging after formal objection had elicited from the state of New Jersey only a "naughty! naughty!" Representative Dingell is so fed up with lack of action by the U.S. Public Health Service that he demands that the function of federal water pollution policing be transferred from the Department of Health, Education, and Welfare to the Department of the Interior.

Needless to say, this would not be unpleasing to the latter, but Senator Muskie and Representative Blatnik in the 1965 amended Federal Water Pollution Act have something else in mind. Up to now the U.S. Public Health Service has legally been able to act only in the case of interstate waters or at the invitation of the governor in the internal waters of a single state.

(There appears to be a loophole which has not been fully exploited in that the federal authority also applies to any navigable waters. According to the Supreme Court decision on the Appalachian Coal case and others, a "navigable" stream also means one that was once navigable or could be made navigable by expenditure of funds, and "navigability" means the capability of carrying some kind of commercial traffic; this could mean a loaded canoe.) But the Public Health Service has not been aggressive. The water-pollution authority is buried under layers of bureaucracy, reporting ultimately through the Surgeon General.

Organized like the Army, the Public Health Service officers have military ranks, a strong *esprit de corps*, and a great desire not to make any enemies. Mike Di Salle used to send a friend out to see how some of his field officers were doing. If the report was "Everybody in the community loves him," Mike had the man transferred immediately. This kind of working philosophy has not imbued the present Public Health Service in its water-pollution responsibilities, since it has acted in such cases as the Raritan Bay case, which might well have become a public disaster, with all the resoluteness of a wet noodle. In a recent meeting in Detroit, it has taken with the toothy smile of noble self-control the usual nonsense from the representatives of industries now polluting the Detroit River and Lake Erie. There a new wrinkle was added and one that John Blatnik has warned against: the "grandfather clause." The industries profess no objection to new "reasonable" water-purity standards for future plants but they scream violently at the hint of applying the same new standards to old plants.

Blatnik and the House and Muskie and the Senate disagree only on the matter of setting up of federal standards of water purity, instead of requiring the states to set up their own standards and enforce them. The Senate wants federal standards. Both House and Senate are heartily in favor of transferring authority from the U.S. Public Health Service to a new Federal Water Pollution Control Administration headed by an Assistant Secretary of the Department of Health, Education, and Welfare. The House and Senate agree on increased grants for sewer projects, grants for water-pollution research, and a general stiffening of the federal backbone. At the time of this writing (September, 1965), however, the Senate and House have not got together on the water-quality standards question. A mysterious lapse of several months had followed passage of both Senate and House versions, all the more painful since the House Bill would have started the money rolling on July 1, 1965.

If this bill passes and is signed by the President, is it going to do the job?

Obviously, without much more money than is now in sight, it will not accomplish what must be accomplished. It may prevent some future outright horrors such as Raritan Bay and perhaps conceivably even clean up the Merrimack River, but it is not going to achieve Lyndon Johnson's goal of "preventing pollution before it happens." It does not propose any really basic remedy for industrial pollution, such as President Johnson's suggestion of a "user fee," similar to the brilliantly successful system used in West Germany. It does not tie together a great national water re-use program with massive elimination of all types of pollution. It proposes a police action rather than a really concerted plan. It would add policemen but not planning engineers. It does pull the water-pollution responsibility from under a shabby table and gives it a formidable desk of office. There are hundreds of desks of office in Washington and across most of them passes an interminable correspondence on water. There are still hot-eyed pork sniffers in the Congress and outside it who would rather spend the money on irrigation reservoirs.

What must somehow be pounded into the heads of the people who govern us is that, so far as the eye can see into the future, our *only* big problem in water is the pollution problem. The problem of water shortages is a problem of treating dirty water, whether the dirt is in the form of municipal sewage, industrial waste, salt or silt.

The difficulty is that when one busies oneself with pollution in this necessarily very broad sense as involving, for instance, soil erosion and salt invasion of ground waters, as well as the more obvious and smelly modes of degrading fresh water, one steps on innumerable toes outside the corridors of power set up for a department. The more rationally the Assistant Secretary of Health, Education, and Welfare, in charge of administering the Federal Water Pollution Act, approaches his potentially great job, the more hisses and catcalls he will get. Even the hitherto mild and spiritless activities of the Public Health Service have caused tantrums of rage among the states, among industrial personages, among other departments. Because of its polite remonstrances the HEW Department has been accused of a ravening will to power. If the new Assistant Secretary attempted to promote what is the most promising large solution to great urban problems of water—the combined reclamation of sewage water and sea water (for example, the reclamation of the Hudson River which would end New York City's prolonged agony)—he would be regarded as a veritable demon of impudence. A demon of impudence is precisely what we need—if the President will stand behind him. We need a man tough as an old saddle and fearless as a wolverine.

An alternative to one-department planning on a grand scale has always been a "council" or a committee. (One recalls the old definition of a camel—a horse designed by a committee.) In 1943 the Federal Inter-Agency River Basin Committee ("Firebrick") was created to encourage cooperation between the Army Corps of Engineers and the Departments of Agriculture and of the Interior in studies of multiple-purpose dams. The members sat on their hands. The Corps and the Reclamation

Bureau went ahead building dams as they saw fit and the Soil Conservation people continued their same tours of duty. In 1964 a Federal Inter-Agency Committee on Water Resources ("Icewater") was set up, consisting of representatives of Interior, Agriculture, Commerce, HEW and the Federal Power Commission. These men have harrumphed and yawned suspiciously at each other, but we still have no over-all resources policy. There is no agency in the federal government authorized to determine the policies, make the decisions, and give the supervision required for water-resources development, and in the area of pollution (which underlies water resources) there is not even a shadow of such authority. The 1965 model was the Water Resources Council headed by the Secretary of the Interior and reporting directly to the President. This was a body hastily drafted to give the thirsting voters of the Northeast an impression that their troubles would be ended by virtue of a series of powwows. It shows no signs of establishing before the public the fact that pollution and water re-use are the basic matters of driving urgency.

In the New York predicament the state has shown more insight than the federal government. The Governor's recent $1.7 billion program for abatement of water pollution, if coupled with reduction of losses and installation of full water metering (New York City *loses* twice as much water in its transmission system—400 million gallons a day—as the city of Boston uses) would go further in relieving the local famine than such airily conceived notions as diverting water from Canada. The plan to use salt water to fight fires in New York City will help.

Growing restive under President Eisenhower's "no-new-starts" policy of reclamation projects, a conference of Western congressmen in 1959 had decided to set up a monstrous committee of its own. This was known as the Senate Select Committee and the chairman was naturally the ubiquitous Senator Kerr of Oklahoma. The concepts of this committee were wrong. They recommended research on everything from weather modification to desalting of the ocean but did not realize the overriding importance of pollution in the water-resources picture and, in fact, did not emphasize pollution at all. They did emphasize money. They estimated that $228 billion would have to be spent developing water resources by 1980. The present total investment is about $185 billion.

The report was published in the first weeks of the Kennedy administration and became a part of the executive program. The President also asked the Federal Council for Science and Technology, which is made up of top officials from federal agencies with science functions, to whomp up a study on natural-resources policy, including water-research policy. This ran into delays so prolonged that the President's patience gave out and a special task force was set up under Roger Revelle, then science advisor to the Secretary of the Interior. One assignment was to draw lines of authority more clearly and cut duplications of research. The agencies involved fought like frontier prospectors over a gold claim. One of the sharpest clashes developed over research on water quality between the Interior Department's Geological Survey and the Public Health Service of the Department of Health, Education, and Welfare.

One result of all such goings-on was a bill introduced by Senator Anderson of Arizona to encourage river-basin planning. The states reacted like stuck pigs. The Corps of Engineers was insulted, since it considered itself official river-basin planner. After giving a ritualistic bow to states' rights, a bill of sorts was passed. Shortly afterward Anderson got another bill through— the Water Resources Research Act—to be administered by the Secretary of the Interior, and a new Office of Water Resources Research. This scatters federal research grants to hell-and-gone over the country's land-grant colleges, state universities, foundations, private research firms, making even local governments eligible for sprinkles of manna.

This is a thoroughly demoralizing and mischievous piece of legislation. What is needed, especially for research approaches to the pollution problem, is a close-knit, highly professional group. What we get from this bill is 50 water research centers varying from a man and two boys in a cow college to part-time consulting from a university professor. Competent hydrologists are only too few, as it is, without encouraging them to scatter all across the country on random, often unrelated projects of their choosing.

It is not unfair to state that the majority of the people and even the majority in the Congress still do not understand the gravity of our water-pollution problems. Cleaning up the rivers is viewed by many as part of the "beautification" program, like getting the automobile junk piles out of sight, and probably something to be handled by a president's wife in her spare time. There is now ethereal talk of the "New Conservation" and of landscaping the Hudson River banks, as if improving the scenery would purge the water. It would seem to be one of the major proofs of insight and resoluteness on the part of the League of Women Voters that it has placed water pollution high on the League's list of "National Continuing Responsibilities," instead of regarding it in the same category as flower arrangement.

As for the implementation of the mighty pushes needed in water re-use, desalting, soil control, etc., there will be an inevitable and justified assumption of federal responsibilities, since the scale of the problem is too huge for the states. One might as well leave to the states the job of getting men to the moon. We need a crash program exceeding the magnitude and pace of the Manhattan Project which developed the nuclear bomb. This is even more true in the research and development aspects of antipollution than in full-scale implementation. There are some tremendous gaps in our knowledge and know-how that must be filled by an immense acceleration of research.

As a professional chemist, I cannot resist the temptation to point out one promising approach to the problem of organic chemical pollution which is receiving no federal money at all. This is the development of strains of bacteria or ferments that would selectively digest the trace poisons in industrial effluents. There has been a recent trend in private chemical and petroleum industries to work along such lines for their own purposes. Standard Oil of New Jersey, for example, has developed a microbiological process for converting petroleum into food. There are known strains of microflora that will selectively chew the wax out of crude oil or will chew the sulfur out of it. Dow Chemical Company, indeed, uses selected bacteria to destroy phenolic chemical wastes. Maybe there are bugs that could be grown which would even thrive on minute but still toxic concentrations of endrin, DDT and the other pesticides that are killing our fish and probably degrading our own livers. There could certainly be developed special microbic scavengers that would do a faster and better job in our municipal sewage plants.

Research work of this kind needs to be done intensively and patiently with astronomical numbers of time-consuming experiments. And yet to my knowledge a system of experiments has not even been started with the specific goal in mind of controlling water pollution. We leave it to Nature to provide the bacteria for sewage treatment, but Nature is not a sanitary engineer and Nature is a great believer in time. One blink of her world-heavy eyelids has seen the human species develop from a hitter of the mammoth and the deer to a dropper of atomic bombs, and, before another blink, she had as soon see this species gone from the earth. Time, however, is of our essence. We run all kinds of races against disaster. Certainly not the least of these is that race against disease and ugliness—the race to clean up our once sweet waters.

BIBLIOGRAPHY

1 LORDS OF THE ANCIENT WATERS

1) *History of Technology:* Vol. 1, *From Early Times to Fall of Ancient Empires*; edited by CHARLES SINGER, E. J. HOLAYARD, and A. R. HALL. Oxford University Press, New York and London, 1954.
2) BREASTED, J. M., *Ancient Records of Egypt*. University of Chicago Press, 1907.
3) BROWN, SIR (ROBERT) HANBURY, *Irrigation, Its Principle and Practice as a Branch of Engineering*. Constable, London, 1920.
4) CLARK, J. G. D., "Water in Antiquity," *Antiquity, 18*, 1, 1944.
5) HARTMANN, F., *L'agriculture dans l'ancienne Egypte*, Imprin. reunie. [Geuther] Paris, 1923.
6) IONIDES, M. G., *The Regime of the Rivers Euphrates and Tigris*. Chemical Publishing Co. of New York, 1937.
7) LANE, W. H., *Babylonian Problems*. Murray, London, 1923.
8) MACKAY, E. J. H., *Early Indus Civilizations*. Luzac, London, 1948.
9) WILLCOCK, SIR WILLIAM, and CRAIG, J. J., *Egyptian Irrigation*. Spon, London; Spon and Chamberlain, New York, 1913.
10) WILLCOCK, SIR WILLIAM, *The Irrigation of Mesopotamia*. Spon, London; Spon and Chamberlain, New York, 1917.

2 THE WETNESS OF WATER

1) HENRICKS, STERLING B., "Necessary, Convenient, Commonplace," *Water*, U.S. Department of Agriculture, 1955.
2) SYKES, JOSEPH F., "Animals, Fowl and Water," *ibid.*
3) SOUDER, ARTHUR M., "The Forked Stick," *ibid.*
4) ROBERTS, KENNETH, *Henry Gross and His Dowsing Rod*. Doubleday, New York, 1951.

5) ELLIS, ARTHUR J., *The Divining Rod, A History of Water Witch-ing.* U.S. Geological Survey, 1938.
6) *Isotopic and Cosmic Chemistry,* edited by H. CRAIG, S. L. MILLER, and G. J. WASSERBURG. North-Holland, Amsterdam, 1964.

3 DEAD WATERS THAT KILL

1) BABBITT, HAROLD I., and BAUMANN, E. ROBERT, *Sewerage and Sewage Treatment.* John Wiley and Sons, Inc., New York, 1964.
2) *History of Technology:* Vols. I–IV, edited by Singer *et al.* Oxford University Press, 1954.
3) "Spraying Waste Woes Away," *Chemical Week,* June 19, 1965.
4) "Epidemic May Affect Water Testing," HARRY NELSON, Los Angeles *Times,* June 15, 1965.
5) DOUGLAS, WILLIAM O., "A Wilderness Bill of Rights," *Encyclopaedia Britannica Book of the Year,* 1965.
6) "Chicago's Struggle for Clean Water," *Business Week,* Oct. 24, 1964.
7) Hearing before a Special Subcommittee on Air and Water Pollution of the Committee on Public Works, United States Senate, 88th Congress on S. 649, S. 1118 and S. 1183, June 17 through June 26, 1963.
8) A Study of Pollution—Water, a Staff Report to the Committee on Public Works, United States Senate, June, 1963.
9) Water Quality Act of 1965, Hearing before a Special Subcommittee on Public Works, United States Senate, 89th Congress, Jan. 18, 1965.
10) "Reclamation of Sewage Water," *Chemical and Engineering News,* Aug. 2, 1965.
11) GARVER, HARRY L., "Water Supplies for Homes in the Country," *Water,* U.S. Department of Agriculture, 1955.
12) Great Lakes Ship Pollution Act, SENATOR GAYLORD NELSON, *Congressional Record,* May 6, 1965.
13) "Milwaukee Beach Pollution," *The American City,* April, 1963.
14) Statement to the House Public Works Committee in Support of Federal Water Pollution Control Act Amendments by MRS. HASKELL ROSENBLUM, Director of the League of Women Voters of the United States, Dec. 6, 1963.
15) Detroit River Pollution Study, SENATOR PHILIP A. HART, *Congressional Record,* May 14, 1965.
16) SCHWOF, CARL I., "Pollution—a Growing Problem of a Growing Nation," *Water,* U.S. Department of Agriculture, 1955.
17) SHEED, WILFRID, review of Brecht's "Baal," *Commonweal,* June 18, 1965.

18) "How Pure is Your City Water?" *U.S. News and World Report*, Feb. 29, 1960.
19) "Infectious Hepatitis from Oysters," *Motor Boating*, August, 1963.
20) MILLER, PAUL R., and CLARK, FRANCIS E., "Water and Microorganisms," *Water*, U.S. Department of Agriculture, 1955.
21) "Don't Be Just Half-Safe," *The American City*, May, 1963.

4 LORDS OF THE MODERN WATERS—ASIA AND AFRICA

1) McNEIL, MARY, "Lateritic Soils," *Scientific American*, November, 1964.
2) *History of Technology:* Vol. II, *The Mediterranean Civilization and the Middle Ages.* Oxford University Press, 1954.
3) *Ibid.*, Vol. III, *From the Renaissance to the Industrial Revolution.*
4) GARBELL, MAURICE A., "The Jordan Valley Plan," *Scientific American*, March, 1965.
5) DE CORVALBO, GEORGE, "Desperate Arab-Israel Struggle for Scarce Water," *Life*, June 18, 1964.
6) REVELLE, ROGER, "Water," *Scientific American*, September, 1963.
7) SWAIN, PAUL, "Strange Things Happen to Drillers," *Oil and Gas Journal*, Feb. 24, 1964.

5 LORDS OF THE MODERN WATERS—EUROPE AND THE U.S.

1) *History of Technology:* Vol. III, *From the Renaissance to the Industrial Revolution.* Oxford University Press, 1954.
2) *Ibid.*, Vol. IV, *The Industrial Revolution.*
3) *Ibid.*, Vol. V, *The Late Nineteenth Century.*
4) LANGBEIN, W. B., and WELLS, J. V. D., "The Water in the Rivers and Creeks," *Water*, U.S. Department of Agriculture, 1955.
5) RENFRO, GEORGE M., "Applying Water under the Surface of the Ground," *ibid.*
6) DULEY, F. L., and COZLE, J. J., "Farming Where Rainfall is 8–20 Inches per Year," *ibid.*
7) WOOTEN, HUGH M., and JONES, LEWIS A., "History of our Drainage Enterprises," *ibid.*
8) DONNOR, WILLIAM W., and BRADSHAW, GEORGE B., "Disposal of Seepage and Waste Water," *ibid.*
9) GREENSHIELDS, O. L., "Expansion of Irrigation in the West," *ibid.*
10) BAMESBERGER, J. G., "Preparing Land for Efficient Irrigation," *ibid.*
11) MUCKEL, DEAN C., and SCHIFF, LEONARD, "Replenishing Ground Water by Spreading," *ibid.*
12) THOMAS, HAROLD F., "Underground Sources of Our Water," *ibid.*

13) "All About Water," League of Women Voters of the United States, May, 1963.

14) "Water, Increase in Interest and Activity," League of Women Voters, May, 1963.

15) "Know Your River Basins," League of Women Voters, 1958.

16) BOWEN, WILLIAM, "Water Shortage Is a Frame of Mind," *Fortune,* April, 1965.

17) EWELL, RAYMOND, "Famine and Fertilizer," *Chemical and Engineering News,* Dec. 14, 1964.

18) REVELLE, ROGER, "Water-Resources Research in the Federal Government," *Science,* Nov. 22, 1963.

19) *U.S. Army Corps of Engineers, Department of Defense* (Flood Control and Watershed Development: Water Supply and Water Quality; Parks, Recreation and Open Space; Navigation; River Basin Planning).

20) *Bureau of Reclamation, Department of Interior* (Flood Control and Watershed Development; Water Supply and Water Quality; Fish and Wildlife Protection and Wetlands Preservation; Irrigation and Drainage; Research and Data Collecting).

21) *Soil Conservation Service, Department of Agriculture* (Flood Control and Watershed Development; Water Supply and Watershed Development; Water Supply and Water Quality; Parks, Recreation and Open Space; Fish and Wildlife Protection and Wetlands Preservation; Irrigation and Drainage; Research and Data Collecting; River Basin Planning).

22) *Farmers Home Administration, Department of Agriculture* (Water Supply and Water Quality; Flood Control and Watershed Development; Parks, Recreation and Open Space; Irrigation and Drainage).

23) *Water Supply and Pollution Control Division, U.S. Public Health Service, Department of Health, Education, and Welfare* (Water Supply and Water Quality; Fish and Wildlife Protection and Wetlands Preservation; Research and Data Collecting; River Basin Planning).

24) *Bureau of Sports Fisheries, Wildlife Service, Department of the Interior* (Water Supply and Water Quality; Flood Control and Watershed Development; Fish and Wildlife Protection and Wetlands Preservation; River Basin Planning).

25) *Agricultural Stabilization and Conservation Service, Department of Agriculture* (Flood Control and Watershed Development; Irrigation and Drainage).

26) *U.S. Geological Survey, Department of the Interior* (Flood Control and Watershed Development; Research and Data Collecting).

27) *Bureau of Land Management, Department of the Interior* (Flood and Watershed Development; Parks, Recreation and Open Space).

28) *Forest Service, Department of Agriculture* (Flood Control and Watershed Development; Fish and Wildlife Protection and Wetlands Preservation; Research and Data Collecting; Parks, Recreation and Open Space).

29) *Bureau of Outdoor Recreation, Department of the Interior* (Parks, Recreation and Open Space).

30) *Agricultural Research Service, Department of Agriculture* (Research and Data Collecting).

31) *Weather Bureau, Department of Commerce* (Research and Data Collecting).

32) *National Park Service, Department of the Interior* (Parks, Recreation and Open Space).

33) *Water Resources Research Department, Department of the Interior* (Research and Data Collecting).

34) *Housing and Home Finance Agency* (Parks, Recreation and Open Space; Irrigation and Drainage).

35) *Tennessee Valley Authority* (Flood Control and Watershed Development; Parks, Recreation and Open Space; Research and Data Collecting).

36) *Migratory Bird Conservation Commission* (Fish and Wildlife Protection and Wetlands Preservation).

37) *General Services Administration* (Parks, Recreation and Open Space).

38) *International Boundary and Water Commission, for U.S. and Mexico* (Water Supply and Water Quality; Flood Control and Watershed Development).

39) *International Joint Commission, for U.S. and Canada* (Water Supply and Water Quality; Navigation).

40) *St. Lawrence Seaway Development Corporation* (Navigation).

41) *Office of Saline Waters, Department of the Interior* (Research and Data Collecting).

42) *Bureau of Indian Affairs, Department of the Interior* (Irrigation and Drainage).

6 WATER FOR LAWYERS

1) BUSBY, C. E., "Regulation and Economic Expansion," *Water*, U.S. Department of Agriculture, 1955.

2) HUTCHINS, WELLS A., "History of Conflict Between Riparian and Appropriation Rights in Western States," *ibid.*

3) ROHWER, CARL, "Wells and Pumps for Irrigated Lands," *ibid.*

4) BYLIN, JAMES, *Wall Street Journal*, April 22, 1965.

5) CARR, HARRY, *Los Angeles, City of Dreams*. D. Appleton-Anbury Co., New York, 1935.

6) CARR, HARRY, *The West Is Still Wild.* Houghton Mifflin Company, Boston and New York, 1932.
7) KING, LAWRENCE T., "Water, Water," *The Commonweal,* Feb. 21, 1964.
8) "Deductible Water," *Time,* July 9, 1965.
9) "Illinois Leads Midwest Against Water Pollution," SENATOR PAUL DOUGLAS, *Congressional Record,* May 24, 1965.
10) "Lake Michigan Water Controversy," REPRESENTATIVE EDWARD J. DERWINSKI, *Congressional Record,* June 16, 1965.
11) "What Lake Michigan Diversion Means to the Chicago Area," SENATOR EVERETT DIRKSEN, *Congressional Record,* May 21, 1965.
12) "Kansas, Colorado Prepare for Water War," Associated Press, June 3, 1965.

7 WATER FAMINE

1) "Drought Impact," *Wall Street Journal,* Nov. 12, 1964.
2) "Drought in Korea," *New York Times News Service,* July 5, 1965.
3) "Drought in Tokyo, Rome and Hong Kong," Associated Press, Aug. 19, 1964.
4) Bechuanaland, *New York Times News Service,* July 4, 1965.
5) THOMAS, HAROLD E., *The Conservation of Ground Water.* McGraw-Hill Book Co., Inc., New York, 1951.
6) MALDO, HAROLD E., "Environment and Man in Arid America," *Science,* July 10, 1964.
7) "Water Shortage and Pollution of the Potomac River," SENATOR DANIEL B. BREWSTER, *Congressional Record,* July 6, 1965.
8) "Water Crisis in the Northeast," SENATOR ROBERT F. KENNEDY, *ibid.,* June 25, 1965.
9) "War on Drought," SENATOR JACOB B. JAVITS, *ibid.,* July 15, 1965.
10) "Water Crisis—USA," Caterpillar Tractor Co., 1962.
11) "Inland Shippers Thirst for Water," *Business Week,* Jan. 23, 1965.
12) "Water Low, Costs Up," *Chemical Week,* Sept. 12, 1964.
13) "Drought Dries up Business, Too," *Business Week,* July 17, 1965.
14) "Dipping Deep into the Gulf Stream," *ibid.,* July 31, 1965.
15) BOWEN, WILLIAM, "Water Shortage Is a Frame of Mind," *Fortune,* April, 1965.
16) "The Land Goes Thirsty," *Business Week,* Nov. 2, 1963.
17) TANNER, JAMES C., "Waterless Plains," *Wall Street Journal,* April 13, 1965.

8 FLOODS

1) RUHE, ROBERT V., "How Water Shaped the Face of the Land," *Water,* U.S. Department of Agriculture, 1955.

2) SALMOND, G. A., and CROFT, A. R., "Management of Public Watersheds," *ibid.*
3) FORD, ERWIN C., COWAN, WOOD L., and HOLTAN, H. N., "Floods —and a Program to Alleviate Them," *ibid.*
4) ANGUSTADT, WALTER W., "Drainage in the Red River Valley of the North," *ibid.*
5) OSBORN, BEN, "How Rainfall and Runoff Erode Soil," *ibid.*
6) STEELE, HARRY A., and SANDALS, KIRK M., "A Law Puts Responsibility at Home," *ibid.*
7) MATSON, HOWARD O.; HEARD, WILLIAM L.; LAMB, GEORGE E., and ILLCH, DAVID M., "Possibilities of Land Treatment in Flood Prevention," *ibid.*
8) "Floods," *Encyclopaedia Britannica,* 1960.
9) "Ohio River Basin," League of Women Voters of the United States, 1964.
10) "Flood Control," REPRESENTATIVE GLENN R. DAVIS, *Congressional Record,* June 22, 1965.
11) "Damage by Floods in Colorado Tops $100 million," *Wall Street Journal,* June 21, 1965.
12) "Flood Disaster Relief," SENATOR WILLIAM PROXMIRE, *Congressional Record,* May 27, 1965.
13) "Red River Basin of the North," Red River Basin Committee, League of Women Voters of Minnesota and North Dakota, September, 1959.
14) "The Susquehanna, A Study of the River Basin," League of Women Voters of Pennsylvania, May, 1962.

9 TREES AND OTHER WATER HOGS

1) HIND, HARRY YOULE, "Reports of Progress, Together with a Preliminary and General Report on the Assiniboine and Saskatchewan Exploring Expedition," Her Majesty's Stationary Office, London, 1860.
2) BERNSTEIN, LEO, "Needs and Uses of Water by Plants," *Water,* U.S. Department of Agriculture, 1955.
3) WADLEIGH, CECIL H., "Soil Moisture and Plant Growth," *ibid.*
4) FLETCHER, HERBERT C., and ELMERDORF, HAROLD B., "Phreatophytes," *ibid.*
5) MUSGRAVE, G. W., "How Much of the Rain Enters the Soil?" *ibid.*
6) HAYES, G. L., and BUELL, JESSE H., "Trees Also Need Water at the Right Time and Place," *ibid.*
7) BARNES, CARLETON F., "What Research Is Doing on Problems of Water in Agriculture," *ibid.*
8) FRIEDRICK, C. ALLAN, "Fire on the Watersheds of the Nation," *ibid.*

9) SCHLANDT, E. A., "Drainage in Forestry Management in the South," *ibid.*

10) GOODELL, B. C., and WILSON, H. G., "How to Get More Snow Waters from Forest Lands," *ibid.*

11) THORNWAITE, C. W., and RATHER, J. A., "The Water Budget and Its Use in Irrigation," *ibid.*

12) DUNFORD, E. G., and WEITZMAN, SIDNEY, "Managing Forests to Control Soil Erosion," *ibid.*

13) RENNER, F. G., and LORE, L. D., "Management of Water on Western Rangelands," *ibid.*

14) RETZER, J. L., and COLMAN, E. A., "Soil Surveys on Forest and Rangelands," *ibid.*

15) WENT, F. W., "Fog, Mist, Dew," *ibid.*

16) DUVDEVANI, S., "Dew Gradients in Relation to Climate; Soil and Topography, Proceedings of Desert Symposium," Jerusalem, 1953.

17) GEIGER, RUDOLF, *The Climate Near the Ground,* Harvard University Press, Cambridge, Mass., 1950.

18) STONE, E. C.; WENT, F. W., and YOUNG, C. L., "Water Absorption from the Atmosphere by Plants Growing in Dry Soil," *Science,* Vol. III, p. 546, 1950.

10 SILT AND SALT

1) GOTTSCHALK, L. C., and JONES, VICTOR H., "Valley and Hills, Erosion and Sedimentation," *Water,* U.S. Department of Agriculture, 1955.

2) "The St. Louis Problem of Siltation," *Business Week,* Jan. 23, 1965.

3) "The Potomac is a Neglected Patient," SENATOR DANIEL B. BREWSTER, *Congressional Record,* June 4, 1965.

4) "Story of the Delaware River Basin," League of Women Voters of the United States, 1959.

5) LANGER, ELINOR, "A View from the Bridge," *Science,* Nov. 1, 1963.

6) FIREMAN, MILTON, and HAYWARD, H. E., "Irrigation Water and Saline and Alkali Soils," *Water,* U.S. Department of Agriculture, 1955.

7) PARKER, GERALD C., "Encroachment of Salt Water into Fresh," *ibid.*

8) MACINKO, GEORGE, "Saturation: A Problem Evaded in Planning Land Use," *Science,* July 30, 1965.

9) "Keystone Dam—Arkansas River," SENATOR MIKE MONRONEY, *Congressional Record,* May 24, 1965.

10) "Salt Threat in Delaware River," *Chemical and Engineering News,* July 19, 1965.
11) "A Pinch of Salt," *Time,* Feb. 28, 1964.

11 POLLUTION IS GOOD BUSINESS

1) Hearing Before a Special Subcommittee on Air and Water Pollution of the Committee on Public Works, United States Senate, 88th Congress on S. 649, S. 1118 and S. 1183, June 17 through June 26, 1963.
2) Water Quality Act of 1965, Hearing before a Special Subcommittee on Public Works, United States Senate, 89th Congress, Jan. 8, 1965.
3) FUHRMAN, RALPH E., "Treating Waste Water for Cities and Industries," *Water,* U.S. Department of Agriculture, 1955.
4) JORDAN, HARRY E., "Increasing Use of Water by Industry," *ibid.*
5) KINNEY, GENE T., "Pollution: Congressional Target for Oil to Watch," *Oil and Gas Journal,* May 24, 1965.
6) "Multibillion Dollar Fight Against Pollution," *Dun's Review and Modern Industry,* March, 1963.
7) ENGDAHL, RICHARD B., and CROXTON, FRANK C., "Pollution: A Problem in Economics," *Battelle Technical Review,* August, 1962.
8) "Stream Pollution Abatement," REPRESENTATIVE WILLIAM S. MOORHEAD, *Congressional Record,* June 10, 1965.
9) "Controlling Water and Air Pollution," REPRESENTATIVE ROBERT N. GIAIMO, *ibid.,* July 22, 1965.
10) "Gulf States Paper Corporation Pollution," REPRESENTATIVE ARMISTEAD I. SELDEN, JR., *ibid.,* July 27, 1965.
11) "Clean up the Great Lakes," REPRESENTATIVE LYNN E. STALBAUM, *ibid.,* June 28, 1965.
12) "Weirton Steel Co. Air and Water Pollution," SENATOR JENNINGS RANDOLPH, *ibid.,* May 6, 1965.
13) "New Attack on Wastes," *Chemical Week,* June 12, 1965.
14) BOWEN, WILLIAM, "Water Shortage Is a Frame of Mind," *Fortune,* April, 1965.
15) "Ohio River Basin," League of Women Voters of the United States, 1964.
16) "Heat Poses New Pollution Puzzles," *Chemical Week,* Feb. 8, 1964.
17) GUSHER, DAVID E., "Foam Fractionation in Water Ecology," *Industrial Engineering Chemistry,* May, 1965.
18) "Lifesaver for Sick Streams," *Chemical Week,* Jan. 23, 1965.
19) "Slim Margin for Error," *ibid.,* Aug. 22, 1964.
20) "Lake Michigan Contaminants," *Chemical and Engineering News,* Feb. 8, 1965.

21) "Ruhr Valley Pollution Control," *Business Week,* April 24, 1965.
22) "Ruhr River Purification," *The German Tribune,* July 26, 1965.

12 WHITE BEER

1) Hearing Before a Special Subcommittee on Air and Water Pollution of the Committee on Public Works, United States Senate, 88th Congress on S. 649, S. 1118 and S. 1183, June 17 through June 26, 1963.
2) Water Quality Act of 1965, Hearing Before a Special Subcommittee on Public Works, United States Senate, 89th Congress, Jan. 18, 1965.
3) "Third Generation Surfactants Based on Fats," *Chemical Week,* Sept. 5, 1964.
4) "Test Compares Detergent Degradabilities," *Chemical and Engineering News,* July 27, 1964.
5) "Fatty Alcohols Poised for Growth," *ibid.,* June 8, 1964.
6) WINTON, JOHN, "The Detergent Revolution," *Chemical Week,* May 30, 1964.
7) BRANDSTADT, DR. WAYNE G., "Foamy Detergents Endanger Water," Newspaper Enterprise Association, July 15, 1964.
8) Banning of Nondegradable Detergents in Wisconsin," *Chemical Week,* Nov. 30, 1963.
9) "Chemical Process Offered to Reduce ABS," *Chemical and Engineering News,* April 15, 1963.
10) HATCH, LEWIS F., "Can Syndet Shift Beat Foam Problems," *Hydrocarbon Processing and Petroleum Refiner,* June, 1962.
11) "Materials Producers Go to the Field for Biodegradability Testing," *Industrial and Engineering Chemistry,* January, 1965.
12) "Confidence is Still Lacking in Biodegradability Methods," *Chemical and Engineering News,* Feb. 15, 1965.
13) WAYMAN, COOPER H., "A Hard Look at Soft Detergents," *Bulletin of the Atomic Scientists,* April, 1965.
14) "Testing for Surfactant Biodegradability," *Industrial and Engineering Chemistry,* March, 1965.
15) "Foam Fracas Boils Up," *Chemical Week,* March 27, 1965.
16) KNAGGS, EDWARD A., "The Detergent Dilemma," *International Science and Technology,* May, 1965.
17) "Split over Syndet Softness," *Chemical Week,* May 22, 1965.
18) "Detergent Makers Finish Switch to Biodegradables," *Wall Street Journal,* July 1, 1965.
19) "Europe Swinging to Biodegradable Syndets," *Chemical and Engineering News,* Dec. 21, 1964.

13 WATER FOR FISH, FOWL AND FUN

1) SIECKER, JOHN H., "Planning for Recreational Use of Water: A Plan," *Water*, U.S. Department of Agriculture, 1965.
2) SHAW, SAMUEL P., and CRISSEY, WALTER F., "Wetlands and Management of Waterfowl," *ibid.*
3) OLSON, HERMAN F.; CLARK, O. H., and O'DONNELL, D. JOHN, "Managing Watersheds to Provide Better Fishing," *ibid.*
4) SHRADER, THOMAS A., "Waterfowl and the Potholes of the North Central States," *ibid.*
5) Hearing Before a Special Subcommittee on Air and Water Pollution of the Committee on Public Works, United States Senate, 88th Congress on S. 649, S. 1118 and S. 1183, June 17 through June 26, 1963.
6) Water Quality Act of 1965, Hearing Before a Special Subcommittee on Public Works, United States Senate, 89th Congress, June 18, 1965.
7) "Puget Sound Pollution," *Chemical and Engineering News*, March 28, 1965.
8) MARTIN, JOHN STUART, "Rebirth of the Shad," *Atlantic Monthly*, June, 1965.
9) "Fake Streams for Pollution War," *Chemical Week*, May 15, 1965.
10) DOUGLAS, WILLIAM O., "A Wilderness Bill of Rights," 1965 Yearbook, *Encyclopaedia Britannica*.
11) "Pesticide War Rumbles On," *Chemical Week*, April 18, 1964.
12) "Pesticide Levels Low in West Coast Fish," *Chemical and Engineering News*, April 20, 1964.
13) "Water Reclamation Test Scores Success," *ibid.*, Oct. 21, 1963.
14) "Lithium Injury to Citrus, Avocados and Grapes," *ibid.*, March 25, 1964.
15) "Pollution Conference Blames Endrin for Fish Kills," *ibid.*, May 18, 1964.
16) "Freeman Says Farm Use of Pesticides Not to Blame for Massive River Fish Kills," *ibid.*, June 8, 1964.
17) LANGER, ELINOR, "Pesticides: Minute Quantities Linked with Massive Fish Kills," *Science*, April 3, 1964.
18) BARDACH, JOHN E.; FUJIYA, MASARU, and HALL, ARTHUR, "Detergents: Effects on the Chemical Senses of the Fish Ictalurus Natalis," *Science*, June 18, 1965.
19) "Instant Fish," Associated Press, June 18, 1965.
20) "Power Plants on Untouched Upper Missouri River," *New York Times News Service*, July 6, 1965.
21) "Conservation, Protection and Propagation of Certain Wildlife," SENATOR WARREN G. MAGNUSON, *Congressional Record*, June 29, 1965.

22) "Water Pollution Problems and Federal Agencies," SENATOR J. CALEB BOGGS, *ibid.*, July 7, 1965.
23) "Proposed Addition to the National Wild Rivers System Amendment," SENATOR EDMUND S. MUSKIE, *ibid.*, May 27, 1965.
24) "Kimberly-Clark Builds Pollution-Free Papermill," REPRESENTATIVE JOHN W. BYRNES, *ibid.*, June 23, 1965.
25) "A Brighter Future for Conservation," REPRESENTATIVE FRED B. ROONEY, *ibid.*, June 28, 1965.
26) "Conservation of Producing Areas for Migratory Waterfowl," SENATOR ROMAN L. HRUSKA, *ibid.*, June 8, 1965.
27) "Water Projects Recreation Act," SENATOR HENRY M. JACKSON, *ibid.*, June 25, 1965.
28) "Plenty of Water, Few Good Places to Swim," REPRESENTATIVE RICHARD D. McCARTHY, *ibid.*, June 2, 1965.

14 THE UNKNOWN

1) WHITE, RAYMOND L., "Review of American Medical Association Conference on Environmental Health Problems," *Science*, Aug. 14, 1964.
2) "Big Push on Pesticides," *Chemical Week*, Oct. 10, 1964.
3) "Safer Pesticides," *Wall Street Journal*, Aug. 6, 1965.
4) "Possible Hazards of Undiluted Pesticides," *Chemical and Engineering News*, July 5, 1965.
5) "Effects of High Energy Ionizing Radiation on Colloidal Systems and Suspensions," *Water and Sewage Works*, July, 1965.
6) WARREN, HARRY V., "Multiple Sclerosis and Lead in Soil," *Nature*, Aug. 15, 1959.
7) TATSUMOTO, M., and PATTERSON, C. C., "Lead Content of Rural Snow," *Nature*, July 27, 1963.
8) CHOW, TRAIHWA, and JOHNSTONE, M. S., "Lead Isotopes in Gasoline and Aerosols of Los Angeles Basin," *Science*, Jan. 29, 1965.
9) PATTERSON, C. C., "Contaminated and Natural Environments of Man," *Archives of Environmental Health* (in press).
10) HIRSCHLER, D. A., and GILBERT, L. F., "Nature of Lead in Automobile Exhaust," *Industrial and Engineering Chemistry*, July, 1957.
11) POKOTILENKO, L., "Vitamin B$_6$ Therapy in Lead Poisoning," *Farmakol. i Toksikol.*, 27, 88, 1960.
12) CONNOR, HELEN, and BOWLES, JESSIE, "Presence of Lead in Vegetation," *Science 137*, 765, (1962).
13) WARREN, H. V., and DELAVAULT, R. E., "Lead in Vegetation," Transactions of Royal Society of Canada *54*, 11, 1960.

14) DOROTEVIC, V., and STANKOVIC, J., "Communal Saturnism in Village of Malo Rudare," *Higijena* (Belgrade) *12*, 35, 1960.
15) WARREN, H. V., and DELAVAULT, R. E., "Lead in Some Food Crops," *J. Sci. Food Agric. 13*, 968, 1962.
16) BAETJER, E., "Intraperitoneal Injection of Lead in Mice," *Archives of Environmental Health 1*, 463, 1960.
17) KIKYO, M., "Chronic Lead Poisoning Symptoms," *Acta Petrol. Japan 8*, 917, 1958.
18) UNGHER-NESTIONE, L., "Chronic Saturnism," *Minerva Med. 1957*, 1361.
19) ESYNTINA, F., "Development of Cancer from Lead Poisoning," *Trudy Inst. Kresevoi 4*, 55, 1956.
20) GOMEZ, V., "Lead as a Toxic Metal," *Chemical Abstracts 41*, 5999.
21) VAHLQUIST, B., and SALDE, HENRY, "Lead Poisoning in Children," *ibid., 41*, 3861.
22) FENSTERMACHER, W., "Lead Poisoning of Cattle," *ibid., 42*, 6006.
23) WILLIAMS, HUNTINGTON, "Lead Poisoning in Children," *Public Health Reports* (U.S.) 67, 230, 1952.
24) HERTZ, I., "Poisoning in Storage-Battery Workers," *Chemical Abstracts 48*, 12312.
25) TOLGSKAYA, M., "Changes in Nervous System in Lead Poisoning," *Chemical Abstracts 50*, 2861.
26) VALYI-NAGG, B., "Effect of Lead Poisoning in Sterility," *Chemical Abstracts 49*, 1201.
27) GIBBS, M., and MACMAHON, G., "Arrested Mental Development Caused by Lead Poisoning," *British Medical Journal 1955*, 320.
28) KOPPICH, V., "Stages of Chronic Lead Poisoning," *Chemical Abstracts 50*, 14147.
29) CHEFTEL, V., "Tables of Lead Content in Foods," *ibid. 45*, 5329.
30) COVALLAZZI, B., "Family Destroyed by Tetraethyl Lead Poisoning," *ibid. 41*, 4231.

15 PORK IS SOLUBLE IN WATER

1) DOUGLAS, WILLIAM O., "A Wilderness Bill of Rights," *1965 Year Book, Encyclopaedia Britannica.*
2) PETERSON, ELMER T., *Big Dam Foolishness.* Devin-Adair, 1954.
3) Statement for Association of American Railroads at Public Hearing at Ada, Oklahoma, Nov. 18, 1958.
4) HAVER, CECIL; BACK, W. B., and SJAASTAD, L. A., "An Economic Analysis of the Navigation Proposal for the Arkansas River and Its Tributaries," copyright 1959.
5) "U.S. Army Corps of Engineers," *Encyclopaedia Britannica*, 1960.
6) WHEELER, KEITH; SNYDER, HENRY; RITTER, NORMAN; WISE, BILL,

and SOCHURET, LEON, "Now—See the Innards of a Fat Pig," *Life*,
Aug. 16, 1963.

7) BROOKS, PAUL, "The Plot to Drown Alaska," *Atlantic Monthly*,
May, 1965.

8) "Is the Bureau of Reclamation Guilty of Illegal Activities?"
REPRESENTATIVE JOHN P. SAYLOR, *Congressional Record*, June 7,
1965.

9) "Lake Powell—Jewel of the Colorado," SENATOR FRANK E. MOSS,
ibid., June 9, 1965.

10) "Garrison Diversion Project," REPRESENTATIVE ODIN LANGEN,
ibid., June 16, 1965.

11) "Additional Authorization for Certain River Basin Plans to Cover
Fiscal Year 1966," REPRESENTATIVE ROBERT E. JONES, *ibid.*,
May 12, 1965.

12) "Western Dams Generate Recreation as Well as Electricity,"
REPRESENTATIVE COMPTON I. WHITE, JR., *ibid.*, June 16, 1965.

13) "Flood Control Act of 1965," SENATOR WILLIAM PROXMIRE,
ibid., July 27, 1965.

14) "Amendment of Small Reclamation Project Act of 1956," SENATOR
FRANK E. MOSS, *ibid.*, June 25, 1965.

15) "Bureau of Reclamation Misrepresents the Truth about the
Solvency of its Program," REPRENSETATIVE JOHN P. SAYLOR, *ibid.*,
July 29, 1965.

16) "Authorization for Secretary of the Interior to Construct, Operate
and Maintain a Third Powerplant at the Grand Coulee Dam,"
SENATOR HENRY M. JACKSON, *ibid.*, July 10, 1965.

17) "Flaming Gorge and Reservoir," SENATOR GALE W. MCGEE, *ibid.*,
June 28, 1965.

18) "The Plot to Strangle Alaska," SENATOR ERNEST GRUENING, *ibid.*,
June 28, 1965.

19) "Establishment of National Recreation Area, Armistead Reservoir,
Texas," SENATOR RALPH YARBOROUGH, *ibid.*, June 21, 1965.

16   HOW TO MAKE SWEET WATER

1) SINGER, S. FRED, "Satellite Meteorology," *International Science
and Technology*, December, 1964.

2) Special Report: Weather Bureau, *Missiles and Rockets*, Nov. 30,
1964.

3) TANNEHILL, IVAN R., "Is Weather Subject to Cycles?" *Water*,
U.S. Department of Agriculture, 1955.

4) FLETCHER, N. H., *The Physics of Rain Clouds*. Cambridge University Press, London, 1962.

5) BOWEN, E. G., "Meteors and Rainfall," *Nature 177*, 1121, 1956.

6) FLETCHER, N. H., "Freezing Nuclei, Meteors and Rainfall," *Science*, Aug. 11, 1961.

7) BRADLEY, DONALD A., and WOODBURY, MAX A., "Lunar Synodical Period and Widespread Precipitation," *Science*, Sept. 7, 1963.

8) WYLER, JOSEPH L., "Who's Who in Weather," UPI, July 9, 1965.

9) GARDNER, CHARLES, "Hauling Down More Water from the Sky," *Water*, U.S. Department of Agriculture, 1955.

10) WORKMAN, F. J., "The Problem of Weather Modification," *Science*, Oct. 19, 1962.

11) WALSH, JOHN, "Weather Modification: National Academy of Science Panel Report," *ibid.*, Jan. 15, 1965.

12) "Scientific Problems of Weather Modification," National Academy of Sciences, 1964.

13) "Needed: Facts on Cloud Seeding," *Chemical Week*, June 19, 1965.

14) BATTAN, LOUIS J., "Changing the Weather," *International Science and Technology*, August, 1963.

15) "New Nucleating Agents," *Chemical and Engineering News*, Dec. 9, 1963.

16) SIMPSON, R. H., and MALKUS, JOANNE S., "Experiments in Hurricane Modification," *Scientific American*, December, 1964.

17) JENKINS, DAVID S., "Conversion of Saline Waters," *Water*, U.S. Department of Agriculture, 1955.

18) "Fresh Water from the Sea," *Dechema Monographs*, Vol. 47, 1962.

19) *The Sea: Vol. II, The Composition of Sea-Water; Comparative and Descriptive Oceanography*, M. N. HILL, editor, Interscience Publishers, Inc., New York, 1963.

20) TALLMADGE, J. A.; BUTT, J. B., and SOLOMON, HERMAN J., "Minerals from Sea Salt," *Industrial and Engineering Chemistry*, July, 1964.

21) CODWALLADER, E. A., "Domestic Desalination Units," *ibid.*, March, 1962.

22) COOPER, DAN, "Destinations: Washington and Moscow," *International Science and Technology*, September, 1964.

23) ABELSON, PHILIP H., "Desalination of Water," *Science*, Dec. 18, 1964.

24) PETERSON, ARTHUR E., "Desalination and Agriculture," *ibid.*, March 5, 1965.

25) WALSH, JOHN, "Desalination: Emphasis is on Dual-Purpose Nuclear Power and Desalting Plants," *ibid.*, March 5, 1965.

26) "The Hard Facts behind Production of Soft Water from the Sea," *Chemical Week*, June 24, 1961.

27) "New Gains in Sea-Water Desalting," *ibid.*, Jan. 11, 1964.

28) "Water: Third Source," *ibid.*, Nov. 14, 1964.
29) "Nuclear Power—Water Desalting Combinations Possible by 1975," *Chemical and Engineering News*, April 13, 1964.
30) "Reverse Osmosis Enters Desalination Picture," *ibid.*, July 20, 1964.
31) "Coal Producers Hit Desalination Proposal," *ibid.*, Aug. 10, 1964.
32) "U.S. Pushes Nuclear Desalting Plans," *ibid.*, Dec. 28, 1964.
33) "Pace Quickens at OSW Test Station," *ibid.*, Jan. 4, 1965.
34) MROZ, EDMUND A. J., "Pure Water from Waste Water," *ibid.*, Feb. 22, 1965.
35) "Reverse Osmosis Plant Begins Operation," *ibid.*, June 21, 1965.
36) "Bechtel Foresees 30-cent Potable Water," *ibid.*, July 19, 1965.
37) BYLIN, JAMES E., "Water from the Sea," *Wall Street Journal*, April 29, 1965.
38) "NAWAPA," North American Water and Power Alliance, Brochure 606-2934-19, Ralph M. Parsons Co.
39) "Expansion of Saline Water Conversion Program," SENATOR CLINTON P. ANDERSON, *Congressional Record*, June 16, 1965.
40) "Proposed Mexico-U.S. Saline Water Conservation Program," SENATOR MIKE MANSFIELD, *ibid.*, June 17, 1965.
41) "The Saline Water Act," SENATOR GEORGE A. SMATHERS, *ibid.*, June 24, 1965.
42) "The Water Problem," SENATOR CLINTON P. ANDERSON, *ibid.*, July 14, 1965.
43) "Proposal for New York Sea Water Conversion Project," SENATOR JACOB K. JAVITS, *ibid.*, July 14, 1965.
44) "Saline Water Conversion Program," REPRESENTATIVE ED REINECKE, *ibid.*, July 15, 1965.
45) "California Finds Key to Future World Water Supply Using Economic Nuclear Power for Sea Water Conversion," REPRESENTATIVE EDWARD R. ROYBAL, *ibid.*, July 23, 1965.
46) "Need for Expanded and Accelerated Saline Water Research," SENATOR GEORGE A. SMATHERS, *ibid.*, July 27, 1965.

17 WHO WILL DO THE JOB?

1) "All About Water," League of Women Voters of the United States, May, 1963.
2) KINNEY, JOHN E., "Our Fictitious Water Famine," *The American City*, April, 1963.
3) KOHLER, KARL O., "Trends in Utilization of Water," *Water*, U.S. Department of Agriculture, 1955.
4) BROWN, CARL B., and MURPHY, WARREN T., "Conservation Begins on the Watersheds," *ibid.*
5) Water Quality Act of 1965, Hearing before a Special Subcom-

mittee on Public Works, United States Senate, 89th Congress, Jan. 18, 1965.

6) Hearing before a Special Subcommittee on Air and Water Pollution of the Committee on Public Works, United States Senate, 88th Congress, June 17 through June 26, 1963.

7) "National Continuing Responsibilities, 1962–1964," League of Women Voters of the United States.

8) BROWN, WILLIAM, "Water Shortage Is a Frame of Mind," *Fortune*, April, 1965.

9) WOLF, LEONARD, "Cleaning up the Merrimack," *Bulletin of the Atomic Scientists*, April, 1965.

10) "Abolition of Department of the Interior is Proposed by Senator Frank E. Moss," *Chemical and Engineering News*, July 12, 1965.

11) "Water Bill Without Sting," *Chemical Week*, March 13, 1965.

12) "Pollution: Appeal to Reason," *ibid.*, June 26, 1965.

13) WALSH, JOHN, "Water Resources: Congress Votes Research Centers for States," *Science*, Sept. 4, 1964.

14) ABELSON, PHILIP H., "Water for North America," *Science*, Jan. 8, 1965.

15) "NAWAPA," *ibid.*, July 19, 1965.

16) "Hudson River—New Conservation Challenge," REPRESENTATIVE RICHARD L. OTTINGER, *Congressional Record*, May 27, 1965.

17) "Pollution Control Key Factor in Water Supply," REPRESENTATIVE RICHARD D. McCARTHY, *ibid.*, May 28, 1965.

18) "State Expenditures are Inadequate for Combating Water Pollution," REPRESENTATIVE ROBERT E. JONES, *ibid.*, June 3, 1965.

19) "Bill to Amend Title II of Water Resources Research Act," REPRESENTATIVE THOMAS L. ASHLEY, *ibid.*, June 9, 1965.

20) "Water Quality Act," REPRESENTATIVE JOHN C. KUNKEL, *ibid.*, June 14, 1965.

21) "The Potomac," REPRESENTATIVE CHARLES McG. MATHIAS, *ibid.*, June 23, 1965.

22) "Let Us Protect our Natural Resources," SENATOR FRANK E. MOSS, *ibid.*, July 1, 1965.

23) "Development of the Nation's Natural Resources—Conference Report," SENATOR THOMAS H. KUCHEL, *ibid.*, July 14, 1965.

24) "Water—Water," SENATOR EUGENE J. McCARTHY, *ibid.*, July 15, 1965.

25) "Planning for Water Conservation," SENATOR CLINTON P. ANDERSON, *ibid.*, July 30, 1965.

26) "Water Pollution Control," SENATOR FRANK E. MOSS, *ibid.*, July 30, 1965.

27) "The Water Shortage: Present and Future," SENATOR ROBERT F. KENNEDY, *ibid.*, Aug. 5, 1965.

INDEX

Index

253

Thames River, 42–45
Thoreau, Henry David, 167; *quoted,* 168
Tigris-Euphrates Valley, 58
Tigris River, 18–25
Timber, *see* Logging
Tiros, 202
Toshers, 44–45
Townley, Richard, 69
Toynbee, Arnold, 24
Transpiration, plant, 111–13, 118, 221; and ground-water level, 114
Treatment, sea water, nuclear, 216
Treatment, sewage: bacteriological, 45, 54, 155; chlorine, 45; modern, 44; nuclear, 216; of Thames River, 44
Treatment, water: ancient, 28; chemical, 28; chlorine, 163; technology of, 154–55; *see also* Activated sludge; Aeration; Chlorination; Filtration
2,4-D: and vegetation control, 114–15; and water pollution, 115

Udall, Stewart, Secretary of the Interior, 88
United Mine Workers, and desalinization plants, 214
United States Army Corps of Engineers: and Alaska dam projects, 195–96; Board of Rivers and Harbors, 180; bookkeeping of, 194, 198; and chemical pollution, 182; and dam-building, 179–80; and flood projects, 109–10; and Missouri River Basin System, 198; and multi-purpose dams, 227–28; origin of, 192–93; and Potomac River, 220
United States Bureau of Reclamation: bookkeeping of, 196–98; and dam-building, 228; and Frying Pan Water Diversion, 191–92; and Marble Canyon Dam, 196–97; and Missouri River Basin Power System, 198; restrictions on, 192
United States Code on lobbying, 196
United States Department of Agriculture, 36; cloud-seeding research of, 205; and conservation, 105; and dam projects, 199; and multi-purpose dams, 227–28; and over-irrigation, 221; and pesticides, 175; soil conservation policy of, 79; and wetlands drainage, 176–77; *see also* Soil Conservation Service
United States Department of Commerce, *see* Weather Bureau
United States Department of Defense, cloud-seeding research of, 205
United States Department of Health, Education, and Welfare: cloud-seeding research of, 205; and interstate pollution, 145; and pesticides, 175; and water pollution, 227; and water-purity standards, 225–26; *see also* Public Health Service
United States Department of the Interior: and cloud-seeding research, 205–6; flash distillation plant of, 213; and multi-purpose dams, 227–28; Office of Saline Water of, 210, 211; Office of Water Resources Research of, 229; and pesticides, 175; wildlife conservation policy of, 79; *see also* Fish and Wildlife Serv-

ice; Fisheries, Bureau of Commercial; Geological Survey
United States Federal Power Commission, 79
United States Food and Drug Administration, 163; chemical tolerance standards of, 181
United States Forest Service, and power company regulation, 179
United States government: untreated sewage at installations, 50–51; water resources policies of, 79–80
United States National Science Foundation, and weather modification, 79
United States Senate Public Works Committee, 218
United States Soil Conservation Survey, 79
United States and Soviet Russia, desalinization efforts of, 217
United States Steel Corporation, pollution by, 151
United States Surgeon General, 185
University of California at Los Angeles, 26
Uranium, cost of, 214
Urban redevelopment, and sewer systems, 42

Vanadium Corporation of America, radioactive pollution by, 182
Vegetation: dew absorption of, 123–25; lead concentration in, 186; and salt incursion, 131–38; water consumption of, 111–26
Venus, water on, 34
Vitamin industry, and pesticides, 175
Vitruvius, 27
Volta River, 64
Vonnegut, Bernard, 205

Walton, Izaak, 39
Warren, H. V., 185, 186
Washington, D.C., *see* Potomac River
Washington, George, 44, 72
Water: biological analysis of, 44; composition of, 30–32; connate, 133; consumption of, 69; consumption *versus* use, 140; cost of, 208–9, 212; depletion allowance for, 105; desalinization of, 97, 207–18; industrial consumption of, 139–40; juvenile, 133; lead content of, 186; metering of, 97, 228; military use of, 23; molecular speed of, 33–34; oxygen content of, 45; plant consumption of, 111–26; policing of, 97; purity standards for, 225–26; qualities of, 30–32; recreational use of, 165–80; saline, 132–34; shortages of, 227; testing of, 48–49; *see also* Desalinization; Dew; Ground water; Rivers; Runoff; Sea water
Water closets, 42; ancient, 38; valved, 41
Water contamination, *see* Contamination
Water-main systems: constant-pressure, 69; dual, 68
Water management, 35; by the clergy, 66–68; federal agencies for, 79–80; and fish kills, 104–5, 166; medieval, 66–68; municipal, 68, 69; in Netherlands, 67–68; Sumerian, 19–21
Water Pollution, *see* Pollution